200 Letters For Job Hunters

by
William S. Frank
President, **CareerLab**®
Denver, Colorado

Ten Speed Press

Ten Speed Press
P O Box 7123
Berkeley, California 94707

Library of Congress Cataloging-in-Publication Data

Frank, William S.
        200 letters for job-hunters / William S. Frank.
        Indexed.
        p. cm.
        ISBN 0-89815-558-4
        1. Job-hunting.
        2. Letter-writing.
        3. Employment references.
        4. Applications for positions.
        5. Thank-you notes.
            I. Title.
            II. Title: Two hundred letters for job-hunters.

HF5382.7.F72   1993   93–26780
808'.06665––dc20   CIP

3 4 5 — 97 96 95

PRINTED IN CANADA

For my family

My parents, Scott and Ruth
My brother and sister, Brad and Sherry
My young-adult children, Kenny and Brandon
and especially for
My sweet wife, Beverly

CONTENTS

Acknowledgements & Credits

Craig Lincoln, Director of our Marketing/Communications Group at CareerLab®, was the inspiration for this book. Five years ago, on my birthday, Craig surprised me with a cover design for the book—long before I ever began writing. Then he met with me weekly to help make it happen.

Thanks to George Young, Christine Carswell, Hal Hershey, and all our friends at Ten Speed Press, for their wisdom, advice, and encouragement. They're the very best.

Ongoing appreciation to those whose letters appeared in the first edition. Special thanks to the new contributors to the second edition: Jim Adams, Bryan Bechtold, Jean Creasy, Edward D. Bales, Keith Bennett, John Doyle, Michael A. Duncan, Robert C. Froetscher, David J. Hansen, Robert W. Jones, Mary Kouri, Ph.D., Jay Conrad Levinson, Pat Nichols, William E. Powell, Ralph Poucher, Ben Reding, Rod Richmond, Michael R. Walker, Gary G. Sullivan, and John Wren. Thank you for sharing.

These artists and cartoonists brought happiness and light into my life, and into this revision: Charles Barsotti, Ashleigh Brilliant, Tom Cheney, Phillip Jewell, and Eli Stein.

I'm grateful to friends in high places who gave permission to use their licensed materials: Jeanne DeSimone, NEA/United Media; Denice Bornander, King Features Syndicate/North America Syndicate; and Jim Cavett, Tribune Media Syndicate.

Cam and Barb Scott and Mitzie Testani and Jeff Mlady at Scott Group, our typesetters, always bring art, beauty, and perfection to their work. As you see, it makes a big difference.

CareerLab® staff, friends, and associates provided advice, critique, and support (and laughed at me from time to time): Alan Forker, MBA, Vice President; Linda Bougie, Consultant; Fred Holland, MBA, Financial Planning Consultant; Scott Howard and Jennifer Craig, Reid Merrill Brunson & Associates, Career Testing Experts; Dr. Jim Jonell, Psychologist; Diane Sears, Director, Client Service; Marilynn & Lin Ellis; Phyllis Record, Kathy Miller and Bernice Leinweber, Record Services.

My wife, Beverly, is my special friend, and she's given me freedom to be myself, as well as great support to follow my direction—whatever it might be on any given day. That's a great blessing.

Heartfelt thanks to you all!

PART ONE

WHAT TO DO FOR A QUICK JOB SEARCH

What to Do for a Quick Job Search

If you're in a hurry—and most job-hunters are—you'll make the best time if you do things in exactly this order:

1. Make sure your telephone is always answered. Get a telephone answering machine (about $50-$100), use an answering service, or subscribe to an electronic voice mailbox (about $13 per month). Some voice mail services give you a new phone number which you can use on letters and resumes as your "office" number, if you're unemployed. Put a businesslike message on your recorder or voice mailbox (no cute messages featuring your kids).

   If you're based at home, you might want to add a second line for business calls. If your home office line doubles as a FAX line, indicate that on your stationery and correspondence.

   AT&T has inexpensive residential 800 service which might help if you're relocating. You can keep the number wherever you go. The monthly charge is $5.50 plus a toll for incoming calls. Contact AT&T Signature 800℠ Service at 1-800-327-9700.

2. Get stationery, envelopes, and business cards printed on white or off-white paper. No "parchment." Five hundred of each should be plenty. Use an "executive"-looking type style, like a lawyer might have—nothing fancy and no large computer fonts.

3. Get set up with a secretarial service, or with your own word processor. Don't try to type correspondence on your dad's old Underwood, unless that's your only choice. Don't do your own letters, unless you're a good typist. Even then, make only six to twelve originals. (Don't force your spouse to type for you, either, unless he or she really loves the idea.)

   If you can afford it, use a secretarial service for mailings of 12 or more pieces. Repeat letters normally cost about $1.00-$1.50 each, which is cheap compared to the value of your time. Your time is better spent on the telephone or in face-to-face meetings.

4. Read the section in this book called "The most important letter you will ever write," pages 7-12. Take great pains remembering the names of everyone you've met.

5. Send a "friendship letter" like Dale Kreeger's to close personal friends (see page 11), and include a resume. (Since 75% of all good jobs come from friends—or friends of friends—this is the single most important strategy you can follow.)

6. Call your friends after they've had a chance to review your letter. Ask them if they got it and what they think of it.

   You'll be amazed at how many "have been meaning to call you," but didn't quite get around to it. You'll also be amazed at how many are actually glad to hear your voice.

   Begin to set face-to-face informational meetings with anyone who seems interested or especially helpful. Follow up on every lead you get, no matter how "silly." Don't prejudge what others will say before you call them.

7. Write a series of tailored "friendship letters" to the most powerful and influential people you know: your banker, your stockbroker, your former employers, your spouse's friends, and so on. (See pages 57-74.)

8. Contact search firms, also known as recruiters and headhunters. (See pages 75-102.)

9. Write to members of your professional association(s) or organization(s). (See pages 71-72.)

10. Develop a generic letter and begin to answer want ads. Customize the letter for important ads, but only devote 5 percent of your effort to answering want ads—not 95 percent, as is all too common.

11. Select a mailing list and write a high-powered sales/marketing letter. Mail 50-100 pieces as a test with no resume included. Mail on Mondays, telephone two days after the letter is received. Record your results, then adjust the letter and the list and mail again if necessary.

12. Send a thank-you letter after every marketing contact, social occasion, telephone call, and personal visit—no matter how insignificant. Job-hunting is a public relations campaign, and you're trying to build good will.

13. Look through this book to find clever ways to introduce yourself to companies, and begin some one-shot, highly targeted mailings. Follow as many letters as possible with phone calls.

14. Once calls start coming in, keep meticulous records to be certain nothing falls through the cracks. Review your records every few days to be sure you haven't missed anything.

15. Continually reprioritize and devote time to only the most important people. As management expert Peter Drucker says, "Do first things first, and second things not at all."

16. Spend as much time as you can talking on the phone or visiting with others. Letters are useful, but it's not wise to try to conduct an entire job-search through the mail. Real opportunities come in face-to-face meetings, because as theologian Martin Buber said, "All real living is meeting."

17. The letters in this book are available as IBM-PC software called INSTANT Job Winning Letters. If you're really in a hurry to get a job, this is the fastest way to go. For information about INSTANT Job Winning Letters, turn to page 347.

PART TWO

HOW TO WRITE A GREAT LETTER

How to Write
a Great Letter

Why this book?

Most job-hunters want a job *fast*, and few have the luxury of time. Even senior executives with large severance packages are often panicked at the thought of being unemployed, no matter how briefly. There's something inside us that says, "I have to be working."

Interviews produce job offers, but letters produce interviews. Well-worded letters will get you talking to more people quicker than any other method. That's why no job-search campaign is complete without them.

A sales or marketing letter is the quickest, surest way to reach a decision-maker, short of calling that person on the telephone.

A letter is fast. It goes right into the employer's office and requires less courage than the telephone. Most importantly, it's efficient. You can't call two hundred people per day, but you can mail to that many. Letters can be sent out by the hundreds.

Best of all, a well-written letter gets results. I've never seen a job-hunter with a superb letter fail. Even if a manager doesn't need you immediately, a really good letter will usually be kept, or passed to another decision-maker. Your letter may have long-term effects you never imagined.

Most job-hunters don't write well

Most job-hunters have trouble writing. They dislike it and agonize over it. Either they didn't learn the craft in school, or they're rusty.

Executives and professionals don't write well, either. In fact, they often write poorly, because they haven't had to do it themselves. Their secretaries write for them, their spouses help them, or they delegate writing to subordinates. No one seems to like to write.

Think about it. It's rare to receive a polished, well-thought-out letter, isn't it? Most business letters are routine, unimaginative, and dull.

If you send an exceptionally good letter, you stand out. If your letter is excellent, it will be read. And if it's especially good, or if it's timely, you'll get a phone call.

The most important letter you will ever write

All job-hunting correspondence is important, but the letter you send your friends is absolutely critical.

Here's why: When you're in a job-hunt you're selling personal services—what you can do—something intangible. People buy services based on trust. Marketing personal services is not like marketing a product. Shoppers buy products knowing they can return them if dissatisfied. But companies can't return employees who fail on the job. They have to terminate them and start over, both of which are costly. That's why employers are so cautious.

Crucial hiring decisions are generally made by a team. Key managers meet to define the duties and responsibilities and decide what sort of person they want. Then they ask, "Who do we *know* that could fill this slot?" Most of the time, someone in the group knows someone. That candidate is interviewed first, given preferential treatment, and usually hired.

The moral of the story is that managers hire their friends—known quantities, not shots-in-the-dark. No one likes to hire strangers—there's too much at stake. One wrong employment decision can ruin a manager's career.

What does this mean to you?

It means your next job is probably going to come from one of your personal friends or business acquaintances—or else from one of their friends. Not from a recruiter. Not from a newspaper ad. Not from knocking on doors or pounding the pavement.

Your friends are your strongest marketing allies. That's why it's important to *involve* them in your campaign, not just *notify* them. Most job-seekers simply call and say, "I've lost my job. Let me know if you hear of anything." The friend says, "Sure I will." And that's the end of it. The phone never rings. Friends want to help, but they have to know exactly what kind of help you need. Tell them in a "friendship letter."

Who are your friends?

When I say "friends," I mean "everyone you know." Not just your closest friends, but anyone who knows your name. I mean your contact network, both personal and business—especially people you've worked with on projects. Begin your marketing campaign by making a list of your friends. Use the following checklist to help you remember names. Record all names. Don't prejudge people, guessing which ones can help you (you'll often be wrong). Don't rule anyone out prematurely.

The Friendship Checklist

- ⇨ Family (uncles, aunts, cousins, distant relatives)
- ⇨ Your significant other's family and friends
- ⇨ Close personal friends
- ⇨ Builders, plumbers, electricians, other tradespeople
- ⇨ PTA members
- ⇨ Students, fellow classmates, former college professors
- ⇨ Parents of your children's friends
- ⇨ Organizational groups
- ⇨ Professional societies
- ⇨ Club officers
- ⇨ Hobby groups
- ⇨ Social groups
- ⇨ Headhunters
- ⇨ Church groups
- ⇨ Religious leaders (pastor, priest, rabbi)
- ⇨ Current and former employers
- ⇨ Fellow jurors
- ⇨ Fellow employees (your peer group)
- ⇨ The staff, editors, and reporters of your local newspaper
- ⇨ Former clients, customers, buyers, suppliers, and sales representatives
- ⇨ Librarians
- ⇨ Consultants you've used

- ⇨ Professionals
  - ⇨ Dentist
  - ⇨ Doctor
  - ⇨ Attorney
  - ⇨ CPA
  - ⇨ Financial Planner
  - ⇨ Psychologist
  - ⇨ Banker
  - ⇨ Veterinarian
  - ⇨ Realtor
  - ⇨ Insurance Agent
- ⇨ Fellow vacationers or travelers
- ⇨ Chamber of Commerce members
- ⇨ Store owners
- ⇨ Former cellmates (just kidding)
- ⇨ Ex in-laws
- ⇨ High school buddies
- ⇨ Fraternity brothers/sorority sisters
- ⇨ Friends of your parents
- ⇨ Favorite waitpeople, bartenders, and hosts
- ⇨ Secretaries
- ⇨ Security guards
- ⇨ The person at the dry cleaners
- ⇨ Your hairdresser
- ⇨ Neighbors
- ⇨ Parents (yes, your parents!)

Go as far back as high school, even grade school. List your old college classmates and roommates. Look at your Christmas/Chanukkah card list. Write names until your mind goes blank. Then stop and rest, and begin again.

Common objections

Many job-hunters resist doing this exercise. They don't see the point. They find it time-consuming and come up with a variety of objections, like these:

Objection	Answer
I don't want to use my friends.	Contact them and give *them* something: a journal article, an idea, an invitation to lunch, a compliment, a good listening. Find out how they're doing.
All my friends are in Chicago and I want to work in Dallas.	People in Chicago have family and friends in Dallas.
I hate to call people and ask for favors.	Read answer number one, above.
I can't remember all these people.	Yes you can. You just don't want to.
I would be embarrassed to say I'm unemployed.	Say something like "I have some great news. I'm finally leaving HighTek—it's about time. Their accounting system is snarled up, and I want to get into a company where I can bring the latest computer solutions into the picture. This is great! I've never been more excited in my life. I can't sleep at night. I feel like a kid again."
I would feel funny writing a letter to people I see in person all the time.	Don't write them a letter. Talk with them face-to-face.

The following stories show the importance of collecting the names of friends, even if it doesn't make logical sense.

It doesn't matter where your friends live

Ken Granger was a senior data processing manager in Denver. He wanted to relocate to Dallas because his wife had family there. I asked Ken to list his friends so he could send them something. He resisted doing the assignment.

His reasoning went like this: "All my friends live in Chicago. I want to work in Dallas. Why should I write to people who can't help me?"

Finally, after three weeks, Ken made his list. We sent a letter, and guess what? One of his contacts in Chicago had a brother who was president of a data-processing company in Dallas. Ken flew down to interview and was hired. That's the kind of thing that often happens in networking.

"You never know how many friends you have until you rent a place at the beach."

Quoted by Wayne Norris in
*You Don't Have to Be Crazy to Work Here . . .
But It Sure Helps* (Price/Stern/Sloan).

Don't guess who your friends are

I've seen hundreds of people contact their network to ask for help, and I see two patterns.

First, friendship letters *always* work. You get *some* positive response from *some* of your friends. That's a big boost when you're feeling down. Second, it's impossible to accurately predict who will help you and who won't. You'll be wrong 50 percent of the time—maybe more.

It's interesting, and sometimes disconcerting, to find out who can be counted on when you need a helping hand. Some of your "dearest friends" will let you down, and some people you have written off will come out of the woodwork and shower you with badly needed love and attention.

Your friends will always help

I contacted my friends—especially former clients—in writing this book. I was announcing the project, asking for permission to use their materials, and looking for advice and ideas. I was reaching out for support.

I was surprised at the positive responses. They really lifted me and made me feel the whole project was worthwhile. There was one letter I will never forget.

Kay Tubbs said, "My advice: Go for it! It's perfect. I would buy it (and recommend it) in a heartbeat. It would also solve a personal problem I have, of not being physically close enough to utilize your services. (It's probably a good thing—I'd be tempted to mortgage the house to hire you as a permanent 'life consultant.')" That felt really good.

You'll find that most of your friends will help you, too, and their heartfelt response may surprise you.

The world's greatest letter

I've always encouraged clients to contact their friends to ask for advice and ideas. They used a variety of letters, and I'm certain many of them worked. But one day in a workshop, I found the ultimate "friendship letter." It was a work of art.

The tone was right: It was warm and friendly and not too pushy or boring. It made you want to help.

I began distributing Dale Kreeger's letter in my classes. Students used it as a guide. (As you will see, many of the letters in this book take off from Dale's.)

Dale was an accountant in a large oil company. At age 55 he was asked to take early retirement before he was ready. Here is what he wrote:

DALE M. KREEGER
6950 South Olive Way
Englewood, Colorado 80112

March 5, 19—

Mr. Mike Roberts
Arthur Andersen & Co.
717 Seventeenth Street, Suite 1900
Denver, Colorado 80202

Dear Mike,

As friend to friend, I want to let you know that I plan to accept the
voluntary early retirement package offered by Worldwide Oil Company as
of March 31, 19—; however, I do not plan on moving out to pasture for at
least another five to ten years. Consequently, I have updated my resume
to begin marketing myself for what I believe will be the most exciting and
productive years of my life.

I am totally open not only to an industry change but also to relocating
if necessary—naturally Thelma and I both prefer to remain in Denver!

Should you be aware of any friends or business associates who may be in
the market for new blood and innovative thinking, I would truly appreciate your slipping them the attached copy of my resume or giving me their
names to contact personally.

Any assistance or advice you can give me at this special crossroads period
of my life will be greatly appreciated.

Very best regards,

Dale M. Kreeger

DMK:df
Enclosure

What makes this letter work?

It's warm.
It's friendly.
It's interesting.
It's not begging.
It's enthusiastic.
It's humorous ("not ready to be put out to pasture yet...").
It's short.
It's everything a great letter should be.

But as good as it is, it can still be improved. The letter doesn't specify exactly what kind of job Dale wants. Friends can't help very well unless they know exactly, clearly, and specifically what kind of help you need. The more specific, the better. As an example, here's a career counselor's "what I want" paragraph:

"I'd like to work for outplacement firms coaching their consultants in career counseling and marketing techniques. I'd like to live somewhere remote and travel to major cities—but no more than 25 percent travel. I want to spend 50 percent of my time consulting and selling, and 50 percent writing and researching." That's a lot to ask, and maybe he won't get it. But on the other hand, maybe he will.

Some job-seekers object to being specific. They want to keep their options open. They reason this way: "If I tell people exactly what I want, I might miss out on other things I might like."

That's true. But, on the other hand, if you tell people exactly what you want, you might get your ideal job. Wouldn't that be better?

The anatomy of a friendship letter

If you write a letter to your network, limit yourself to about 100-150 words. You can use Dale's letter as a model or you can invent your own. If you do your own letter—and I recommend that—here are five steps you should take:

1. *Establish rapport (about 20 words)*
   Rebuild old fences. Make your reader feel good. Make them glad you're writing.
   "I can't help remembering the fun we had last time in Atlanta..."
   "New York hasn't been the same since you left town. We've missed you."
   "You've played a major role in my career development, and I can't thank you enough."

2. *Explain the situation (about 30 words)*
   "I've decided I need more responsibility; so I'm seeking to move out of sales into sales management."
   "Sally's health is not good, and we feel we must leave Wisconsin to find a warmer climate."

Don't simply say, "I left," "I resigned," or "My boss and I didn't see eye to eye." Those answers leave too many unanswered questions. The reader's mind will automatically think the worst: "Was she fired?" or "Is he a troublemaker?"

Even if you left under the most unpleasant circumstances, try to frame the change in a positive light: "We were purchased by a Fortune 500 company, there was considerable overlap in staffing, the company was reorganized, 20 managers were laid off, and I lost my job at the end of December."

3. *Tell them what you want (about 30 words)*
   This is your chance to paint a clear but brief picture of your ideal, perfect job. The more detail the better. Mention possible job title, size and philosophy of company, management style, preferred industries, duties and responsibilities, geographic preferences or restrictions—in short, anything that clarifies. Your friends can't help you unless they know what fits; and they don't know what fits unless you tell them!
   For example: "My expertise would best fit the high-reliability electronics industry, such as medical, automotive, industrial, or computers—although I also have considerable background in the metals and machining industries. Most of my experience with Boeing was related to electronics, but included materials such as glass and graphite epoxy composites, adhesives, coatings, and plastics.
   "I would prefer to remain in the Chicago metro area or relocate to the Pacific Northwest. I am most interested in a company in the startup phase or in a period of rapid growth. My recent experience with ChicagoTek during a 400% increase in business was very rewarding, and I find myself looking for another similar company."

4. *Ask for advice and ideas (about 20 words)*
   "Your words of wisdom have always meant a great deal to me over the years."
   "I've always counted on you to spark my creativity."
   "Would you mind reviewing my resume and letters and giving me some honest opinions? Could you call me or jot some notes in the margins?"

5. *End on a warm, friendly, enthusiastic note*
   "Should you be free in the near future, Jim and I would like to have you come to dinner."

Writing to strangers

After you've mailed to your friends, you'll be mailing to "strangers," and that's a much tougher sell. To many of them, you're just a number, an interruption, a salesperson.

In trying to reach outsiders, you have a lot of competition. You'll find commercial television and cable channels, radio stations, metropolitan dailies, national media, billboards, and ads on shopping carts all vying for attention.

Nationally, we spend $68 billion a year on advertising (more than $800 per household). Network television features 600 commercials per day. There are at least 1,500 advertising messages sent directly to you. That's a lot of hype.

During a recent recession in Denver, the Colorado Association of Realtors spent $250,000 to promote only three words: Take Another Look. (Meaning, the real estate market may be better than you think.)

When you market or advertise yourself (that is, when you try to find a job), you're competing for attention with well-capitalized corporations. So you and your message may easily get lost.

The only marketing lesson you'll ever need

Right after college I had a "marketing lesson" I've never forgotten; it has shaped much of my business success. Here's what happened: I decided to teach a personal growth workshop, printed several hundred flyers, and passed them out like handbills.

After about an hour of walking, I faced a dilemma: should I continue putting out flyers or go home to answer the phone? I knew it would be ringing off the hook.

When I couldn't wait any longer, I raced home, and guess what? The phone never rang. Not even once. I call that my "Marketing 101" lesson: customers (employers) don't really care about our great stuff and nifty ideas. They're busy people. In marketing—the job-hunt—we have to grab their attention before someone else does.

Drawbacks to letter writing

A well-written letter can break through the "communications jungle" and lead to interviews, but there are definite pros and cons to writing sales and marketing letters. Here are just a few:

Plus	Minus
They're fast.	They're hard to write. They take brain power. They take time.
They're personal.	A letter must be extremely well-written or it will fail.
They take less guts than a cold call.	They're somewhat costly (versus the telephone, which is virtually free).
Once you have a letter that works, you can send it out hundreds of times and multiply your efforts enormously.	A bad marketing letter can make you look like a real loser or an egomaniac and, therefore, blow your future chances.
The letter can be selling while you are doing something else.	If you send a poor marketing letter and don't get any response, it can be quite depressing.
If you write a good letter, you may be perceived by the recipient as extremely creative.	The average letter gets between three and ten seconds of attention on the way to the trash can. (How fast do you open your own mail?)

A well-written letter *always* gets responses.

My world famous junk mail lecture

Do you save the junk mail that comes to your house? If not, perhaps you should. Businesses spend hundreds of millions of dollars each year designing direct mail pieces and testing the results. Obviously, some of it works or they wouldn't keep using it. In direct mail, nothing is sacred—results are the only things that count. If a mailing doesn't pay for itself, it's discontinued.

Years ago, I started collecting junk mail and advertising gimmicks: door hangers, table top tent cards from restaurants, all kinds of direct mail—especially letters. And I learned to write letters that always get results.

13

My own letters have landed more than 100 major corporate accounts, built a thriving consulting business, gotten me interviewed on television, collected delinquent bills, and secured a publisher for this book—plus much more. With a little research and planning, yours can do the same.

Look at a few direct mail letters from your mailbox. What do you notice about them? For one thing, no two are alike. Sure, there are similarities, but each letter is essentially one of a kind. Some are amateurish, some are great. Some turn you off, some pull you in.

Examine the format and you'll see a lot of white space on the page. That's visual appeal—the letters look good. Also, they're fun to read—not dull, boring, or routine. They offer something. They're loaded with benefits for the reader. They tell you exactly what you're going to get, and precisely how it will help you.

The words and sentences are short and easy to understand. You seldom see jargon or buzzwords—unless the offer comes from a specialized industry source.

Here's a project that will help your letter writing: Collect your junk mail for a week. Look at it. Study it. Critique it. See how you could improve it. Rewrite it. Play with it.

Try to incorporate some of it in your writing. If you can, most of your letters will be winners. (You don't want your letters to seem to *be* "junk mail," though.)

What is advertising appeal?

I once noticed a restaurant billboard that said, "We welcome tour buses." Why do they want tour buses? I wondered. And then it dawned on me: Tour buses are full of hundreds of customers. I watched the signs. They changed slightly, but most sounded alike: "Bus Drivers Welcome." That sort of thing.

Then I saw a sign that accomplished what all the other signs had merely tried to do. *It stopped the buses.* What did it say? "Bus Drivers Eat Free." That's advertising appeal: finding the right message for the right crowd.

Why write emotional copy?

John Caples, author of *Tested Advertising Methods,* says, "If you write with the prejudices and preferences of other people uppermost in your mind, you will produce copy as correct as a school child's essay, but utterly lifeless . . .

"Get excited! Get worked up! . . . Then start to write," Caples says. "Write fast. Write furiously. Write as if you had to catch a plane. Write as if you had to put all your thoughts on paper in the next five minutes or lose them forever . . .

"Action—that's the vital quality that emotional copy possesses and that 'reason why' copy lacks.

"Everybody knows that you can tame a wild horse and make the animal useful. But it is impossible to put life into a dead horse. The same is true of advertising copy. An advertisement that has been pounded out in the white heat of enthusiasm can be tamed and made effective. But it is impossible to put life into dead copy."

The best emotional copy I ever read appeared in an ad for Boeing. Picture this: an empty beach, white sand, bright sunlight. A young couple—no children around—walking away arm-in-arm. Then the words . . .

"SOMEDAY"

We'll take off. Just the two of us.
No kids. No pets. No worries. We'll
lie on a lonely beach. And plan
another 100 years together.

"Remember the first time you mentioned going away? How many somedays ago was that? Is your warm and wonderful someday really ever going to happen? Right now, your travel agent or airline can arrange especially good values in air travel on Boeing jetliners. To anywhere in the world. So go. Before your someday slowly slips away."

BOEING

Isn't that wonderful? Nothing logical about it—it's all emotion, all persuasive. Doesn't it make you want to go to the beach?

Show your excitement and enthusiasm

A big part of letter writing is attitude. If you have a positive attitude that comes through in your words, you shouldn't have any trouble getting the right response.

The best letters are "heartfelt"—not academic or strictly logical. Good ones have feeling; they move you.

Be brave. Yes, if you're too aggressive you run the risk of "turning them off," but if you write too carefully, you run the risk of being totally ignored. And being ignored is the fate of most job-search letter writers—I can say that from experience.

If you like people, tell them so. Don't be afraid to show honest feelings. Here's an excerpt from one of my own sales letters: "Great meeting you! You sound like a very positive, upbeat, helpful person—just the kind I like to work with."

Here's something else I used: "You really got me off to a great start last week. I think Saturday was the most exciting day of my life. Almost too exciting."

Make your letters electric. Don't hide your feelings, and don't play "hard-to-get." Your words should feel fresh and alive, interesting and intriguing, different, creative, and thought-provoking. Let the reader feel your emotions. Does that seem like a tall order? It is, but you can do it.

How to collect your ideas

When you begin to write, your mind may give you random, disjointed thoughts. Your ideas probably won't come out logically or sequentially, but write them down as they appear, without worrying about order or logic. Don't judge and evaluate, simply collect them. Later you'll evaluate, sort, and organize them. At this stage you just want to get them down on paper, on tape, or on computer disk.

It is easier for most people to write this way, because the creative part of your brain isn't very logical, and the logical part of your brain isn't very creative. Don't expect your mind to perform both functions at once (although some can).

Use the "card trick" to organize your thoughts

Sometimes it helps to put all your thoughts on individual index cards, exactly as they come to mind. Later, you can sort the cards to get a finished product, eliminating cards that don't fit.

This is also a beautiful way to write a magazine or journal article with very little stress—and very little "writer's block," because nothing you write down has to be said perfectly or accurately. Everything can be sharpened up later. Your first goal is simply to collect your rough thoughts. Once you've accomplished that, here's what to do next:

1. Spend some time on your letter. Someone once said, "With part-time effort, you get part-time results." This is especially true in letter writing. You can expect to spend several hours, or even several days, on a letter.

2. Write a draft, then let it cool off overnight.

3. Rewrite if necessary.

4. Use a strong close, like these:
   "After you have had a chance to review this letter, I will call you to get your reactions."
   "I will call your office next week to arrange a time when we might be able to get together. If you have any questions before that, please call me at (510) 771-4357."

5. Avoid weaker endings like these:
   "Please call me at your earliest convenience."
   "I believe that a meeting could prove to be mutually profitable, and ask that, if you agree, you contact me so that we can arrange a convenient time."
   "Thank you for your consideration. I am available for a personal interview at your earliest convenience and look forward to hearing from you."
   "In the next week or two when your schedule permits, let's meet and discuss my aspirations in more detail. Please give me a call."
   "I look forward to your reply."

6. Ask for opinions, advice, and feedback from friends, and from sales, marketing, and advertising experts.

7. Mail a small sample to test your letter. This is important. A consultant friend once mailed 76,000 brochures at a cost of nearly $15,000, and only got three responses. What a shame! The material was poorly written, badly designed, and poorly tested. Test your letters before you roll them out on a large scale.

8. If you're getting the kind of response you want, mail larger numbers.

9. Enclose a *response form* to increase your response. (See pages 183-197.)

10. Remail the same letter to the same people two or three times. Repetition often helps.

11. Don't mark letters "Personal and Confidential," unless there's a solid reason why they can't be opened by a secretary. If the letter is persuasive enough, it will get through.

Give yourself time

You can't expect to produce an exceptional document overnight. Letter-writing is actually harder than resume-writing because you're starting with a clean slate. In resume-writing at least you have your background—which is definite—to work with. In letter writing, you start with nothing. Letters can be about *anything*. That's why they're so difficult.

I once took a class called "How to Market a Book." The class focused on writing query letters to publishers to get a book contract. The course lasted six weeks and met for two hours each week. I spent several hours per week on homework—staying up all night several nights—and the end product was a one-page sales letter to publishers. Lots of work for just one letter.

I mailed the letter to about 30 publishers and got 13 responses. No one bought the book, but one publisher did offer to publish it for royalties only (no advance), which I declined. That book was the forerunner of this one.

Writers often say, "I don't like writing, but I like having written." That's how many of us feel. Writing can be hard work. Don't take it lightly, and don't feel bad if you can't write a high-impact marketing letter in half an hour. Neither can professional copywriters! Writing is a profession, like rocket science. Don't expect to learn or perfect it overnight.

Don't copy someone else's letter

Take these letters as samples and modify them to fit yourself, but don't copy them verbatim. I've found that people who copy someone else's letter seldom get a good response, regardless of how good the letter is. Be original.

It *would* be easy to take the letters in this book and use them word-for-word. That would be quick, but probably not effective. Your letter has to be "you." It should sound like you, feel like you, read like you—because *you* have to follow it with a phone call, or answer questions about it.

So, don't send a really "hot," aggressive letter if you're introverted and laid-back. You'll have trouble following up on the letter and you may not come across well. Send a letter that mirrors your style—and only you can write that letter.

Get professional help

If you're a skilled writer, fine. The project may be easy for you. But if you're not, you may need help. Consider hiring a professional freelance writer to help you compose and edit your letters, but not to do them for you.

Where can you begin to look? Call your local ad club for the names of direct mail freelance writers. Read the classifieds in *Writer's Digest*. Check the *Yellow Pages* under "Writers." Contact your local writers' guild. Check with local advertising and PR firms. They use lots of freelancers. Newspaper and magazine editors know writers too.

Twenty-eight common mistakes

If you've ever seen a batch of letters sent in response to a want ad, you know they can be hysterically funny. A random sampling usually demonstrates every mistake in the book (like sending the letter to the wrong company). Here are twenty-eight common errors to avoid:

1. Addressing letters, "Dear Sir:" or "Dear Sirs:" As you know, many readers today are women. If gender is unclear, the salutation should be something like "Dear Hiring Manager," or "Dear Human Resources Manager."

2. Addressing letters, "To whom it may concern." Find out who will receive the correspondence, and address it personally. We received a letter addressed to "Dear Whomever," to which one consultant replied, "I'll answer to anything but this!"

3. Enclosing a photo. Skip the photo unless you're a model or an aspiring actor.

4. Handwriting or typing over an old resume or letterhead. If you've moved, start over. Changes on old documents aren't acceptable.

5. No signature. Even if you type your name at the end of correspondence, you should sign the page in your own handwriting to give it a personal touch.

6. Spelling errors. One applicant said he was well suited for "writting and editing chores . . . contac t (sic) me at the adrwss (sic) below." Would you give him your editing work? Another writer said she would enjoy "hearing form (sic) us." Word processing spell checkers make mistakes; so proof everything.

7. Not checking grammar. One person wrote, "It sounds exciting and give me (sic) the opportunity to use my skills." Check your letters for correct sentence structure. Have friends review them too.

8. Handwriting letters. Brief 30-word thank you notes can be handwritten, if legible. All other correspondence should be typewritten or word processed, even if you have to borrow a word processor or pay a secretarial service. Handwritten letters don't say "business."

9. Using a Post-It™ Brand Note as a letter. Post-It Brand Notes aren't letters. Using one says, "This isn't important. I was too busy to write a real letter."

10. Using the word "I" too much. Some letters are filled with 20 or 30 Is. Make sure yours aren't. Advertising is about "you." Emphasize "you" rather than "I."

11. FAXing letters unexpectedly.

12. Forgetting to include your phone number. One woman wrote, "Please call me at home," but didn't include a phone number. That looked bad.

13. Cluttered desktop publishing. With the advent of PCs, some job seekers feel the urge to "be creative" using various type sizes and fonts. Avoid this in business correspondence. Except in rare cases, business letters should look conservative. If you want to be creative, do so in your choice of words. Save Ventura Publisher and Aldus Pagemaker for your Christmas cards.

14. Using a post office box as an address. Except in rare cases, such as conducting a confidential job search, use a street address. Post office boxes seem "transient."

15. Oddball phrasing, such as "an opportunity to expand my strengths and delete my weaknesses . . ." Or, "You may feel that I'm a tad overqualified." Or, "Enclosed herewith please find my resume." Do you talk that way? You should write the way you talk. Avoid bad phrasing by having others critique your letters.

16. Typos, like "thankyou for your assistance."

17. Mailing form letters. Some letters contain "fill in the blanks." Generic forms don't work well.

18. Not saying enough. One want ad letter read, "Please accept my enclosed resume for the position of Executive Director. Thank you." That's too short. A letter is an opportunity to sell. So *say something* about yourself.

19. Ending with "Thank you for your consideration." EVERYONE ends their letters this way, so please don't.

    Try something different, like "I'm excited about talking further," or "I know I could do a good job for you." The same goes for "Sincerely," and "Sincerely yours." EVERYONE uses them. Find something different like "Good wishes," "With best regards," or "With great enthusiasm."

20. WRITING IN ALL CAPS. IT'S HARD TO READ. DON'T DO IT.

21. Abbreviating Cir., Ave., Dec., and all other words. Take time to spell words out. It looks so much better.

22. Forgetting to enclose your resume. If you say you're enclosing one, then do.

23. Justifying right margins. When you "justify right," you create large gaps between words inside your sentences. See?

24. Forgetting the date and/or salutation.

25. Using dot matrix printers. Most are hard to read and they make you look like an engineer. Whenever possible, use a laser printer, even if you have to borrow one.

26. Talking nonsense. "I work in instilling proper conduits for mainstream educational connections while also encouraging individual creative forms." What? Run that one by me again.

27. Forgetting to put the letter in the envelope. (I received an empty FEDEX package yesterday.)

28. The 300-word paragraph. The worst mistake in marketing is writing too long. Limit sentences to seven or eight words, and limit paragraphs to four or five lines. In letter writing, short is usually better. I try to limit my own letters to one page, seldom two. I believe if I can't say it well in one page, I probably can't say it well at all.

More about endings & avoiding "Sincerely"

"Thank you for your time and consideration" appears too often and sounds like a form of begging. "Sincerely" is generally a poor close to a letter, because nearly everyone uses it. Why should you? This is your chance to be "new and different"—and employers like that.

"Very truly yours" is nearly as bad, because it's used almost exclusively by lawyers. After threatening to sue you, they close with a coldhearted "Very truly yours."

World-famous photographer Ansel Adams was a great letter writer. (See *Ansel Adams: Letters and Images 1916-1984*, Little, Brown and Company.) We can take a lesson from him. Some of his letters ended with humor: "Cheeriow, luff and all that," "LET'S GO!!!," and "Whoops." Others ended with heart: "All best, always," "With all best wishes," and "Warmest greetings to all."

Business letters can be warm and friendly as long as they're not too personal. You have to sense the character of your audience and write accordingly. Some readers can stand more warmth than others. In general, it's better to be too warm than too distant.

Phyllis Record sent me a thoughtful note that ended with "Thinking the best for you." That heartfelt note encouraged me to renew an old friendship—and hire her again!

This year Howard Edson wrote his own Christmas card, a small booklet of his thoughts on life. He signed it "Season's blessings"—quite striking compared to the usual "Merry Christmas, Happy New Year!"

After an eight-hour job interview, Steve Jorgensen wrote a thank you note that ended "With kindest personal regards." It was the perfect touch.

Next time, instead of closing with "Sincerely," "Best regards," or "Very truly yours," let yourself risk a better ending. Two of my personal favorites are "Enthusiastically," and "Good wishes, always." You could try something like:

All best wishes,
Best wishes for your future,
With confidence,
Just to keep in touch with you,
More shortly,
Warmest greetings to all, or
Yours always.

Remember, the ending of a letter is just as important as the beginning and the middle. It's your one chance to make a strong lasting impression.

Try using stamped reply envelopes

If you're doing a small mailing to a carefully selected list of important contacts, say to thirty recruiters in your targeted geographic area, it might be worthwhile including a self-addressed stamped envelope. It's a convenience to the reader, and it may increase your response dramatically. I would try this tactic with any important letter where I definitely want an answer.

Advantages of the plain white envelope

I always open envelopes with no return name or address. I'm afraid not to. Who knows what's in them?

I once received a mailer that looked like junk mail. It was one of those envelope-like packages you pull apart at the seams to expose the contents, like the things your bank sends at the end of the year for tax purposes. I opened it on the way to the trash can. And surprise! It was a $5,000 check for a consulting assignment. Since that time I seldom throw away unopened "junk mail." There are some real treasures in there.

I never throw plain envelopes away unopened, either—especially if the name and address are handwritten or typed onto the envelope (mass-produced labels and bulk postage are a tipoff that this could be junk mail). Try some different mailing approaches and see what results you get.

Personal and confidential

Never mark an envelope "personal and confidential," unless it really is. Yes, you may fool the secretary and get the letter to the right person. But if they open it expecting something extremely urgent—perhaps an emergency—only to find a job-seeker, the results can be negative. Most people don't like to feel they've been tricked.

It's like getting an executive on the phone by saying his house is on fire. It works. You do get the targeted person on the phone, but the rest of the conversation can only be disastrous.

There are times when "personal and confidential" is appropriate, such as when security would be breached, in an emergency, or when time is of the essence. In these cases, use the notation without worrying. That's what it's for.

How to select a mailing list

List selection is critical to a successful mailing. It just doesn't make sense to send a sales letter to someone who couldn't possibly be interested.

Where do you get the right names?

First of all, you compile them yourself. Begin with your own contact network. That's the most important list you could ever get your hands on, because those people know and trust you. You're a known quantity to them. (Remember, the business world is suspicious of "strangers.") Your friendship list will be your biggest ally in your search for new employment.

Get other lists from:
Professional organizations
  (names of their members)
Telephone directories
Contacts Influential
Your city directory
The newspaper (business section, special inserts)
Chambers of commerce
Directories In Print (a directory of directories)

Lists you can buy

I've found the best lists are those you create and verify yourself, but if you're in a hurry, or want to do a mass mailing—say 1,000 pieces—you can buy or rent names. These list compilers will send you free catalogues:

1. Dun & Bradstreet, Inc., 3 Sylvan Way, Parsippany, New Jersey 07054; 800-526-0651.

2. Hugo Dunhill Mailing Lists Inc., 630 Third Avenue,
    New York, New York 10017; 800-223-6454.

3. PCS Mailing List Company, 85 Constitution Lane, Danvers, Massachusetts 01923; 800-532-LIST.

4. Ed Burnett Consultants, 100 Paragon Drive South, Montvale, New Jersey 07645; 800-223-7777.

Be a list-monger

Be on the lookout for lists and directories. Get your hands on them and don't let go. If they're affordable, buy your own directories so you can mark them and reuse them.

Some directories are free. Get them. Some cost as little as $5 or $10. Grab them. Some cost $25-$35. Buy them if you will need them often. Borrow expensive directories from the library. Copying names and titles from the library is the worst-case scenario because it's slow and boring. I prefer to find smaller directories I can buy and own—usually those under $25. I have a filing cabinet full of them.

Don't forget that some associations sell their membership lists on pre-printed labels, so you can buy the labels and skip the data entry—a big time-saver, although labels tend to look like "mass mailings."

Some lists come on computer disk, a great idea if you need a lot of names—and if the list is current. Some list services offer their names "on line" so you can access them over a modem.

Where to get the names of executive recruiters

1. Buy a copy of *The Directory of Executive Recruiters* published annually by Kennedy Publications, Templeton Road, Fitzwilliam, NH 03447; 603-585-6544, FAX 585-9555, $39.95. All listings in the directory are available on pressure-sensitive labels (but look mass-mailed).

2. Contact Ken Cole, publisher of "The Recruiting & Search Report," and author of *The Headhunter Strategy*. P.O. Box 9433 Panama City Beach, FL 32407; 800-634-4548 or 904-235-3733. Ken publishes directories of executive search firms by industry, functional specialty, and geographic location.

   Directories are revised quarterly. General lists are $9.00 each with a minimum order of three. Mention this book and get a FREE directory with purchase of three at the regular price. For an extra charge, you can get a custom geographic printout of all the recruiters in your area.

Verify all names, titles, and addresses

My definition of a directory is "something that's obsolete the day it comes off the press." Why? Because people move so often.

Every time you use a list, verify names and titles. Call the company and ask, "Is Marcia Cooke still in charge of accounting?" Five times out of ten they'll say, "No, Marcia has left the company. Ron Black is now in charge of accounting."

Verifying names is a lot of work, but it's worth it. Letters that don't go to an identifiable person are useless. People don't like to receive mail addressed to someone else, especially their predecessor. Readers like their mail personalized. I think you're better off sending 50 letters to the right people than mailing 500 pieces to an outdated list.

Follow up. Follow up. Follow up.

An extremely well-written and timely letter will get response automatically. People will call you. But, you'll improve your odds dramatically if you follow your letters with a phone call. (Even a great letter can sit unanswered on the reader's desk for weeks.)

In nineteen years as a marketer, I've followed dozens of letters with phone calls. It's not at all uncommon to hear something like this: "I've got your letter right here. I've been meaning to call you."

Yes, they've been meaning to call me, but there's a 98 percent chance they never would have called, had I not called them first. Why? Because they're too busy.

How to follow a letter with a phone call

It took me years, and lots of calls during which my hands were shaking, to decide what to say after I'd sent a letter. (I always use first names when I phone, but you may prefer Mr. or Ms. for those one or more steps above you in a business setting.) The script I settled on after a decade of agony goes something like this:

"Hi Tom, this is Bill Frank calling you from Denver. I sent you a letter last week and wanted to find out if you've received it."

Simple, isn't it?

I've found that once I ask this question, two things happen. Number one, they say they've received the letter, and they launch into a fifteen-minute response to it. They tell me everything I need to know, and then they let me ask questions.

Number two, they haven't seen the letter or the mailing. If they haven't seen the letter, I tell them I'll send another one immediately and that I'll follow up after they've received it.

If they want to know what the letter is about, I don't tell them, unless I feel absolutely confident I can sell myself over the phone. Usually, I don't try it. That's why I wrote the letter in the first place. I needed an icebreaker. I want them to have some background information—exactly the right information—before we talk.

I loaded the document with crucial information. It has exactly the right appeal. It's concise and well written. It's polished. It creates a highly favorable impression. It makes me something of a known quantity instead of a complete stranger, so it's usually to my advantage to wait until the reader sees the letter before trying to sell myself.

To repeat: if they ask what the letter is about, I say, "If it's okay with you, I'd rather let you see the letter. It's complicated. There's a lot in it. I'll give you a call in a few days after you've received it. Is that okay?"

Usually it is. Callers seldom press me to tell them immediately "what this is about." They're too busy. Life is too short.

By the way, most people are friendly on the telephone. I've made hundreds of calls, and all my worst fears about being attacked, sworn at, or hung up on have never materialized. Most people are supportive. They like to help, if given the opportunity. On the other hand, I'm not pushy on the telephone. I'm friendly and helpful myself. For instance, I treat secretaries like "helpers," not like "barriers" or "obstacles to progress." I don't try to "get through them." I ask for their help and advice, and they usually cooperate.

Measure your results

How can you tell if you've truly communicated? You get a positive response. Therefore, if you don't get the results you want, you don't have the letter right yet. Work on it some more.

Avoid mass mailings

I'm not a fan of mass mailings. By "mass mailings" I mean mailing letters by the thousands. I believe in targeted mailing, writing to clearly identified groups for a specific purpose. I can see sending 100 letters to selected search firms. Or 250 letters to targeted companies. Or 300 letters to the members of your personal contact network. I can't see mailing to one thousand companies. To me that means you haven't done your homework and you're really shooting in the dark. Yes, maybe there's a chance one of those letters will hit, but at what cost? Fifteen hundred dollars?

Job-hunters are typically budget-conscious, making every dollar count. I think you're better off writing an excellent letter and mailing it to fewer people than writing a mediocre letter and mailing it to thousands.

"We couldn't ignore your aggressive letter campaign."

What are "formula letters?"

They are letters that are easy to use, because you simply fill in the blanks. Let's take a look at two examples: the problem-solver letter and the accomplishment-oriented letter.

1. *The problem-solver letter*

Here you introduce yourself as the solution to a difficult business challenge. It could be lack of personnel policies and procedures, or low employee morale. It can be *anything*. The important thing is that it's the kind of problem you love solving.

To write this letter, first decide what kind of problem(s) you want to solve. Then ask companies if they have that particular problem—and if they want it solved. (Some companies like their problems.)

Isn't that simple?

The formula for the letter looks like this:

1. Do you have _____ problem?

2. If so, I might be able to help (I'm the solution).

3. Here's why (list key accomplishments).

4. Here's how you're going to benefit by having me around (go heavy on the benefits).

5. Close the sale: After you have had time to review this material, I'll call you to get your reactions.

A real-world example

Nancy Thomas came to see me after graduating from law school. She had written to 250 Denver law firms, and had called the senior partners in all 250 firms. The net result of her effort was two courtesy interviews and no job offers.

Nancy was upset. She had tried everything. She had answered ads in legal journals and newspapers. She had done extensive networking and nothing was working. (Imagine having spent five years and $23,000 on an advanced degree, only to find no job waiting.)

We analyzed the situation. It wasn't that no attorneys needed help. They did. Show me a major law firm that isn't swamped. The real problem was the economy: We were in a recession, and lawyers were afraid to add new staff—and $20,000 to $30,000 in overhead—in uncertain times.

We pictured our ideal "problem situation" graphically, even humorously. This was the "perfect" work environment for Nancy to walk into. And here's what it looked like:

- It's midnight.
- An attorney sits at his desk, still working.
- He's bleary-eyed. He had a couple of drinks at dinner and has now consumed a pot of coffee.
- He has a headache.
- The office is a mess—he's disorganized.
- His tie is loose, sleeves rolled up, shirt wrinkled.
- The desk is stacked with papers.
- His wife has called him three times for help with the kids.
- Tomorrow he has the biggest court case of his life, and he's going up against F. Lee Bailey.

To this imaginary attorney, we sent the following letter:

OVERWORKED? NEED HELP?

Wouldn't it be fantastic to be able to hire a part-time
lawyer when you need help in emergencies?

Nancy Thomas . . .

— Was admitted to the Colorado Bar on October 17, 19—.
— Has a commitment to law.
— Deals well with clients.
— Is eager to learn . . . likes to be "taught."
— Turns out quality work, and
— Is unhappy cutting corners.

She is heavily experienced in . . .

The field of Estates and Trusts; and is very interested in (1) Real Estate,
(2) Natural Resources, and (3) Tax and Corporate matters.

YOUR FIRM WILL GAIN

— Expert help without the cost of a full-time salary.
— Flexibility in your scheduling.
— Relief from pressures and deadlines.
— A co-operative, interested colleague.

I'M AVAILABLE TO HELP YOU NOW

Call 893-7989 and ask for Nancy Thomas
388 South Monaco Parkway
Denver, Colorado 80219

The letter produced instant results. Apparently, we found the right appeal. Within a week, Nancy had two or three part-time legal jobs. She chose her own hours and decided which assignments she wanted to accept. She was her own boss. She became the first freelance attorney in the country, and she still continues as a freelancer today. Nancy has had opportunities to accept full-time assignments, but declined them. Freelancing was too much fun.

Nancy solved her problem—not by focusing on her own needs and frustrations, but by focusing on ways to help others. It was truly a win-win situation. And there's an answer like this to every career problem. The answer may not be obvious at first. It often takes several hours—sometimes weeks—of wrestling with the problem to see the solution. But it's there. And it can often be implemented with a well-planned letter.

Take action

Think about yourself for a moment. Do you want to solve accounting problems? If so, exactly what kind? Do you want to solve marketing problems? If so, where?

List some of the kinds of problems you'd like to solve, and be as specific and detailed as you possibly can.

1. _____

2. _____

3. _____

4. _____

Now, picture a company badly in need of your services. What does it look like inside? What's happening? Exaggerate the situation greatly so that everything seems larger than life. Write down the particulars.

1. _____

2. _____

3. _____

4. _____

5. _____

6. _____

Next draft your letter. You'll be on the way to some well-deserved interviews (where you'll often be the only candidate for the job).

2. The accomplishment-oriented letter

The word resume means "summary," and resumes began as biographical sketches. They listed hobbies and interests, and things like your height and weight.

Today, resumes are more sales- and marketing-oriented. They have become sales tools. Some are so accomplishment-oriented ("at my last job, I worked a miracle") that they bear almost no resemblance to the modest resumes of the past. If you have an accomplishment-oriented resume, it's easy to cut and paste a marketing letter. The two-step formula for this letter is:

1. I hit home runs at my last job, so . . .
2. I can hit home runs for you.

Here is the text of an excellent accomplishment-oriented letter that was sent to me:

Maurice M. Bordeaux
4421 Oak View Road
Sioux Falls, South Dakota 57103

May 24, 19—

William S. Frank
President
CareerLab
9085 East Mineral Circle, STE 330
Englewood, Colorado 80112

Dear Mr. Frank:

For some time my wife and I have been discussing a move from the South Dakota prairie to Colorado, and my research shows CareerLab to be active there. In eleven years with Northern Bank, I have developed skills in managing people, budgets, products, and services. These skills work well in any organization or profession.

Here are some of my accomplishments:

o   As Director of Consumer Loans, I successfully managed 20 loan officers in 8 locations. In four years we tripled our outstandings ($15,000,000 to $45,000,000) and profits, while keeping our delinquencies at the same low of 1.0%-1.3%.

o   As Retail Manager of our largest branch, my staff was motivated to increase deposits 30% ($73,000,000 to $90,000,000) over the last three years. I accomplished this with measurements, rewards, and enthusiastic training sessions.

o   In the last three years I reduced my branch staff from 30 to 23 (23%) by implementing automation and reorganization. This saved us $70,000 annually.

o   I developed our large line revolving credit product and also developed new fee income which is now 20% of total fee income.

Since my training has been in the banking profession, that is where I will concentrate my search. However, I think you will agree that the skills I have developed are adaptable to other situations. I will be home for two weeks beginning May 24th. I would like to visit with you and look forward to hearing from you some time then.

With best wishes,

Maurice M. Bordeaux

Steven crafted a thoughtful, persuasive letter. I could tell by reading it that he got some phone calls. Well-written letters always do.

To summarize

As a general rule, a marketing letter is:
1. addressed to a specific person by name and title;
2. brief, short, and direct—seldom more than one page;
3. intriguing, never boring;
4. written by you, never canned;
5. tailored to the audience;
6. warm and personal, not cold and analytical, and
7. infused with energy, excitement, and enthusiasm.

What do conservative people say?

Some conservative businesspeople resist writing "sales letters." They say, "That's fine for salespeople, but it really wouldn't work for me. I'm an accountant (or a lawyer or an engineer . . . or whatever) and we're very conservative."

That's true. Some businesspeople are conservative, but not all of them. If you're an executive or a professional, all this means is that you have to tone down your sales letter to meet your market. You have to tailor your approach to your recipient (choose the right appeal).

There are at least five kinds of letters:
1. Hot
2. Warm
3. Neutral
4. Cool
5. Cold

When you draft your thoughts, think about who will receive them. A doctor? A lawyer? A union steward?

If you're conservative, you can still use a marketing letter, but cool it off to match your audience. It's still a sales letter, because it's selling, but it's a subtle soft-sell. It's less obvious, but it's loaded with benefits for the reader.

As you page through this book, you'll find examples of soft-sell letters that any professional could feel comfortable sending.

About the examples that follow

This book consists of letters I wrote myself, letters that were written to me, and letters my clients and I created for their job campaigns. I know the reactions they got: I know they worked. These are the best job-search letters I've seen. So if you read and study them, you'll know everything you need to know about letter-writing. You'll open doors that have been closed to you before.

And that's a promise.

Anonymity and fictitious names, places, and companies

I've printed the real names of friends who wanted to see themselves in print. All other names, companies, addresses, telephone numbers, situations and events in this book are fictitious to preserve the privacy of the contributors. Any similarity to any real person, living or dead, or any company or business unit is strictly coincidental.

How the letters are arranged

The letters which follow are filed by "main theme"—their central idea. However, many letters have several themes in them. This has made organizing difficult.

For example, reply letters are really a form of self-introduction. So are sales letters. Thank you letters are often sales letters in disguise. Announcements and thank you letters are also PR/relationship-building letters. You get the idea.

Therefore, don't look for letters in only one place. Browse through the material. The letter you want may be filed elsewhere in the book.

If you're an accountant, read letters to and from marketing people. If you're an engineer, read letters by geologists. You'll miss a lot if you confine your reading to only examples from your own profession or specialty. Read all through the book. See what you can discover.

You may want to cut-and-paste to get the letter that's ideal for you. By the way, that's how I wrote the query letter that produced a contract for this book.

Why I break my own rules

In the letters that follow, I've occasionally broken my own rules. For example, some of them lack a date, telephone number, return address, secretarial initials, or enclosure notations—or they are crammed onto the page. Usually, that's because I've condensed a two-page letter onto one page to save space. Normally, a long letter would go onto the next page, and all the proper data would be included.

How to read the page notations

The bottom of every page lists the section number, the page number, and the kind of letter you're looking at. For example:

15.1   SELL YOUR ACCOMPLISHMENTS   244

Section   Kind of letter   Page
Number   Number

What the footnote means

When the footnote symbol appears on a page, it means the letter is discussed in the notes and comments, beginning on page 323. A letter is featured because it:
1. is easy to adapt for a quick job-search;
2. produced an interview;
3. resulted in a job offer (or desired result); or
4. involves an interesting story.

Final note: Mail your letters

In the early 1980s I worked with my first oil and gas geologist. Randy's background was solid, but his attitude was negative. He was full of reasons why things wouldn't work.

Randy *did* put a lot of energy into writing a sales letter, and it came out very well. Then he put a lot of time and effort into collecting a list of names to mail that letter to. Surprisingly, after all that work, he never mailed his letters. I'm not sure why. Maybe he was afraid they wouldn't work.

Direct mail is an interesting business. You never know what the results will be until after you mail the letters. Guesses as to what will happen are often wrong. So don't second guess yourself.

Mail your letters!

PART THREE | 200 OF THE WORLD'S BEST LETTERS

1

Copyright © 1993 Eli Stein. Reprinted with permission.

Announcements

The world economy is uncertain, and for many people job-hunting has become a lifestyle. With mergers, takeovers, bankruptcies, and new government legislation, you could be unemployed overnight—even if you own the company!

Make it a priority to let your network of recruiters, personal friends, and business acquaintances know where you are and what you're doing, at all times, especially when you change jobs or addresses. Announce changes even if it's an intercompany move.

Once they land a job, ex-job-hunters tend to forget those who've helped them. They get busy packing, moving, tying up loose ends, and taking on the duties of the new assignment; but that's a mistake. Remember, your first duty is to your career. This doesn't mean your new assignment isn't important. It means your friendships and your personal future are equally important.

The quickest way to handle the thank-you task is to give your letter and mailing list to a secretarial service. Let them type and address the letters; you sign them. This requires very little time and energy, probably less than two hours. Believe me, it's time well spent.

The letter on page 31 is a good model. It's a combination newsletter, change of address, and thank-you, all in one—and it's limited to one page.

The best time to find a new job is when you don't need one, and the best time to cultivate business relationships is when everything is going smoothly.

GEORGE L. OCHS
6031 West Rowland Place
Littleton, Colorado 80123
(303) 979-9293 (H)
(303) 629-6653 (W)

November 14, 19—

William S. Frank
President
CareerLab
9085 E. Mineral Circle, Suite 330
Englewood, Colorado 80112

Dear Bill:

After spending nearly three years consulting for Urban Investment and Development Company, I will be moving on to a new assignment. Effective December 2, 19— I will be consulting for The Prudential Insurance Company, Denver Real Estate Investment Office. The past three years were very exciting, being part of a team which managed the construction, lease-up and tenant build-out of City Center 4. Your support throughout these past few years is greatly appreciated. Please keep in touch, as I'm not moving out of town. I'll be just a few blocks down the street. Starting Monday, December 3, 19— I can be reached at:

> The Prudential Insurance Company of America
> Denver Real Estate Investment Office
> 1050 17th Street, Suite 2501
> Denver, Colorado 80265
>
> (303) 629-6653

With many thanks,

George L. Ochs

/cb

Michael R. Walker
7606 Rock Falls Court
Houston, Texas 77095

February 23, 19—

Mr. Alan Forker
Vice President
CareerLab
9085 E. Mineral Circle, Suite 330
Englewood, CO 80112

Dear Al:

Isn't life amazing! Just when you think you have things pretty well figured out, new opportunities come breaking through. A little over six years ago, my career path in Baker Hughes brought us from Oklahoma to Houston, Texas. Just when we were finally getting semi-adjusted to the traffic, crowds and heat, a merger within the corporation landed us in a position that we never expected— unemployed. Now, thanks to my many friends, business acquaintances, and a lot of aggressive networking, we find that our new career opportunity is taking us to Green Bay, Wisconsin, a smaller city that enjoys long winters and short springs!

I'm excited and happy to tell you that I've accepted the position of Vice President, Human Resources and Organizational Development with Employers Health Insurance in Green Bay. Employers is a $1 billion plus company with 2500 employees and is a part of the Lincoln National Corporation. Employers is a pro-employee, quality oriented company that has developed the culture and the customer orientation that allows them to be a leading player in their markets. I'm looking forward to moving back into the insurance and service industry. My official start date is March 1, 19—.

One of the things that I've learned in this transition is the importance of staying in touch with friends, business associates, and my network contacts. Therefore, I wanted to give you my new address and telephone number, in the hope that at some point in the future, I will have the opportunity to repay your friendship and consideration:

> Michael R. Walker
> Vice President, Human Resources and
>   Organizational Development
> Employers Health Insurance
> 1100 Employers Blvd.
> Green Bay, Wisconsin 54344
> (414) 336-1100

Again, I want to thank you for your support, interest, and encouragement. I look forward to staying in touch with you and if I can ever be of any assistance, don't hesitate to call me.

Your friend,

Michael R. Walker

Neil B. Stein
Agent
Michael L. Johnston and Associates
1872 South Bellaire Street, Suite 600
Denver, Colorado 80222
(303) 691-5150

June 13, 19—

Mr. William S. Frank
President
CareerLab
9085 East Mineral Circle, Suite 330
Englewood, CO 80112

Dear Bill:

I'd like to share some very exciting news with you.

As of June 1st, I've established an insurance practice affiliated with
Connecticut Mutual Life, a highly respected "blue chip" company for the last
142 years.

Although I firmly decided before going to work for Connecticut Mutual that I
would never use friendship for business purposes, I feel that it would be
appropriate to at least make you aware of my career change and to offer my
services should your situation warrant it. I would be happy to make an objective appraisal of your present life or disability insurance situation at some
time in the future.

I'm sure you'll agree that because we are friends, you would receive a more
accurate appraisal of your insurance situation from me that you would from a
total stranger who may not have your best interest at heart. I realize the
mere fact that we are friends is no reason why you should buy insurance
from me. On the other hand, it's no reason why you shouldn't, either.

I'll be moving into my new office by the time you receive this letter. My new
address and phone number is above. If you're in the neighborhood, please stop
in and say hello.

Enthusiastically,

Neil B. Stein

NBS/daf

BIG CHANGE!

Please note the following change of business address:

FROM: James L. Rasmus
Manager, Communications and Human Resources
United Technologies Microelectronics Center
1575 Garden of the Gods Road
Colorado Springs, Colorado 80907

TO: James L. Rasmus
Manager, International Personnel
United Technologies Automotive
Avenue Du Tribunal Federal 34
1005 Lausanne
Switzerland
Telephone: 041-21-208614

Thank you for noting this change. Please update your mailing lists
and stay in touch.

Jim Rasmus

FROM:
Norman A. Newton
4505 South Yosemite
Denver, Colorado 80237
Daytime: (303) 771-4357

STARTING DATE: NOW

ENDING DATE: JAN. 31, 19—

NEWS RELEASE

Norman Newton has joined McDATA Corporation as Vice President of Manufacturing. In this capacity, Newton will be responsible for overseeing all manufacturing operations for McDATA's network communication product lines. Prior to joining McDATA, Newton worked for Samsonite Corporation as Vice President of Operations. Other positions at Samsonite included Director of Special Projects and General Manager of the El Paso/Juarez operations. Newton has also worked for Atari Inc. as Managing Director of European Operations. Newton brings 25 years' experience in managing industrial manufacturing operations to McDATA Corporation.

Career Direction

The first part of any job-hunt is figuring out where you're going. As Dick Bolles, author of *What Color Is Your Parachute?* says, "The more time you spend in preparation, the less time you spend on the pavement."

Take a sheet of paper for each job title you've had. On the left side of the page, write all the things you liked about the job. On the right side, list the things you disliked. Nothing is too silly to mention. If you disliked the army-green color of the carpet, say so. If you disliked reporting to two bosses at the same time, list that. Once finished, look for patterns. Design your "likes" into the new job, and design your "dislikes" out.

Then make a four-column shopping list: 1) things I want in the new assignment; 2) things I don't want; 3) things I must have; and 4) things that would be fun, but frivolous, like a car phone or window view of the ocean.

Once that's complete, write an essay about your ideal first month on the new job. Describe each day in depth. On your first day of work, the boss hands you six file folders with problems to solve. What's in the folders?

Your friends and acquaintances know you well, perhaps better than you know yourself. They can give you valuable information about the business world and about your skills and abilities. If you're feeling uncertain about your career path, seek their advice and ideas. You might be pleasantly surprised by their creative suggestions.

Reprinted with permission.

Ramona M. Vargas
11726 San Vicente Blvd.
Los Angeles, CA 90049
(310) 207-1963 (o) • (310) 207-2438 (h)

May 18, 19—

Carol Shannahan
655 Redwood Highway
Mill Valley, California 94941

Dear Carol,

My present position with the National Management Association is part-time, and I'm trying to define my career goals. I have a clear idea how I would like to proceed, but I'm not sure what position or department within a company that fits.

Enclosed is a scenario of how I want to spend the next five years. It is obviously idealistic. (The scenario was an exercise of envisioning what my future might look like if I "had a magic wand.") I seek your help to make it realistic.

Following the scenario are two lists—one telling what I've done, and one telling some of what I can do—as well as a letter describing how some people perceive me. I am asking you to respond to some or all of the following questions:

1. How can I make this scenario more realistic?
2. What beginning position in a company am I describing?
3. Who, if not the CEO, is the logical person for me to report to?
4. What is the career path to move to external and international areas?
5. Is it appealing to a company to have me on retainer?
6. Where are the holes in my logic?
7. What training do I need to support these goals?
8. Is there someone else you think might help me clarify these goals?
9. Do you have suggestions as to what company/industry might have such a position, and/or at what level I should make contact to pursue such a position?
10. Any other suggestions/direction?

I realize every organization is different, but I respect your insight and experience, and believe your suggestions would be applicable.

As with anyone in the job market, my internal time line is short, so a quick response would be greatly appreciated. A self-addressed envelope is enclosed for that purpose, or if it's more convenient for you to call me, please do.

You have my sincere gratitude for helping me to pursue my career goals, Carol.

Ramona

January 15, 19—

Mr. Richard R. Nelson
President
REMAX
P.O. Box 255
Ft. Collins, Colorado 80522

Dear Mr. Nelson:

I was in the audience last Thursday when you spoke about Just
In Time (JIT) and Total Quality Management (TQM). Your talk was
inspirational—I took five pages of notes—and I enjoyed meeting you.

Because you are a leader in the Ft. Collins business community, your
advice and ideas are of value to me. After 13 productive years here
(summary of accomplishments enclosed), I am seeking to make contact
with other Ft. Collins business executives who may be in a position to
provide me with advice regarding my next career step.

I will call you next Thursday between 3:00 and 4:00 p.m., and I would
appreciate hearing your thoughts about where you think someone with
my skills and abilities might be needed. Please note, I will not be asking you for a position in your firm. I ask only for five minutes of your
valuable time, and the benefit of your experience.

Many thanks!

Douglas P. Arnold, Jr.

Enclosures

Mr. Richard P. Riley, Jr.
4353 Roswell Road
Atlanta, Georgia 30342
(404) 342-9865

December 1, 19—

William S. Frank
President
CareerLab
9085 E. Mineral Circle, Suite 330
Englewood, Colorado 80112

Dear Mr. Frank:

I am interested in entering the outplacement field and would appreciate any assistance you might be able to offer.

As my enclosed resume outlines, I have had considerable experience in the Human Resources function. I have done extensive training of managers on the job search process and have lectured on the subject before university groups and professional associations. It is my intent at this time to devote my career to this area.

If your professional practice involves activities in which I might be of assistance, I would welcome the opportunity to speak with you. I would be interested in working with you on a permanent or contract basis if your workload requires additional professional assistance.

I have attached a copy of my resume and an article I wrote which appeared in the Wall Street Journal's "National Business Employment Weekly."

I look forward to hearing from you.

Sincerely,

Richard P. Riley, Jr.

RPR:sh
Enclosure

RICHARD E. HART
2700 Valley Drive • Hermosa Beach, California 09254 • (213) 376-3897

November 23, 19—

<u>PERSONAL AND CONFIDENTIAL</u>
Nancy K. Turner
Pacific Bell
11882 West Olympic Boulevard
Los Angeles, California 90064

Dear Ms. Turner:

Since you are legal counsel to one of the largest corporations
in California, I am writing you hoping to obtain some information
pertaining to practicing law as an "in-house" attorney. You are ideally situated to help me gain some insights into corporate practice.

I am writing you this letter because, after seven years of building a
law firm from three employees to twenty, I have rethought my lifetime
objectives, and have decided to change the direction of
my career. I am not writing you seeking employment from Pacific
Bell, as it is my understanding that you are not currently hiring;
however, I am seeking any information which you might have regarding
my job search.

In this effort, I am enclosing my resume, from which you can see that
I have had my share of successes, not only in contributing
to the building of a $1 million-plus-a-year business, but also in the
practice of law. For a variety of reasons, I have decided to make a
career change and have determined that I shall move into an "in-
house" corporate practice.

I would appreciate the opportunity to discuss with you several questions which I have about corporate practice. I will be calling you
in the next few days. For obvious reasons, I must request absolute
confidentiality.

Thank you for your attention.

Very truly yours,

Richard E. Hart

David J. Hansen
6023 S. Eudora Way
Littleton, CO 80121
Residence: (303) 796-9429
Ans. Serv.: (303) 757-2590

August 15, 19—

Mr. William S. Frank
President
CareerLab
9085 E. Mineral Circle, Suite 330
Englewood, CO 80112

Dear Mr. Frank:

Bob Schulz at Jones Intercable suggested I contact you. I am seeking information from individuals active in promoting growing firms, or firms undergoing transition.

I do not expect you to have or know of any "openings" at this time. Rather, I am seeking expertise and guidance in becoming acquainted with one or more firms seeking an experienced manager.

I would like to become associated with a small or mid-sized firm starting up or making the transition to a professionally managed organization. My background includes strategic planning and tactical problem solving that would contribute to any organization needing an experienced and versatile manager. An association with a firm requiring interim or full-time management would be welcomed. My qualification summary is enclosed.

May I have the favor of a brief meeting with you to discuss planning, development and management in small and mid-sized firms? I am told that there are any number of new firms with great ideas that only need good management to establish themselves. I would welcome your ideas on how to contact these firms.

I will contact you by phone on Tuesday, August 20, to arrange a meeting. Thank you for your attention.

Warmly,

David Hansen

Mitchell Dunhill
Senior Geologist
Rocky Mountain Petroleum
5800 South Quebec Street
Englewood, Colorado 80111

October 10, 19—

Dear Mitchell,

As you may be aware, I am a consulting petroleum geologist with over 11 years
of experience in the Rocky Mountain basins. Most recently I was affiliated with
Ladd Petroleum for almost 6 years, and had approximately 25 wells drilled
with 6 new discoveries in several different areas. I have good, broad Rockies
experience, and feel I can provide a valuable service for your company if
given the opportunity.

Until specific consulting or other opportunities come my way, I plan to actively
generate [oilfield] prospects out of my home, predominantly in areas where I
have past experience. These areas include the Williston, Paradox, Central Kansas,
Uinta, Greater Green River, and Piceance Basins. I will concentrate on one or
two of these areas, but have not yet decided which ones.

I would appreciate your input in this matter, primarily in terms of your
company's needs for prospects or specific interest level in particular areas.
I would like to generate plays [discoveries] in areas where you have a strong
interest, hoping that you will want to see these prospects when completed. Your
input will guide me to these areas with minimal waste of time and effort.

I am planning to follow this letter with a phone call to you in a few days to
hear your thoughts and suggestions. Your input will be greatly appreciated.
Also, should you have specific needs for a consultant or a possible full-time
geologist, I would appreciate your interest for that as well.

Thanks for your help!

Bruce R. VanDeventer
Consulting Geologist

Bud Inzer
237 Acoma Street
Denver, Colorado 80223
(303) 771-3548

March 18, 19—

Mr. William S. Frank
President
CareerLab
9085 E. Mineral Circle, Suite 330
Englewood, Colorado 80112

Dear Bill:

Four years ago I attended one of your seminars and your presentation made a distinct impression on me. Your certainty and belief that it is not only possible but practical to pursue work that is fulfilling validated my own convictions. Your success over the years encourages me to seek you out, for the purpose of learning more about the career development field today. As someone who followed your heart and stayed with it, your experience and opinions are very valuable to me.

Like you, my own career frustrations became a motivation for educating myself in the process of career change. Although, for several years, I developed and led a number of successful workshops and consultations, I became frustrated with the financial position. I am presently running my own small promotions business but am interested in returning to the career development field. My purpose is not to look for a job, but to gain more information.

I would like to call you shortly to arrange a meeting. I know that your time is valuable so please be assured I won't ask for more than 30 minutes.

With warm regards,

Bud Inzer

3

Part-time Employment

Inactivity during unemployment can contribute to depression. Usually, the longer you are unemployed, the lower your self-esteem falls. Therefore, never let yourself be "unemployed" in your mind, even for a day.

Always find something productive to do. If necessary, volunteer a few hours a week or work part-time for a friend. Job-hunters may question this, but almost any work is better than no work at all. Even temporary work provides contact with people and the opportunity to care and contribute.

If you look around, you'll see unmet needs everywhere. If you want to help, the world needs you. That's why you never need to be "unemployed"—especially in your own mind.

Temporary work isn't necessarily a dead end. I call it a career field goal. It isn't seven points, but it isn't zero points, either. What do the successful pro football teams do when they can't score a touchdown? They go for the field goal, knowing they'll attempt the touchdown later.

Pay attention to your language. Don't say things like, "I'm out of work. I have nothing to do. No one wants me." That's not only ridiculous, it's terribly damaging to your sense of self-worth.

In addition, you want potential employers to perceive you as busy and active, not bored and depressed. Rather than say, "I've been out of work for 18 weeks," say, "I've got several things going while I'm in the market. I work part-time for Hewlett Packard on a new product launch, and I'm helping Memorial Hospital set up their SIDS department." Doesn't that sound better? You bet it does.

The attitude that you're working even though not employed communicates action, movement, and momentum! Just what employers look for.

Berry's World

WORKAHOLIC
—
WILL WORK
FOR THE
FUN OF IT.

© 1991 by NEA, Inc. 12B

BERRY'S WORLD reprinted with permission of NEA, Inc.

May 6, 19—

Mr. William S. Frank
President
CareerLab
9085 E. Mineral Circle, Suite 330
Englewood, Colorado 80112

Dear Mr. Frank:

Is you company under PRESSURE?

Are your employees OVERWORKED?

Are DEADLINES difficult to meet?

Wouldn't it be great to have:

```
        *     Experienced     *
        *       Efficient      *
        *   Part-Time Help    *
```

to alleviate the stress!

<u>Nancy Yoshida</u>

— has ten years' experience in accounting
— maintains a high level of productivity and accuracy
— uses superior verbal and written communication skills
— listens effectively
— is self-directed
— likes to learn
— has a valuable ability to organize
— is adaptable
— is cooperative

Nancy enjoys:

— team problem solving and development
— coordinating
— client relations
— staff development
— instructing
— promoting a growth-oriented environment

Let's discuss how we could work together. Call 771-4232.

Sincerely,

Nancy Yoshida

BRUCE D. ROBERTSON, CPA
Assistant Professor

ROBERTS WESLEYAN COLLEGE
2301 Westside Drive
Rochester, New York 14624-1997

(716) 594-9471 x324 (W)
(716) 594-2766 (H)

December 8, 19—

Mr. Bill Frank
President
CareerLab
9085 East Mineral Circle, STE 330
Englewood, Colorado 80112

Dear Bill:

Thank you for your support during my recent job search. As you know, I have accepted a job as Assistant Professor of Business at Roberts Wesleyan College, a small Christian Liberal Arts college founded in 1866. I am really enjoying teaching in the college setting. This semester, my favorite course is Income Tax. Next semester, I will be teaching Micro Economics, Cost Accounting, and Beginning Accounting. I am also involved in developing international courses and working them into the existing curriculum.

I will be expanding my consulting practice in accounting and international business in Denver during breaks from school.

I plan to be consulting in Denver on the following dates:

— Friday, December 18th through Sunday, January 10th
— Friday, February 12th through Monday, February 22nd
— Thursday, March 31st through Monday, April 11th
— Monday, May 16th through Friday, August 18th

If you know of companies that might need tax, accounting, international or financial help, I would like to know about them.

Thank you for your continuing help and support.

In friendship,

Bruce D. Robertson, CPA

BDR:bl

BRUCE D. ROBERTSON, CPA

3182 South Holly Street
Denver, Colorado 80222

(303) 756-7434 (H)
(303) 779-1417 (W)

March 6, 19—

Ms. Loretta B. Hazen
Vice President Administration
The Weyerhauser Corporation
6000 Stewart Street
Seattle, Washington 98101

Dear Ms. Hazen:

<u>Do you have a one-time overload project</u>?

— An accounting crisis?

— A new computer system?

— A new European operation?

<u>Would you like to hire a part-time financial expert</u>?

Someone who . . .

— Established an international consulting firm.

— Was number two man in a European operation which grew
from $5 million in sales to $55 million in sales in
two years.

— Has 17 years of experience in administration and finance.

I'm in the process of a full-time job search, <u>but I would be interested in
helping you part time in overload situations</u>.

Please call me at your earliest convenience at (303) 779-1417, or return the
enclosed postage-paid questionnaire.

Many thanks,

Bruce D. Robertson

BDR:bl
Enclosures

January 11, 19—

Bill:

Congratulations!

By re-entering the workplace you certainly have rewritten the book on "Great Ways to Retire!"

Despite its many problems, steering the university battleship through choppy waters has got to be more satisfying than running a major bank—and trying to collect from all the countries south of the border.

I have ended my Lone Ranger counseling act, and am negotiating on a corporate finance job back in Peru and I'm also talking to one of Denver's larger law firms. Neither idea is going to crystallize for a while, however, so I've got several weeks of time on my hands.

Could you use any emergency help from a local citizen—who also served time in Missouri?

Best regards,

Dick Ruby

ARE YOU UNDERSTAFFED?

Do you have full-time secretarial needs,
but only a part-time budget?

Wouldn't it be great to have a part-time secretary with all the skills and experience of a full-time secretary? Here are some of my skills and abilities:

- Get things done and handle a variety of tasks EFFICIENTLY.
- Organize my time and complete tasks quickly and ACCURATELY.
- Work very well independently—am an ambitious SELF-STARTER.
- Have extremely good PEOPLE SKILLS.
- Am super CONSCIENTIOUS.
- Will turn in work that is neat and PICTURE PERFECT.
- Am a skilled typist—90 WORDS PER MINUTE.
- Am thorough in RECORD KEEPING.
- Show painstaking attention to DETAIL.
- Am attractive and WELL-GROOMED.
- I have a STRONG and very COMPETENT secretarial background, as well as experience in SUPERVISION.
- I have worked as a secretary/administrative assistant in a variety of areas, including STOCK BROKERAGE FIRMS, OIL AND GAS, LAW and CONSTRUCTION MANAGEMENT.
- I have two years experience as a legal secretary, having done bookkeeping, payroll, journal and general ledger posting, quarterly reports, client billings, as well as the typing of all legal documents.
  —BONUS: I love to be BUSY.

I AM LOOKING FOR PART-TIME SECRETARIAL WORK
AND WILL PROVIDE YOU WITH TOP-NOTCH, QUALITY SERVICE.
IF YOU ARE LOOKING FOR THE BEST, WHY NOT GIVE ME A CALL?

Bobbi Gutentag
100 Reed Street, Lakewood, Colorado 80215

You can reach me weekdays between 8:00-10:00 a.m. at 231-4765.

LAI NAM PHAN
ONE POST OFFICE SQUARE
BOSTON, MA 02109
617-423-4114 (O)
617-227-1584 (H)

May 21, 19—

William S. Frank
President
CareerLab
9085 E. Mineral Circle, Suite 330
Englewood, Colorado 80112

Dear Mr. Frank:

I would like to provide your firm with a convenient, high-quality, low-cost training alternative. I excel in this work and enjoy offering training:

— as short-term or long-term repetitive assignments
— as a substitute for unavailable staff (vacation, illness, travel)
— to enhance current staff temporarily for special projects
— <u>without adding to your headcount or benefits costs</u>

As head of a management consulting firm, are your talents needed more for marketing and directing? Are you and your staff of consultants less inclined to do the daily grind of standup training? My interest and expertise is stand-up training for all areas of business management from new-hire orientation to outplacement. I specialize in flexibility, short notice, and teaching those basic, repetitive courses frequently requested by new or smaller firms.

My training expertise focuses in the areas of management and professional development. I've had over 10,000 adult classroom training hours in business. I'm a highly experienced trainer with top-notch group facilitation skills.

My background includes start-up companies, large multi-national and high-tech firms, as well as the public sector. With my word processing equipment I can tailor my materials (or yours) to meet client needs.

Keep me in mind. Don't turn down a strategically important or profitable opportunity because it's too basic for your firm to handle. When you need some temporary help, I'm available. I'll bet a need will arise soon.

Let's talk,

Lai Nam Phan

Clinton D. Jones
1330 Marion Street
Denver, Colorado 80218
(303) 861-7356

November 3, 19—

Mr. William S. Frank
President
CareerLab
9085 E. Mineral Circle, Suite 330
Englewood, Colorado 80112

Dear Bill,

I have begun to market myself as a personnel manager on a permanent part-time basis to small firms (25-75 employees) in the greater metro area. I am open to any type of organization or industry, but I prefer professional firms such as:

> Law
> Medicine
> Engineering
> Accounting
> Financial Planning
> Dental
> Architecture

Should you be aware or become aware of any of your business associates, friends, or acquaintances who may be considering the need for a part-time Personnel Manager, I would appreciate your giving me their names to contact personally.

Any assistance or suggestions that you can give me will be appreciated.

Your friend,

Clinton D. Jones

CDJ/
Enclosure

January 25, 19—

Ms. Pat Jones
Robert Half, Inc.
2000 College Parkway
Ft. Collins, Colorado 80522

Dear Ms. Jones:

Having completed the financial turnaround of Ft. Collins Manufacturing,
I am now seeking a regular full-time position. I'm sending you my current
resume and a summary of my recent significant accomplishments as
an accounting, finance and computer systems manager.

I would like to call your attention to the fact that I am particularly
strong in working with computerized accounting systems.

Having been a resident of Ft. Collins since 19—, I am aware that locating
a suitable full-time position may take some time. I would appreciate
being considered for appropriate Robert Half temporary assignments.
I am available to interview at your convenience and can begin work
immediately.

Yours truly,

Douglas P. Arnold

DPA/
Enclosure

4

No Resume?

Everyone knows it's a good idea to keep an updated resume, but few people actually do. We're just too busy.

Suppose your resume is outdated and a headhunter calls and requests it overnight for an important high-paying job. What do you do? Should you send an old, incomplete resume—one with 300-word paragraphs? Absolutely not!

Remember, you never get a second chance to make a first impression. An outdated, poorly drafted resume will not sell you well, because it doesn't show you at your best.

Your competitors' resumes will come in looking clean, crisp, and tightly written. Yours will look weak by comparison. How will you compete? Do you think you'll be interviewed? Perhaps . . . but maybe not.

Regardless of what the books say, you can't draft a good resume overnight, especially if you're a well-experienced pro. It just doesn't happen.

What's the answer? Send a tightly written, power-packed, results-oriented letter that tells potential employers what they want to know—no more, no less. While they're reviewing the letter, you update your resume, load it with accomplishments, and overnight it to them. Presto! You come across as a busy, success-ful candidate. You may be perceived as loyal to your present employer, too, and that could be a plus. Why? Because you didn't have a loaded resume lying in your desk drawer.

"As you go through life, my boy, you must remember one very important rule—always keep your resume updated."

TWO THOUSAND OAKS TOWERS • 2000 WEST FEDERAL STREET • BOSTON, MASSACHUSETTS 02110 • (617) 765-9898

September 4, 19—

Mr. William T. Dewar
Executive Vice President
U S WEST Inc.
7800 Orchard, Suite 200
Englewood, Colorado 80111

Dear Mr. Dewar:

I understand that you are looking to fill a key management position in your Controller's department. I would like to be considered for that position.

The enclosed excerpt from *Fortune* magazine describes what I am doing now and how I got there. My investment advisory practice is successful and growing, but it does not use enough of the skills and competencies I have spent a lifetime building.

My background is in finance. I earned an MBA in finance from Stanford in 19—. Upon graduation, I went to work for Amoco in a small group that did strategic planning, capital budgeting, and merger and acquisition work. Amoco, at that time, was a leader in this area, and we completed some very significant acquisitions during this period.

From this position, I went to Collins Chemical, Amoco's fertilizer subsidiary, where I was a principal architect of the strategy that brought the company from an $11 million loss to profitability. Then in 19—, I moved to Denver to take charge of the administrative, financial and later, the domestic and international acquisition areas, for Amoco's Minerals department.

After Amoco was acquired by Dow Chemical Company, I became Executive Assistant to the Chairman of Bender Coal, where I worked on problems in the capital expenditure and cash flow areas that arose from the merger. In late 19—, I left Amoco to join InTek as Executive Vice President in their troubled oil and gas operation. Later, I became President of this company. The *Fortune* article sets out the rest.

Mr. William T. Dewar
September 4, 19—
Page Two

My experience in finance, organization and business has been both extensive and varied. I am a "pro." My background is finance, but my success has been due to my ability to work well with people, whether negotiating with officials of foreign governments or leading management teams in turnaround situations.

I have a lot to offer, and would like to put it to better use. Even if my information is wrong about the position in your Controller's department, I would like to meet you and get your advice. I will be in touch with you in the next few days to ask if I might schedule a few moments with you.

Yours truly,

Michael D. Burns

Enclosure

Todd R. Kliebstein
2 North Park East
Dallas, Texas 75201
(214) 374-4858

April 24, 19—

Thomas Blackman
Russell Reynolds Associates
320 Grand Avenue, Suite 4200
Los Angeles, California 90071

Dear Mr. Blackman:

Confirming our telephone conversation of this date, I am including my resume which is current up until 19—. In April of 19— I resigned my position with Texaco Oil Company to accept a position as Vice President of Supply and Distribution with Gulf Oil (U.S.), Inc. in their San Francisco office. In addition to being responsible for all of Gulf's crude oil activities, I was Vice President of Gulf Pipeline, Inc., a subsidiary company for Gulf's pipeline activity.

In November 19— I resigned my position at Gulf—along with seven other employees—to set up a crude oil purchasing and gathering operation for a company, Petrol, Inc., operating out of Houston, Texas. By March of 19— Petrol, Inc. had a change of heart, shut down the Houston operation and I was laid off.

During my employment at Texaco, the natural gas sales function reported to me and I supervised a gas sales contract person. Hopefully, the foregoing will be a sufficient update of my resume to acquaint you with my background and experience in the oil industry. My contacts and associations throughout the oil and gas industry are strong assets.

I'll call you Monday.

Sincerely,

Todd R. Kliebstein

TRK/dl
Enclosure

5

*"Care for an hors d'oeuvre, Mr. Macklin,
or a copy of Ed's resume?"*

Friends

Fifty to seventy-five percent of good jobs come from friends—and friends of friends—by word of mouth. The higher the level of the job, the more that rule applies. At the senior executive and professional level, for example, as many as 90 percent of good jobs come through personal friends.

Therefore, it's urgent to *involve* your friends in your job-search, not just *notify* them of your plight ("I'm out of work. Let me know if you hear of anything.").

Job campaigns often stall because job-hunters leave their personal networks too quickly to go off into the world of "strangers." Strangers will seldom be as responsive to you as people whom you've met before, even briefly. Surprisingly, your attendance at a trade show can qualify you as a "friend" in someone's eyes.

Make sure you get your job-hunt strongly established with personal friends and business acquaintances before you spend a lot of time answering ads, working with recruiters, or cold calling. Cold calling isn't very appealing—that's why they call it *cold calling*!

JONATHAN P. GREENBERG, J.D., C.P.A.
35 Winchester Way
Englewood, Colorado 80110
(303) 790-1644 (h)
(303) 238-1592 (o)

September 10, 19—

Mr. William S. Frank
President
CareerLab, Ltd.
9085 E. Mineral Circle, Suite 330
Englewood, CO 80112

Dear Bill:

Since we have known each other I have been in private law practice in downtown Denver. Although I have enjoyed the past several years and have found the practice to be both intellectually stimulating and financially rewarding, I've also found myself wanting to put my accumulated experience and skills to work for a single enterprise. I look forward to becoming an integral part of a management team, instead of an outside adviser, and participating in the long-term results of the team effort.

My earlier public accounting experiences with Price Waterhouse and a local CPA firm, together with my law practice with a Denver law firm and my current position as a partner with the Denver office of a national law firm, have given me exposure to a wide range of problems in large and small companies from the perspective of both a CPA and a lawyer. In addition, I have gained management experience through performance of significant administrative duties in each of the law firms.

I am excited about stepping into a position in which I will be able to utilize my legal, accounting and administrative skills, and at the same time experience new challenges and opportunities. I would like to be associated with an established, growing company, privately or publicly held, which is in need of an executive to take responsibility for its legal, financial, operational or other general management activities. Although I do not have a preference as to industry, I do prefer a company based in the metro Denver-Boulder area.

I've enclosed a copy of my résumé for your perusal. Please feel free to pass along copies to any of your business associates that you think may have an interest.

I plan to call you within the next 10 days to be sure you received this letter and to ask if you have any thoughts or ideas about people I should contact, or specific positions or opportunities I should pursue. I appreciate your taking the time to consider my situation, and I look forward to talking to you soon.

Best personal regards,

Jonathan P. Greenberg

John H. Norris
2894 S. Lima Street
Aurora, Colorado 80014
(303) 755-8880

April 14, 19—

Ms. Tamara Swift
Vice President Finance
Transamerica Financial Services
1225 17th Street, Suite 3000
Denver, Colorado 80202

Dear Tamara:

I'm looking for some advice and counsel from people I know and trust.

Rocky Mountain Bank, the firm I worked for the last five years, was sold at
year-end and merged with another financial institution. As a result, my job
was eliminated. The Federal Savings and Loan Insurance Corporation, receiver
for Rocky Mountain Bank, asked me to remain and assist in managing the
real estate loan/asset portfolio. The position was temporary, as a relocation
would be required to make it permanent. I've completed that assignment and
I'm ready to move forward with something more long-lasting.

I'd like to continue to be a manager in a financial services company (bank,
savings and loan, credit union, insurance company, etc.). I'm good at managing people and other resources to attain corporate profits. I've also managed
data processing installations of all sizes. I like being a part of a dynamic
organization, and I am looking for that next opportunity.

You're a successful person with friends who are also successful. Perhaps you,
or someone you know, are aware of a firm that needs someone with my capabilities. If so, I'd appreciate your giving them a copy of the enclosed resume,
and I'd like their name so that I can contact them personally.

The past few months have been exciting, but the next few years hold even
more promise. I'm enthused about the prospect for change and I hope that
you can help me make sure it's a positive change.

I'd appreciate your thoughts and ideas. Please contact me at (303) 755-8880.
Thanks for your help.

Best regards,

John H. Norris

MICHAEL D. BURNS

TWO THOUSAND OAKS TOWERS • 2000 WEST FEDERAL STREET • BOSTON, MASSACHUSETTS 02110 • (617) 765-9898

January 16, 19—

Mr. Richard C. Forest
President
California Oil & Gas
330 Primrose, Suite 310
Burlingame, California 94010

Dear Richard:

The years since Stanford Business School have been varied and fulfilling for me, and I hope they have been the same for you. The enclosed excerpt from *Fortune* magazine and the copy of my resume will give you a snapshot of what I have been doing until recently. In late 19—, I left the investment advisory business to begin marketing myself for re-entry into the corporate world.

Since leaving Amoco, I have found that I greatly enjoy working in smaller, more entrepreneurial businesses and that's what I am looking for now. My job target is a position with a high management content, either in operations or in the financial area. Ideally, it would be with a company that is two to ten years old and has sales of $5-$50 million. Although I am not looking for investment opportunities, I might consider a limited investment in the right situation. Geographic location is not a major consideration.

I have some preference to stay in the oil business, but I am not limiting my search to this area. A favorite alternate industry of mine is hazardous waste, however I am open to any situation that is challenging and will make adequate use of my skills.

Should you become aware of any of your business associates, friends, etc., who might be interested in my abilities, I would appreciate your sending them a copy of my resume or letting me have their names so I can contact them personally.

Richard, any assistance or advice you can give me would be greatly appreciated and I look forward to hearing from you.

Best regards,

Michael D. Burns

Enclosures

Rao Phaisawang
13050 North 40th Street
Paradise Valley, Arizona 83606
(602) 555-3832 Office

September 24, 19—

Tracey Lammers
1140 Fairfield Drive N.W.
Sioux Falls, South Dakota 57117

Dear Tracey,

I am in the process of making a job change and am writing to college friends whose opinions and insights I value.

Thirteen years ago I joined Beco-Med, a small-but-gaining medical products company. Over that period its size has tripled and its sales quadrupled. In the process it has moved away from the dynamic let's-make-something-happen-today operation that I thoroughly enjoyed. Now the company has been merged with a competitor to form an organization three times the size of Beco-Med.

Reorganization and downsizing of the management staff are not uncommon activities following a merger of this sort. I have accepted an attractive severance package and am now searching for another small company. I once again want to enjoy the feeling of "making something happen today."

During my working years I have acquired considerable knowledge and experience of manufacturing operations. This, coupled with BSME and MBA degrees, strong organizational skills and leadership abilities, makes me a candidate for consideration in a wide variety of operations management positions.

I realize that you are not an employment office. However, I also know that only 20% of positions filled are listed in the employment ads. The rest are filled by people being in the right place at the right time.

I would really appreciate your reviewing the enclosed résumé. If you know of anyone that might be looking, now or in the future, for someone with my background, please contact me. Or if you have any ideas as to where I should direct my search, please let me know that also. With your help I might just be in that right place at the right time!

Thanks!

Rao

DOUGLAS P. ARNOLD, JR.

295 TREETOP LANE N.W. • FT. COLLINS, COLORADO 80521 • (303) 578-2929

January 7, 19—

Ms. Roberta Martin
University of Denver, MBA Program
University at Evans Avenue
Denver, Colorado 80210

Dear Ms. Martin:

You may remember me in connection with SunTek Industries, last spring. At that time, I was the Controller of Robertson Manufacturing. I am writing to you as I am presently seeking a new position and realize you may be able to help.

I have enclosed two copies of my current resume, and would appreciate it very much if you could make me aware of any interesting situations that come to your attention. Please note that my skills are not restricted to financial accounting. Related administrative positions, such as computer systems management are also of interest, expecially as my MBA degree emphasis is MIS [Management Information Systems].

In addition, I am also looking for temporary and/or part-time work.

I was impressed with you as an instructor, and since you awarded me an "A" in your course, I presume you might not be uncomfortable recommending me as a first-class accounting professional.

Thank you for your attention. I am aware that you must be very busy, and I appreciate your consideration.

Yours truly,

Douglas P. Arnold, Jr.

Enclosures

DOUGLAS P. ARNOLD, JR.

295 TREETOP LANE N.W. • FT. COLLINS, COLORADO 80521 • (303) 578-2929

January 7, 19—

Dr. Randolph Moore, DDS, MPH
1000 Medical Towers, Suite 3200
Ft. Collins, Colorado 80521

Dear Randy,

I resigned my controllership of Robertson Manufacturing last week. My work there is completed, and I have ridden off into the sunset toward "Happily Ever After Land." However, in order to be happy when I get there, I'll need to find another position.

As a fellow professional, you are no doubt aware that networking is the only way to make the contacts necessary to build a successful practice, or to find a good job in this town. You may be in a position to help me.

I have enclosed a copy of my current resume, and would appreciate it very much if you could make me aware of any interesting situations that come to your attention. Please note that my skills are not limited to finance and accounting. Related administrative positions such as computer systems management are also of interest, expecially since my MBA area of emphasis is MIS [Management Information Systems]. I am also seeking temporary work while conducting this job search—and yes, I do taxes too.

Thank you for your attention. I am aware that you are busy, and appreciate your consideration. Should you wish to know more about this situation before my next appointment, please feel free to telephone.

Best regards,

Douglas P. Arnold, Jr.

Enclosure

DOUGLAS P. ARNOLD, JR.

295 TREETOP LANE N.W. • FT. COLLINS, COLORADO 80521 • (303) 578-2929

January 8, 19—

Dr. Pamela Swanson
Director, MBA Program
University of Denver
Evans at University Boulevard
Denver, Colorado 80210

Dear Dr. Swanson:

A few weeks ago, a D.U. seminar entitled "How to Conduct a Professional
Job Search" was cancelled. This was something of a disappointment
since I had just left my position as Controller of Robertson Manufacturing,
and was ready to begin just such a search. Fortunately, Lee Thomas
recommended a consultant who provides excellent advice, so the search
is under way.

Networking is the key concept used to locate opportunities in Denver.
I would very much appreciate it if you would permit me to consider
you part of my network. As Director of the MBA Program, I know you
make contact with many successful business leaders in Denver on a
regular basis. Such contact is invaluable in connection with a professional job search.

Will you please take the time to read my resume? I would appreciate
it very much if you could make me aware of any interesting situations
that come to your attention. Any leads you can provide will be of great
assistance to me. Please keep in mind that my skills are not limited to
financial accounting. Related administrative positions such as computer
systems management are also of interest, especially since my MBA
area of emphasis is Management Information Systems.

Thanks for your interest. I regret imposing upon you for this help—I
know you are very busy. Be assured that any effort you make to help
me will be appreciated.

Sincerely,

Douglas P. Arnold, Jr.

DPA/
Enclosure

MICHAEL D. BURNS

TWO THOUSAND OAKS TOWERS • 2000 WEST FEDERAL STREET • BOSTON, MASSACHUSETTS 02110 • (617) 765-9898

January 2, 19—

Mr. Fred Morris
Occidental Petroleum, Inc.
9900 West 95th Avenue
Los Angeles, California 92715

Dear Fred:

It's been quite a while since we've been in touch, and I hope this letter finds things going well for you.

As for me, these years have been filled with change and I've never been bored. The enclosed resume plus the excerpt from *Fortune* magazine will give you a snapshot of what I've been doing until recently when I left the investment advisory business to start marketing myself for re-entry into the corporate world.

Since leaving Amoco, I have found that I really enjoy working in smaller, more entrepreneurial businesses and that's what I'm looking for now. My job target is a position with a high management content, either in operations or financial areas. It would ideally be with a company that is perhaps two to ten years old and has sales of $5 to $50 million. Although I am not looking for investment opportunities, I might consider a limited investment in the right situation. Geographic location is not a major consideration.

I am focusing my attention outside oil and hardrock mining, and although a current favorite industry of mine is hazardous waste, I am open to any opportunity that has growth potential.

Should you become aware of any of your business associates, friends, etc., that might be interested in my abilities, I would appreciate your sending them a copy of my resume, or letting me have their names so I can contact them personally.

Fred, any assistance or advice you can give me would be greatly appreciated, but regardless of whether you are aware of anything, I'd like to get a note from you to hear how you are. Or better yet, a phone call.

Best regards,

Michael D. Burns

MDB/
Enclosures

SIRIKARN W. KANIKICHIARLA
6667 E. Dorado Avenue
Greenwood Village, CO 80111
(303) 694-6698

March 7, 19—

Mr. Phil Rowley, President
Rowley & Associates
8719 East San Alberto
San Antonio, Texas 78240

Dear Phil,

It's been too long since we've been in touch, and I hope this letter finds things going well for you. Even when we do get together, we seldom talk business, so the enclosed resume will probably fill in some gaps for you on what I've been doing since law school.

As you can see, I've been primarily involved in building new businesses. Two of them have been great successes for me, the other founders, and our investors. I wish I could count on batting .500 forever!

However, I've made a career decision to look for a long-term position with a growing but stable small to medium-sized company. I am totally open to the type of industry since I have worked with companies in such diverse businesses as electronics, health care, telecommunications, and consumer services. Although I am not looking for investment opportunities, I would consider taking an equity position in the right situation.

If you know or become aware of any business associates, friends, or acquaintances who may be in the market for someone with my abilities, please give them a copy of my resume or give me their names to contact personally. Any assistance or advice you can give me would be greatly appreciated.

Regardless of whether you have any leads, give me a call when you have a chance and let me know what you've been up to.

Best regards,

Sirikarn W. Kanikichiarla

Enclosure

BRUCE M. KLEINMAN
335 Sacramento Street
San Francisco, California 94111
(415) 391-2323

February 10, 19—

William S. Frank
President
CareerLab
9085 E. Mineral Circle, Suite 330
Englewood, Colorado 80112

Dear Bill:

It's been some time since we have talked, and I wanted to make you aware of my decision to leave my current position as Vice President of Human Resources for The Health Group (THG). As you may know, during the past years, THG (like the industry in general) has undergone severe economic difficulties resulting in dramatic staff reductions, budgetary belt-tightening and a general slowdown in activity. These factors have contributed to my decision to look for another opportunity where the economic climate and corporate outlook are better positioned to benefit from strategic business partnership utilizing innovative and strong Human Resource Management.

I believe my 15 years experience as a Human Resource and Strategic Business Planning professional and executive has uniquely prepared me to manage state-of-the-art, integrated Human Resources systems.

I am interested in talking to executives of companies who are willing to demonstrate their commitment to expending their Human Resources management capability. If you are aware of challenging opportunities within such companies, I would appreciate the opportunity to share my achievements, experience and ideas directly with them. I am not restricted geographically and am anxious to find an opportunity where my energies and skills in Human Resources Management can be utilized to achieve bottom line results.

I am anxious to talk with you and will call you in the next week or so. I would appreciate your help and look forward to talking with you.

Regards,

Bruce M. Kleinman

BMS/br

December 16, 19—

Mr. Matthew Morris
Merill Lynch Pierce Fenner & Smith Inc.
Colorado Building
Ft. Collins, Colorado 80521

Dear Matt,

Seasons Greetings!

I trust things are going well for you and that you are enjoying settling into your new career. Knowing your professional style, I have no doubt you will be a very successful broker within a short time.

My "executive marketing campaign" is coming together well. It should be in full swing by the new year. I have not yet contacted Ms. Daniels, but intend to do so soon, now that my printed resume is ready, and my beard is off once again.

I have enclosed two copies of my resume, and would appreciate it very much if you could make me aware of any interesting situations that come to your attention. Please note that my skills are not restricted to financial accounting. Related administrative positions, such as computer systems management are also of interest to me.

Once again I'd like to thank you for your help and cooperation in turning around the Robertson situation. While I have received all the credit, I know that without the cooperation of the commercial lending officer, the outcome would have been very different.

Yours truly,

Douglas P. Arnold, Jr.

Enclosures

January 30, 19—

Mr. Paul Robinson
President
Pester Corporation
303 Kensington Way
Des Moines, Iowa   50306

Dear Paul,

Congratulations! *Business Week* wrote an interesting article about you—even the picture was a good likeness.

Will you have your own financial and accounting group, or some part thereof? Consulting is a "feast or famine" profession, and I need to build something for my future.

Your job at Pester to build a retail organization will be an exciting one, and I would be glad to be part of it.

Please think about a way to use my talents, and call me in the next week or two when you have a moment.

Warm regards,

Paul H. Gutknecht

December 15, 19—

Ms. Janet Taylor
MCI Communications
7100 Campus Drive
Ft. Collins, Colorado 80521

Dear Janet:

Thank you for taking the time to speak with me on the telephone two
weeks ago regarding the possibility of finding employment with MCI.

During my tenure at Robertson Manufacturing, I had the opportunity
to interact with many MCI representatives who were working on our
installations. The professional manner in which they dealt with a very
difficult situation has shown me that MCI may be the kind of organization
where I could find a good "fit" and fully utilize my abilities.

Enclosed are two copies of my current resume. Please feel free to
share the information with any employer who may be interested in the
skills and experience I can provide.

Please do not hesitate to telephone should you have any questions or
require additional information. Once again, thank you for your help.

Sincerely,

Douglas P. Arnold, Jr.

Enclosures

Luciano D. Maestas
6148 S. Coventry Lane East
Littleton, Colorado 80123
(303) 794-2465

August 16, 19—

William S. Frank
President
CareerLab
9085 E. Mineral Circle, Suite 330
Englewood, Colorado 80112

Dear Mr. Frank:

HELP A PERSONNEL SOCIETY COLLEAGUE IF YOU CAN!

Do you know of any upcoming HR openings in the Denver area?

My qualifications:

* Ten years Human Resources experience

* Specialties:

> Employment
> Recruiting - including senior level
> Selection testing - assessment
> Management development
> Manpower planning

* MBA education

Should you know of a potential opening, please contact me at (303) 794-2465.

With great thanks,

Luciano D. Maestas

PAUL H. GUTKNECHT

11374 QUIVAS WAY • WESTMINSTER, COLORADO 80234 • (303) 465-1236

March 18, 19—

Mr. Charles F. McCay
Vice President Finance
Bank of America
123 Post Street
San Francisco, California 94104

Dear Mr. McCay:

I am writing to you as a fellow member of the Financial Executives Institute and seeking your advice in my job search. My 30 years of experience includes 3 years of consulting for the top managements and 20 years in top management of two different companies, plus 8 years as a bank director.

Most of my experience is in the petroleum industry; but management, financial and accounting skills are valuable in any industry. Although we enjoy living in Denver, my wife and I would gladly relocate.

Please take a few minutes and think about possible needs among your associates and friends for a man of my talents. You can either give them the enclosed copy of my resume, or give me their names so that I can follow through.

Any assistance or advice that you can give me will be greatly appreciated.

Thank you,

Paul H. Gutknecht

PG/jt
Enclosure

DOUGLAS P. ARNOLD, JR.

295 TREETOP LANE N.W. • FT. COLLINS, COLORADO 80521 • (303) 578-2929

January 8, 19—

Mr. Tom Spaulding, President
Coldwell Banker
4000 North Foothills Road
Ft. Collins, Colorado 80521

Dear Tom,

As a real estate professional in Ft. Collins, I know you're aware that networking is the most effective method of doing business in this town. A case in point is that I chose Coldwell Banker to help me find my home based upon a recommendation from Bill Moore.

Having completed the financial turnaround of Robertson Manufacturing, I am now seeking a permanent position. The Controllership position I held at Robertson has been eliminated as a result of my efforts. Have no misunderstanding—this parting of the ways is by mutual consent. There are no hard feelings between the company and me.

I hesitate to impose upon your good nature, Tom, but unfortunately my network of friends and acquaintances is limited. I believe you may be in a position to help me connect with my next job. I have enclosed a copy of my current resume and would appreciate it very much if you could make me aware of any interesting situations that come to your attention.

Please note that my skills are not limited to financial accounting. Related administrative positions, such as computer systems management are also of interest, especially since my MBA area of emphasis is Management Information Systems.

Thank you for your attention. I know you are very busy and I appreciate your help.

Best regards,

Douglas P. Arnold, Jr.

Enclosure
P.S. I still love my house. Thanks for the flowers!

Dick and Laurie Thomas
435 Mountain Way
Colorado Springs, Colorado 80919
(719) 594-3096

September 24, 19—

John and Joan Emerson
300 Nightingale Street
Hatboro, Pennsylvania   19040

Dear John and Joan,

We are looking for some advice and assistance from friends.

As you may know, on July 1st, Electronics, Inc. sold the Colorado Springs facility to a small company based in California. As a result, Dick's job was eliminated. In addition, Electronics, Inc. is currently going through a major restructuring process which prevents us from continuing his 22 year career with them by relocating to another facility. Consequently, we have made a career decision to enter the job market.

Dick would like to continue his financial management career. Enclosed is an outline of his job preference characteristics. As you can see, he is open to a broad range of industries, and we are willing to relocate to other parts of the country. Please keep in mind that these characteristics are preferences, not absolutes, and therefore Dick and I are open to most opportunities.

If you know or become aware of any business associates, friends, or acquaintances who may be in the market for someone with Dick's abilities, please give them a copy of the enclosed resume, and send us their names so we can contact them personally.

We are excited about the prospect for change and we hope that you can help us make it a positive change. In the meantime, Dick is doing some temporary consulting, Jared has started kindergarten, and we are getting along just fine.

We would appreciate any assistance that you can provide.

Thanks for helping,

Laurie

Employment Agencies

If you earn $50,000+, recruiters and headhunters (also called executive search consultants) should be part of your job campaign.

You must sell yourself to recruiters the same way you sell yourself to employers. Like employment managers, they too are drowning in resumes. The best way to approach unknown recruiters is by mail. Search consultants are usually busy, and they often consider calls from job hunters a nuisance. A high-impact letter will get you in the door.

By reviewing your resume, the recruiter can see what you *have done*. The problem is to determine where you fit next. A well-structured letter will answer five key questions:

1. What two or three job titles would fit you now?

2. If you could design the job yourself, what duties and responsibilities would you choose?

3. Which companies and industries appeal to you? Which don't?

4. Where are you willing—or unwilling—to live?

5. What range of compensation are you seeking?

The example on page 78 is one of my favorites. The first paragraphs explain your situation; then the numbered items address the recruiter's "need to know."

Ken Cole, author of *The Headhunter Strategy*, recommends sending a high-impact sales letter and no resume. That's always a good strategy if you have a terrific sales letter.

Look at the letters here. To learn more about working with recruiters, read *The Headhunter Strategy*, by Ken Cole or *Rites of Passage at $100,000+* by John Lucht.

"My problem is that although you're people-oriented, action-oriented and growth-oriented, you don't seem to be buzzword-oriented."

PAUL L. TURNER
9344 S. Pleasant Avenue
Chicago, IL 60620
(312) 233-7459 (H)
(312) 751-2700 (O)

March 13, 19—

Mr. Kenneth J. Cole, Publisher
THE RECRUITING & SEARCH REPORT
P.O. Box 9433
Panama City Beach, FL 32407

Dear Mr. Cole:

I am writing to you at the suggestion of the University of Chicago Graduate School of Business Executive Program and am a member of the fifty-seventh group. My track record demonstrates the kind of professional growth I've heard you like to recruit.

The president of a $182 million NYSE corporation chose me to head a division because of the contributions I made as a VP of Operations. While Division President, circumstances beyond my control—changing consumer preferences—have made me "Captain of the Titanic."

The significant achievements that led to my selection as President were:

- Reducing administrative expenses $1 million annually by eliminating 26 jobs, consolidating functions, and more efficiently using data processing resources.

- Successfully demonstrating to our union that we must reduce contractual task classifications. This negotiated concession reduced payroll costs by $600,000 in only one year.

- Reducing direct costs 30% from the previous year by shrinking inventory and standardizing production and purchasing processes.

- Improving direct mail profitability $350,000 by eliminating poor performing lists, changing advertising agencies and raising prices.

I will achieve similar results for my next employer.

I will be in my office next week; however, after that I will be traveling extensively. I look forward to your call so that we can begin a fruitful association.

With enthusiasm,

Paul L. Turner

Ali B. Sandtkhah
11726 San Vicente Blvd.
Los Angeles, CA 90049
(310) 207-1963 (o)
(310) 207-2438 (h)

May 27, 19—

Joseph D. Gibson
Executive Search Consultant
Technical Placement
4000 North Belt East
Houston, Texas 77060

Dear Mr. Gibson:

After 20 years with National Laboratories, I have decided to pursue a new career and would appreciate your help in making this transition. I have extensive experience in integrated circuit and computer aided design tool development, and I have served on a number of technical and professional committees and organized and managed a number of large technical conferences. The following profile represents a list of parameters which may be helpful in focusing this search:

1. <u>Desired Positions</u>
   Vice President/Director/Manager—Engineering, Research & Development, Integrated Circuit Design, Computer Aided Design

2. <u>Desired Duties and Responsibilities</u>
   Research and Development, Product definition and development, Integrated Circuit Design, Definition and development of computer aided design tools, Technical Marketing, Strategic Planning.

3. <u>Preferred Companies and Industries</u>
   Profitable Semiconductor Manufacturer, New Start-up with defined market niches and business plans, Large Research and Development Organization.

4. <u>Geography</u>
   West and Southwest preferred (New Mexico, Arizona, Colorado, Southern California, Texas).

5. <u>Compensation</u>
   Salary range: $140K to $200K

Please review my background relative to your current search assignments and contact me if you need additional information. I can be reached at (310) 207-1963.

Let's talk soon,

Ali B. Sandtkhah

Michael Herbert
12021 Wilshire Blvd., Suite 210
Los Angeles, CA 90025
(310) 454-1863 (o)
(310) 454-1320 (FAX)
(310) 452-1893 (h)

April 29, 19—

Ms. Jane Peters
Corporate Search Consultants
324 Wall Street
Princeton, New Jersey 08540

Dear Ms. Peters,

I joined The Worthington Corporation ten years ago when it was a $100 million company and played a major role in its growth to $2 billion.

However, I've progressed as far as possible. (My boss, the Vice President of Finance, is appointed by the German parent company.) As a result, I've decided to seek a new opportunity. Rather than moving into another large organization, I'd prefer a smaller, more entrepreneurial environment. The following profile may be helpful in focusing this search:

1. <u>Desired Positions</u>
    CFO or Vice President Finance and Administration

2. <u>Desired Duties and Responsibilities</u>
    a) corporate finance, including capital markets and bank relations; b) treasury, including cash management and investments; c) tax planning; d) accounting; e) mergers and acquisitions; and f) employee benefits.

3. <u>Preferred Companies and Industries</u>
    $10 to $200 million, public or privately held. Almost any industries, except: a) banking, b) real estate, c) non-profit, and d) financial services.

4. <u>Geography</u>
    Willing to relocate.

5. <u>Compensation</u>
    $125 to $150K, depending upon equity opportunities.

Please review my background in light of your current search assignments, and contact me regarding positions that require my skill sets.

With best wishes,

Michael Herbert

6.1   6.1, p. 324   BROADCAST LETTER TO RECRUITERS

78

T. Craig Lincoln

4720 West 49th Street
Denver, CO 80018
(303) 555-7114 (o) • (303) 555-1682 (h)

April 17, 19—

Mr. Richard Matthews
Georgia Arts Personnel
2584 Peachtree Road
Atlanta, Georgia 30326

Dear Mr. Matthews:

Now and then corporations send out feelers for "just the right type" of creative person. This person must fit very specific criteria. Usually, after all is said and done, the corporation wants a business person who can manage, create and communicate. A seasoned professional who's been around for a while.

If you've been looking for this rare combination of business saavy and design expertise, my background might interest you.

—Twenty-seven years of national experience.

—Solid background in the management of creative up-and-comers.

—Know new technologies that show instant profit, such as computer-aided production via Mergenthaler CRTronic systems augmented with an IBM PC/AT CAD.

—Consistently bring projects in on budget or below budget.

This is but a brief summary of my abilities. And there is much, much more to share.

Presently, my position is contracted through June of this year. I am beginning my search on a local and national level. I feel I have strong marketable skills in which you would be interested.

At your earliest convenience, please contact me if you would like to hear and see more. During the day you can reach me at (303) 555-7114 or in the evening at (303) 555-1682.

Enthusiastically,

T. Craig Lincoln

January 18, 19—

Mr. Richard T. Ferguson
Engineer's Search
300 Winter Street, Suite 320
Boston, Massachusetts 02108

Dear Mr. Ferguson:

Your firm has been recommended to me as specializing in the oil and gas industry and I would like you to be aware of my credentials. Enclosed is a resume and an excerpt from *Fortune* magazine which summarizes my experience and highlights a few of my accomplishments.

Most of my career has been in management and the financial areas. With participation in two turn-arounds and one startup, my experience has been varied and I have built a consistently successful track record. I am adaptable and learn fast as evidenced by my level of accomplishment in jobs that varied greatly in content, and in three different industries. I have found that I enjoy working in smaller, more entrepreneurial businesses and that is what I am looking for now.

My job target is a position with a high management content, either in the operations or the financial area. It would ideally be with a company that has an entrepreneurial outlook, perhaps be five to ten years old and has sales of less than $100 million. The position could be in oil or mining, but that is not a requirement. A favorite alternate industry of mine is hazardous waste.

I am flexible on immediate compensation if there is adequate potential for growth. A chance to earn equity would be attractive. Although I am not seeking investment opportunities, I might consider a limited investment in the right situation. Geographic location is not a major consideration.

Mr. Ferguson, this should cover the key points. I will be glad to provide any other information you may need and can provide strong references when appropriate.

Many thanks,

Michael D. Burns

Enclosures

Rud Bergfeld
274 Madison Avenue
New York, NY 10016
(212) 679-0139

February 20, 19—

Mr. Richard K. Dean
Richard Dean & Associates
1490 Old Toll Road
Madison, Connecticut 06443

Dear Mr. Dean:

Presently, I am concluding a public acquisition for private investors—I selected the prospect, structured financing and negotiated arrangements with previous management, but have declined the permanent CEO position. Instead, I desire to continue to enjoy the "Thrill of the Hunt" in locating, acquiring and building high technology organizations. Several associates have mentioned your firm often represents technology-driven companies with strong growth/acquisition goals, and I understand you are searching now for a CEO or Executive VP who will make your client money.

My diverse background demonstrates exceptional officer-level sales, marketing, financial and leadership abilities in high tech areas:

— The technical, management, and executive team I identified recruited and trained boosted corporate revenues from $11 to $100 million in only five years, increasing ROI by an astounding 300%.

— Created a worldwide sales organization (affiliates and reps) in 40 countries and dominated those markets with new technologies in only 1-1/2 years; it took the competition over 3 years to respond.

— Assembled the capital and designed the equity structure at extremely favorable terms to the founders, completing the project in three quarters of the time called for by the strategic plan.

I enjoy the challenge of creating, building and growing a professional organization. Opportunities and potential are of paramount importance. I would be most pleased to discuss with you and your client how I would quickly duplicate these successes and build on them. Could we talk about it in the next week or ten days? My travel schedule picks up substantially late this month and I'll be much more difficult to reach.

With enthusiasm,

Rud Bergfeld

Steven R. Marinaro
11285 Admiral Road
Albuquerque, New Mexico 87112
(505) 821-5520

February 3, 19—

Ms. Barbara Simms
Director
NYC Executive Search
10 East 21st Street
New York, New York 10010

Dear Ms. Simms:

As a Managing Partner in a $100 million company, as President of a $15 million company and, as Founder and President of a $5 million firm, I know how to manage—people—projects—offices—regions—companies—for a profit. My management and marketing skills have been instrumental in generating profits in the good times, recessionary periods, and now, as the economy slowly recovers.

I am interested in a firm that has plans for growth and/or diversification and which has an executive management position with both P&L and marketing responsibility and an equity potential.

I know that it takes enthusiastic, innovative, and decisive leadership to provide profits in today's marketplace. I have—and can—provide that leadership.

In addition, I have the financial experience to manage and analyze accounting information and negotiate with bankers and other financial groups with respect to long and short-term borrowings, letters of credit, and payroll arrangements.

I would like to meet or talk with you to see if your clients need someone with my capabilities. I'll call you next week to introduce myself.

Yours truly,

Steven R. Marinaro

SRM/bt

Ramon Rodriguez
President
International Search Group
2121 Park Avenue, STE 2500
New York, NY 10012

September 27, 19—

Dear Mr. Rodriguez:

I am interested in teaming-up with your recruiting firm in accomplishing an effective search for a middle to upper-level Marketing Management position. I have recently concluded a ten-year career as a Marketing Manager for the Ampex Corporation, where I enjoyed continuous upward mobility in my career.

By way of introduction, let me outline some of my background:

— Developed and implemented comprehensive marketing and public relations plans covering national and local consumer markets.

— Directed over 90 sales promotion events budgeted at $10MM.

— Managed a Marketing Department with a staff of eight and an annual operating budget of $5MM.

— Consistently achieved marketing objectives within budget as measured by sales, publicity and spin-off opportunities.

If I were to characterize myself, I would say that I have strong communication skills with emphasis on creative writing, sensitivity to the corporate environment and an ability to respond to its demands; good organization and budget management skills; and the capacity to motivate professionals to goal achievement.

A minimum compensation package of $50K plus benefits and a relocation allowance is my goal.

An expression of your interest in my background in view of your client requirements would be appreciated. I certainly would be pleased to meet with your representative to conduct an appraisal interview. As you can see, I am not adverse to travel or relocation.

A resume is enclosed for your additional information. Thank you for your assistance.

Sincerely,

Maureen Hubbs

Thomas L. Bouchard
Five Warren Street
Concord, New Hampshire 03301
(603) 224-3837 (o)
(603) 225-2823 (h)

March 17, 19—

Mr. George R. Reisinger
Managing Partner
Sigma Group, Inc.
717 17th Street, Suite 1440
Denver, Colorado 80202

Dear Mr. Reisinger:

My current position as Executive Vice President of a <u>Fortune 50</u> company
has been an excellent arena to become operationally involved in a variety of
businesses and acquisitions from real estate development to image processing.

As General Manager, Executive Vice President and Chief Financial Officer,
I have played key roles in the execution of successful turnaround situations,
the development and implementation of acquisitions/divestitures and the
design of marketing and operational strategies. The international exposure,
outlined in the resume, includes foreign operations and acquisitions in the Far
East, Australia and Europe.

Please review my qualifications against your current clients' needs. Certainly
most of your placements come from within similar industries, however, many
of my assignments have required fast learning curves and I have consistently
produced results beyond what was expected.

Titles are not always an indicator of the responsibilities of a position.
However, my objective will most likely be met by positions such as President,
General Manager, Executive Vice President or CFO. In recent years my com-
pensation has ranged from $100,000 to $150,000 annually. Although we love
Concord, my family is ready to move for the right opportunity. Location,
equity or stock options will be important considerations in my decision.

I would welcome a discussion regarding any possibilities of which you are
aware.

Most sincerely,

Thomas L. Bouchard

John W. Van Dyke
380 Madison Avenue
New York, NY 10017
(212) 557-3418 (o)
(212) 557-3425 (FAX)
(212) 685-1599 (h)

October 1, 19—

Ramon Rodriguez
President
International Search Group
2121 Park Avenue, Suite 2500
New York, NY 10012

Dear Mr. Rodriguez:

Ten years ago I made a strategic career move to enhance my commercial, international marketing experience with aerospace and electronics technologies while continuing my Martin Marietta education. Today, having earned a 15-year MM "track record," I am ready to make another strategic career move and am exploring new career paths.

My objective is the CEO, COO or immediate successor position in a $50 to $250 million commercial electronics/aerospace business.

I have prepared for this challenge. MM has given me the opportunity to develop key leadership skills—strategic issue resolution, product line restructuring, new business development and day-to-day operations—and apply them with P&L responsibilities in businesses ranging from $10 to $215 million. Personal qualifications include a BSEE, a full complement of MM management training programs and experience in five MM businesses covering commercial, government, U.S. and international markets.

Martin is a great place to work; it's an excellent company and they've invested heavily in my education, relocation and a $100K compensation package including stock options, but I am seeking the dynamic environment of an autonomous, market-driven, engineered products business.

Should you have a current or emerging search for an aggressive general manager, perhaps it would be worthwhile for us to talk and investigate how I might be able to successfully satisfy your client's requirements.

My resume is enclosed for your confidential reference. Your office may reach me during the business day at (212) 557-3418.

Many thanks,

John W. Van Dyke

August 24, 19—

Mr. Howard Welshans
Search Associates
Eagle Square
New Hope, PA 18938

Dear Mr. Welshans:

Your firm, Search Associates, has been most highly recommended by a respected associate for the
excellence of your searches in the financial area. My background (University of Chicago MBA, plus
a CFA) and record with the Amoco Pension Fund qualify me as either an analyst or portfolio manager. Some of my background follows:

o Compiled a seven-year record of 17.1% compound growth compared to the S&P
   growth of 10% compounded;

o Made investment and divestment decisions for up to a quarter of a $450 million fund
   covering over 30,000 employees by using a capital asset pricing model (CAPM), a
   University of Chicago state-of-the-art financial management tool;

o Achieved the best record of five managers in the Amoco Fund which was chosen as
   the No. 1 large in-house managed corporate pension plan in the country for one-year
   and three-year periods ended June, 19—;

o Some of my stock picks: Waste Management, up 138% in 9 months; Newhall Land
   and Farming, up 106% in 3 years; Getty Oil, up 88% in 2 years and 7 months.

We had the best record in the country, and I had the best record in the group. This record is the more
remarkable since I had primarily cyclical areas in a growth-oriented operation. *Institutional Investor*
recognized this accomplishment in an article on the top performing money managers in the country
in November, 19—.

I mainly followed oil and gas production, gas transmission, chemicals, metals and mining, conglomerates
and special situations. I was highly successful in selecting issues that showed special promise for
capital appreciation. I used the Capital Asset Pricing Model, Wall Street research, company management
interviews, trade journals, and industry- and brokerage-sponsored conferences to make security selec-
tions. As a result, I dramatically outperformed bull markets on the upside and declined less than the
average on the downside.

Does your client need someone who can make money for his investment portfolio? Please call me at
312/446-2192 and we can continue our discussion.

Yours truly,

Edward M. Ortt

EMO/jz

Charles D. Waldron
1980 S. Post Oak Blvd.
Houston, TX 77056
(713) 840-1700

July 24, 19—

<u>C O N F I D E N T I A L</u>

Mr. George L. Reisinger
Managing Partner
Sigma Group, Inc.
717 17th Street, Suite 1440
Denver, Colorado 80202

Dear Mr. Reisinger:

On February 22nd, following a change in the ownership of the company, I left my position as President/CEO of National Industries. I had served on the Board of Directors of that company for the past six years and had directed its operations for the past four years. During that time the company gained a significant share of the market throughout the world as a direct result of improved product quality, improved order fill rates, creative marketing programs and new products.

Also, under my direction, two new assembly operations were successfully established in Mexico and the company has nearly completed a major relocation of much of its operations from Denver and Cheyenne to a brand new facility in Atlanta. My total compensation package at National Industries was approximately $250,000 per annum.

I am interested in finding a challenging CEO or Division President position (or CFO with a $500 million plus organization) commensurate with my skills and background, which would offer an opportunity for a meaningful equity participation and/or performance bonus(es). I am a global-thinking executive who believes both in serving the marketplace and in positive cash flow. I would be very valuable to the right organization.

My preference would be to relocate back to Southern California, although I would be receptive to relocation elsewhere for the proper opportunity.

A copy of my resume is enclosed (solely for your internal use), and I was hoping you might have an open search for which I would qualify as a candidate. Please feel free to call should you have any questions.

Best regards,

Charles D. Waldron

ROBERT C. HAYES, JR.
8225 FAIRMONT DRIVE • GLENCOE, IL 60022
(H) 708-835-9247 • (O) 312-987-6000

January 19, 19—

Mark Williams
Executive Placements, Inc.
1825 Marine
Mt. Prospect, IL 60056

Dear Mr. Williams:

This letter is difficult and painful for me to write. It is critical that you do not discuss this contact with anyone until we agree that it's in both our interests. My organization cannot know about this letter.

I build and run world-class marketing and customer service operations. A well-connected colleague (who assured me of your confidentiality), tells me that if anyone has an assignment for a VP-Marketing and/or Customer Service with a solid track record, it would be you. Some background:

- My boss (the COO of this company and president of my division before), attracted me to this high-profile, technology-based startup. I'm VP-Marketing & Client Service. In less than a year (from scratch), I have built an <u>outstanding</u> marketing/service operation that is prepared to support a profitable scale-up and commercialization.

- At my last organization (the Midwest Division of a telecommunications company you know), I also built the marketing department, driving five years of 30+% growth in revenue and volume. My multi-phased marketing strategy (incorporating the latest developments in niching and segmentation), was instrumental in creating a $1 billion (that's a "b", not an "m") business for the corporation. Then, after my appointment as Director of the Midwest Service Center (340 employees, $17 million operating budget, $390 million in revenue), I led the organization from 7th of 7 in productivity to 1st in less than a year.

- While justifiably proud of my operational and staffing record, I am a highly proficient marketer and developer of technological products. The electronic couponing/point of sale products we are about to introduce may revolutionize retail trade in the U.S. — and the world.

Why contact you now? My current firm is a great opportunity and a highly promising technology — It's also a cash-eater. I'm concerned the second round of financing we require shortly may not come as easily as the first did. Can we talk soon? I know you're being swamped with paper in this market, but I suspect your client will want to hear more about me. I am a Northwestern MBA (with distinction) and a Rose-Hulman mechanical engineer (magna cum laude). And, I'll make your client money.

Sincerely,

Robert M. Hayes, Jr.

Steven L. Hargreaves
3548 Bender Trail
Plano, Texas 75075
(713) 385-5733

January 14, 19—

Ms. Anne A. Dexter
Duggan and Company
City Financial Center
10050 North Wolfe Road, Suite 270
Cupertino, California 95014

Dear Ms. Dexter,

When contacted by you in May 19—, I was not interested in making a career change. At this time, I feel changing companies and perhaps an industry change or variation would benefit the long-term growth of my career.

If you are interested in placing me in an executive position in another company, please write to me so that we may discuss the idea further.

With best regards,

Steven L. Hargreaves

SLH/hb

Enclosure

February 25, 19—

Howard Mitchell
Vice President
BankSearch
One Financial Plaza, Suite 1800
Ft. Lauderdale, Florida 33395

Dear Howard:

You heard from me last year, but an updated resume is enclosed to ensure that I am still included in your active file.

My 30 years of experience includes three years of consulting for top management and 20 years in top management at two different companies, plus eight years as a bank director. Most of my experience is in the petroleum industry, but management, financial and accounting skills are valuable to any industry.

I want to get back into the corporate world and make another ten-year contribution to a company's success. My wife and I would cheerfully relocate, if the opportunity were not in Denver.

Please call so that we can talk about your client assignments which could use my experience and talents.

With best regards,

Paul H. Gutknecht

PHG/lg
enclosure

David K. Trujillo
1102 Grand Avenue
Kansas City, Missouri 64106

April 28, 19—

Ms. Sandra D. Wright
Healthcare Recruitment, Inc.
7325 North 20th Street, Suite 4500
Phoenix, Arizona 85020

Dear Ms. Wright:

Kansas City Memorial Hospital has undergone an unexpected reduction in force, and my position was one of many that were eliminated. I did not leave because of performance problems or any other difficulties. All of the administrative team has expressed their sympathy and support, and I am leaving on excellent terms with all of them. Just a few weeks before this, I had received my best performance evaluation ever.

I am now very actively in the marketplace seeking an executive position in <u>Hospital Administration, Information Systems Management, Healthcare Consulting, Strategic Planning, or Management Engineering</u>. My resume is enclosed.

Most recently, I have been responsible for the Information Systems departments: Management Engineering, Patient Care Information System (PCIS), Word Processing, and Data Services liaison (our Data Services department is a corporately provided service and reports directly to the headquarters office in Kansas). The three departments reporting directly to me represented over $.5 million to manage and we came in 5% below budget in 19—.

I am interested in expanding my administrative experience. During the last seven years, I have developed my systems and management skills with a focus on cost efficiency. I have learned effective negotiating skills for contracting and which kinds of automation will generate a substantial reduction in costs or increase in revenue (I have included a summary of the automation savings achieved in 19—). I have also co-developed a successful strategic planning methodology for integrating the hospital's corporate goals with its operational and financial goals as well as its employee performance evaluation program to focus the whole organization on achievement and reward for attaining goals.

I would appreciate the opportunity to work with you. Please call me at (816) 842-2376 or return the enclosed postage paid questionnaire.

Thank you!

David K. Trujillo

RESPONSE LETTER

David K. Trujillo
1102 Grand Avenue
Kansas City, Missouri 64106

Dear David:

_____   Please call me for a telephone interview.
Telephone: (_____) _____

_____   We do not recruit at your level.

_____   We do not recruit for Healthcare or related industries, e.g. State Hospital
Associations, Hospital Information Computer vendors, Healthcare
insurance/consulting/auditing firms.

However, you should talk to the following recruiter who may be interested
in your background.

Name: _____

Street Address: _____

City, State, Zip: _____

Telephone: (_____) _____

_____   I have nothing available now. Please contact me again after
_____(date).

Comments: _____

_____

_____

_____

Sincerely,

_____

_____

Company Name

WILLIAM A. STEINHOUR
35 Glenlake Parkway
Atlanta, GA 30328
(404) 390-1120

June 30, 19—

Mr. James D. Wilson
Executive Recruiters, Inc.
6l00 Lake Forest Drive, Suite 265
Atlanta, Georgia 30327

Dear Jim:

I hope by now you've had a good long weekend with your family in Arkansas and find yourself restored and looking forward to the rest of this short week.

<u>Here are the two documents we talked about:</u>

— My resume (which touches only briefly on my engineering background since my objective is a marketing management position), and . . .

— The professional profile I mentioned, which focuses on what I feel are my strongest suits.

As I mentioned, we are now quite open to relocation, having combed this area pretty thoroughly.

If you have any questions, need references, or want to discuss a potential opportunity to fill a client's requirement, please give me a call.

My very best regards,

W. A. Steinhour

Chang Young Li
212 Old Lake Road
Worthington, Ohio 43085

August 1, 19—

Ms. Sharon King
Management Recruiters of Cleveland
20950 Center Ridge Road
Cleveland, Ohio 44116

Dear Ms. King:

Thank you very much for taking some time with me in our recent telephone conversation. Your advice has been most useful.

I am seeking a position as an R&D/Technology Manager in a large firm or Director or Vice President of Technology for a small firm with a technology-driven product line. My broad technical background, together with marketing and profit center management experience should make me especially attractive to a smaller firm requiring a strategically-minded technical officer.

I have an excellent track record as a turnaround manager. Most recently, I took over a demoralized, moribund $12 million/year profit center and built its profitability from losses in l9— to over 10% net on volume at present while restoring morale. This was done without substantial staff reductions.

My geographic preferences are northeast and northern midwest. The Cleveland area is presently quite attractive because of my wife's employment situation. Compensation should range from the mid-$70s up and is dependent upon the location and nature of the job and the details of the compensation package.

I appreciate your efforts on my behalf.

Very truly yours,

Chang Young Li

CYL/sle
Enclosure

December 1, 19—

Mr. Tom Garber
Tom Garber & Associates
1106 Second Street, Suite 200
San Leandro, California 92024

Dear Tom:

It was a pleasure talking with you this afternoon. Enclosed is a resume which
summarizes my experience and highlights a few of my accomplishments. Although
I started as a geologist, most of my career has been in the financial and management
side of business. With two turnarounds and one startup, my experience has been
varied and I have built a consistently successful track record. I am adaptable and
learn fast as evidenced by my level of accomplishment in jobs that varied greatly
in content, and in three different industries.

As we discussed, I have been working as an investment advisor (sales) since leaving
InTek. In October, having decided to re-enter the corporate world, I transferred most
of my clients to other advisors so that I could pursue my job-search. I was quite
successful in investment sales, designing and implementing a telemarketing approach
that brought about 50 clients in a few months, most with a net worth of at least six
figures. I point this out because I believe successful sales experience is important for
a general manager.

My job target is a position with a high management content, either in the operations
or financial areas. I would ideally be with a company that has an entrepreneurial
outlook, perhaps be five to ten years old and have sales of $14 to $50 million.

Regarding compensation, I have a range of $70,000 to $100,000 in mind. Although
I have earned more in the past, I expect some cost to be associated with an industry
change, and I definitely want to get into the hazardous waste industry. At InTek, my
base salary was $135,000 plus bonuses that ranged from $10,000 to $40,000 per year.
Six years ago, at Amoco my base salary was $85,000 per year.

Mr. Tom Garber
December 1, 19—
Page Two

The potential for growth is as important as immediate compensation. An opportunity to earn equity would be very attractive. Although I am not seeking investment opportunities, I might consider a limited investment in the right situation. Geographic location is not a major consideration.

Tom, this seems to cover the items you mentioned on the phone, and I can provide strong references when appropriate. I'm looking forward to hearing form you in the near future.

With best wishes,

Michael D. Burns

MDB/fd
Enclosure

2001 ROSS AVENUE • DALLAS, TEXAS 75201 • (214) 345-3548

February 3, 19—

Ms. Judith Erickson
Manor Oak 3, Suite 611
1910 Cochran Road
Pittsburgh, Pennsylvania 15220

Dear Ms. Erickson:

Thank you for the opportunity to send my resume for the position you are filling for your Philadelphia client. The position of vice president in a major agency handling high-tech clients certainly would provide the challenge I seek to enhance my career.

I was pleased to learn that Diane Roth, with whom I have worked closely as a fellow officer of the Public Relations Society of America, passed along my name as a potential candidate.

As I mentioned during our telephone conversation, I am entering the job market because of major organizational changes at Ogilvy & Mather.

During my career, I have worked in both agencies and major corporations, so I know the sensitivities and working relationships that exist in both arenas.

I am a "quick study" with the ability to apply my communications and management skills to nearly any industry or discipline. My several years of experience with high-technology firms are shown on my resume. These assignments enabled me to work the entire product spectrum from research and development through manufacturing and marketing.

Two versions of my resume are attached. The shorter one provides a quick overview of my career. The more lengthy version—a dossier, if you will—explains in greater detail exactly what I have accomplished in each of my professional assignments.

As I mentioned, my present salary is $80,000. The responsibilities of the position you described and the necessity to move to the Philadelphia area would place my minimum salary requirements in the upper $80s.

Thank you for reviewing my credentials. Please contact me should you need additional information to assess my qualifications.

Wishing you well,

Mark C. Stankovic, Jr.

AFTER PHONE CALL WITH RECRUITER

MITCHELL B. STEVENSON
3250 Wilshire Blvd., Suite 510
Los Angeles, CA 90010
(213) 386-7689 (o)
(213) 386-6593 (voicemail)

January 5, 19—

James R. Terry
High Technology Executive Search
1900 Embarcadero
Palo Alto, California 94306

Dear Mr. Terry:

A colleague informed me that you are conducting a search for Vice President of Development for an emerging high technology firm.

I am a partner in a law firm where I concentrate on locating capital for clients starting new business ventures or expanding existing product lines. My legal experience enables me to coordinate capital development questions and manage internal legal matters that increase profitability and reduce risk.

Prior to private practice, I was Vice President of Investment Banking for a regional investment banking firm. In a three-year period my group assembled over $1 billion in new capital programs. These programs provided uniform cash flow which saved over $20 million in interest expense, created over 1,000 new jobs and earned our firm $8 1/2 million in management and underwriting fees.

I also directed the first regional development and new product innovation center in the United States. I was selected for this position because of a unique combination of business and governmental expertise. Our initial funding came from several Fortune 500 companies and nationally-recognized private foundations. These efforts resulted in 10,000 new industrial jobs, $300 million in government-assisted financing, over $100 million in private development capital and the development of 37 new companies.

I have helped clients cut their approval time by 50 percent on projects that were affected by environmental and administrative regulations. I have also coordinated and successfully guided legislative programs that improved the business climate in my clients' industry.

I will duplicate these results for your client, and I will make a change quickly for the right opportunity to play a key role in a growing technology-driven company.

Please call me next week.

Sincerely,

Mitchell B. Stevenson

R O N A L D   L .   Y O S H I H A R A
375 Park Avenue, Suite 3201
New York, NY 10152
(212) 688-8585 (o)
(212) 889-1543 (h)

September 16, 19—

Ms. Jan Baxter
Search Alternatives, Inc.
332 Nassau Street
Princeton, New Jersey 08542

Dear Jan:

I want to thank you for all your efforts on my behalf with regards to the L.L. Bean organization. Needless to say, I was disappointed to learn that they selected someone else. I hope it is because they truly felt that the other person was better able to do the job for them, and not merely for economic reasons. If the economics were the deciding factor, I certainly would have entertained a discussion to negotiate an acceptable salary level.

As I have told you, my family and I would like to return to the East. Since both my wife and I were raised in Johnstown, Pennsylvania, we are hoping to relocate somewhere near there. However, it does not need to be within the state itself. I would consider any favorable career opportunity in the East, including states like Indiana, Kentucky, and Virginia.

I'm certain you will be dealing with other new opportunities in the Eastern states. Please keep me in mind when you are evaluating those job orders. Anything you can do for me will be greatly appreciated.

My best regards,

Ronald L. Yoshihara

TWO THOUSAND OAKS TOWERS • 2000 WEST FEDERAL STREET • BOSTON, MASSACHUSETTS 02110 • (617) 765-9898

January 28, 19—

Mr. Allen J. Thomas
International Executive Search
2790 Mosside Boulevard
Monroeville, Pennsylvania 15063

Dear Allen:

It was a pleasure talking to you this morning. A short resume and an excerpt from *Fortune* magazine are enclosed which summarize my experience and highlight a few of my accomplishments.

You stated that Mike Taylor wants to take advantage of today's strong growth climate and build his company into a substantial factor. Helping him achieve this sounds like a challenge I would very much like to meet.

Most of my career has been in management and finance and I have built a consistently successful track record handling situations like this. My personal strengths and abilities have enabled me to work successfully in a variety of industries, as evidenced by my level of accomplishment in jobs that ranged from turnarounds to raising large sums of money for limited partnerships.

With regard to immediate compensation, I am flexible if there is adequate potential for growth. Equity participation would greatly influence my salary requirements. Geographic location is not a major consideration.

Finally, personal chemistry is important for this effort to be successful. An early meeting between Mike and me would be a good way to determine if this chemistry is present, as well as resolve other questions we both may have.

Allen, I very much appreciate your help in all this. After you have had a chance to review the enclosed materials, I would like to call to get your reactions and comments.

Best regards,

Michael D. Burns

Enclosures

February 2, 19—

Mr. Roy W. Laurence
Ward Howell International, Inc.
20 North Wacker Drive
Chicago, Illinois 60606

Dear Mr. Laurence:

Just a brief note to thank you for responding to material I sent you earlier this month. I am glad to hear that you are retaining my resume and hope some assignment in the near future calls for a background and experience that matches mine.

I have strong and well-balanced experience in general management and finance encompassing one start-up and two successful turnarounds. With a track record that was established in three separate industries, I should not be categorized as a one-industry specialist. I can offer a lot.

If I can provide you with any more information or be of any other help, please do not hesitate to call.

Best regards,

Michael D. Burns

MARK C. STANKOVIC, JR.

2001 ROSS AVENUE • DALLAS, TEXAS 75201 • (214) 345-3548

February 20, 19—

Ms. Judith Erickson
Smith Associates, Inc.
Manor Oak 3, Suite 611
1910 Cochran Road
Pittsburgh, Pennsylvania 15220

Dear Ms. Erickson:

It's been a few weeks since we last talked about the public relations position you are filling for your Philadelphia client.

I just wanted to see if you have been in touch with your client and if there is opportunity for further discussions. I will call you on Wednesday to determine the status of the project.

With good wishes, always,

Mark C. Stankovic, Jr.

Want Ads

When you think of want ads, think 5% of your campaign, not 95%. Everyone should answer ads—especially those that are a perfect fit, but answering want ads should generally consume no more than 30 minutes of your day. That's because there are so many other, better ways to job-hunt.

If you plan to answer ads, I suggest you develop a "generic" letter that can be mailed quickly by simply changing names and dates. Use this letter to answer most ads. Photocopy your completed letter and clip the ad to your copy so you'll have a record if and when someone calls (they seldom do). Once you mail the original, forget about it. Get back to doing more productive things.

If you find an ad that is 100% perfect, your ideal dream job, take the time to tailor a letter. Find a business directory, look up the name of the hiring manager—not the personnel director—and write that person a sales letter. That's a letter you can follow up, because you have a name.

By the way, if you find that you're not getting any response from ads, don't be discouraged. That's the rule today, not the exception. Few companies even send rejection letters anymore. It's too costly. Keep answering the ads that fit you, and sooner or later, the phone will ring.

"Didn't you read the ad? They're looking for a specific type."

Robert S. Rosenthal
303 North Central Avenue
Phoenix, Arizona 85012
(602) 264-1488

November 28, 19—

Ms. Janet Campbell
Astronautics Corporation
P. O. Box 587
Orchard Park, New York 14127-0587

Dear Mr. Campbell,

   Subject: Stanford Alumni Employment Bulletin - Advertisement for President

Enclosed is my resume in response to your advertisement. I found the wording
of your advertisement with emphasis on leadership, innovation and change quite
intriguing. It is in response to such challenges that I have excelled during my career.

Most recently, I was President of a troubled subsidiary of InTek which I turned around
and led to the best performance in its history. Previous to that, I worked successfully
in a variety of unusual situations, including the startup of a significant division of
Amoco and the turnaround of Collins Chemical. In each of these situations, the problems (or opportunities) differed widely. They had in common, though, a requirement
of an ability to size up the situation, assess the reasonable alternatives and execute a
plan of action. My track record shows that I am able to do this.

With regard to the requirement for manufacturing experience, I have worked 14 years
in mining and milling operations, where I obtained an in-depth exposure to production problems. Additionally, of course, I was President of InTek with full responsibility
for all operations and financial activities.

I am free to travel and open to relocation. I would welcome the opportunity to meet
you and to further discuss your requirements.

Thank you for you interest.

Sincerely,

Robert S. Rosenthal

BEN REDING
577 Silverton Court
Colorado Springs, CO 80919
(719) 594-8086 office
(719) 598-3422 home

November 25, 19—

Professional Staffing
Applied Materials
M/S 0561/FL
3340 Scott Blvd.
Santa Clara, CA 95054

I was excited to find your advertisement for a Technical Support Engineer in the Oregon State alumni bulletin on November 8th. After 16 years in the high reliability Integrated Circuit industry I am looking for a new challenge with a progressive company. I can bring the following assets to your organization:

YOUR REQUIREMENTS	MY QUALIFICATIONS
Solving complex system-level hardware problems that occur in a production environment. High degree of analytical problem solving and hardware troubleshooting skills.	Hands-on installation of an MRC magnatron sputtering system, SiCr thin film resistor process development, and transfer of process & equipment to production. Also, assisted in the development of an in-house vapor deposition system for R&D.
Skills in one or more areas: Electronics (digital/analog), electrical power engineering, electromechanical engineering, software engineering, ultra-high vacuum systems, and physical vapor deposition process technology.	Assembled and disassembled ultra-high vacuum pumps. Debugged RF plasma deposition. Fabricated in-house deposition targets. Excellent computer hardware/software skills. Designed cooling coils for vapor deposition system. Mechanical tooling and enclosure skills.
3+ years of experience in the semi-conductor capital equipment industry.	Equivalent of six years experience working closely with semiconductor capital equipment industry by working one-on-one during the R&D phase of new semiconductor equipment design.

YOUR REQUIREMENTS	MY QUALIFICATIONS
Advanced degree (BS/MS/PhD) in either Electrical or Mechanical Engineering.	BS in Mechanical Engineering with strong R&D skills.
Program Management skills, highly organized and be able to work on multiple tasks independently.	Program Management planning, scheduling, and budgeting of up to 13 simultaneous programs with both small and large teams, up to 100 people. Accurate forecasting skills with 90% on-time milestones.
Documentation and reporting skills are important.	Excellent written and oral reporting skills. Performed as proposal manager on more than nine contract proposals ranging from 50 to 400 pages. Monthly oral reporting to UTMC's President and Operating Committee on company critical program.
Multiple positions: Santa Clara, two of which will require a 1+ year assignment in either Korea or Japan as well as fluency in those languages.	I am not bilingual but am willing to learn if needed.

The ability to work well with people, to have the drive and interest to get the job done, and several years of stable work experience make me uniquely qualified for this position.

I look forward to meeting with you personally to discuss the opportunity and how I may contribute to the ongoing success of your organization.

Thank you!

Ben J. Reding

Kathleen R. McCormick
7409 Mt. Meeker Road
Omaha, Nebraska 68124
(712) 277-4474

January 25, 19—

Ms. Nancy P. Carson
Employment Manager
Personnel Department
The Alexandria Hospital
4320 Seminary Road
Alexandria, Virginia 22304

Dear Ms. Carson:

The image of Alexandria's stimulating and historic environment caught my imagination when I read about your Director of Planning position in the January career opportunities listing of the Society of Healthcare Planning and Marketing.

I currently hold the position of Director of Marketing at Longmont hospital—a national specialty medical center—which has no planning department, per se. Therefore, institutional planning has, for the most part, been carried out on the basis of market analyses conducted by me and my staff.

This, in addition to my other qualifications, makes me particularly well-suited to your opening. Over the past 16 years I have worked in several progressively more responsible positions within health care. In each position I enjoyed and performed best in the areas of planning and program development.

May I please know more about Alexandria Hospital and its mission? About who the position reports to, and the corporate structure of the hospital? And also the relationship between planning, marketing, and public affairs?

Thank you for you attention.

Sincerely,

Kathleen R. McCormick

John B. Doyle
9142 W. 92nd Avenue
Westminster, Colorado 80021
Home: (303) 420-4428 Work: (303) 231-4307

October 13, 19—

Sentrol Inc.
Attn: HR - Pur.
10831 SW Cascade Blvd.
Portland, Oregon 97223

Dear Human Resources Manager:

I am responding to your October 9th advertisement in <u>The Wall Street Journal</u> for Purchasing Manager. The following comments show how my qualifications match your stated requirements:

<u>YOUR REQUIREMENTS</u>	MY QUALIFICATIONS/ <u>ACCOMPLISHMENTS</u>
1. Electronics and mechanical purchasing background.	1. Ten years in all phases of electro-mechanical assembly, five plus years as purchasing manager.
2. Experience and knowledge of international business and purchasing standards.	2. Familiarity with ISO 9000 Series and the FDA's Good Manufacturing Practices.
3. Experience developing world class supplier relationships to achieve cost delivery and service including implementing JIT and direct to line supply programs.	3. Developed many systems to meet requirements for world class manufacturing in addition to several supplier programs for JIT.
4. Strong communication skills, including negotiation skills.	4. Worked on all major contracts over a five year period resulting in 2-5% cost reductions.
5. Strong management skills and the ability to develop a purchasing team.	5. Excellent leadership abilities and believe in employee participation and empowerment.
6. Must be customer service and team oriented.	6. Total focus for PIC and Purchasing was to satisfy the Customer.

Please contact me to talk further about this exciting opportunity.

Regards,

John B. Doyle

James R. Adams
1038 Oak Hills Drive
Colorado Springs, CO 80919
(719) 593-1576

January 6, 19—

MCNC
Attn: Barbara Ramirez
     Human Resources
P.O. Box 1224
Research Triangle Park, NC 27709

Dear Ms. Ramirez:

I'm responding to your announcement in the January 4, 19— issue of <u>The Wall Street Journal</u> on the opening for Director, Device Fabrication Technology at MCNC. I have been looking for a position where I can continue to grow in my career, and leverage my broad background in microelectronics technology, strategic planning, and marketing to develop high value-added products and technologies. I believe that my qualifications and industrial experience are an excellent match for your stated requirements:

<u>Your Requirements</u>	<u>My Qualifications</u>
1. MS or Doctoral Degree in Electrical Engineering, Physics or Materials Science.	1. PhD EE, University of Nebraska, specializing in Electrical Materials.
2. At least 10 years of management experience in industry.	2. Twenty-three years industrial experience. Thirteen years at the senior management level. Managed cross-functional and line organizations with multi-million dollar budgets.
3. Well known in the microelectronics field for technical and leadership capabilities.	3. Internationally recognized expertise in semiconductor technology and radiation effects in microelectronics. Twenty-six publications, sixteen presentations and three patents. Extensive continuing education in Total Quality Management, teamwork, and leadership.
4. Strong sales and marketing orientation with experience in strategic planning.	4. Director, Strategic Planning, and Program Management, Manager, Strategic Marketing. Developed plans for strategic business relationships and penetration of strategic programs. Extensive customer, university and Government interface experience. Raised venture capital in Europe and the U.S.

There are other accomplishments in my background that are summarized in the enclosed résumé. I have also enclosed a copy of my publications, presentations, and patents, and a list of my continuing education courses. If there is any additional information you require, please do not hesitate to contact me. I am looking forward to talking with you further to discuss this exciting opportunity.

All the best to you,

James R. Adams

BRUCE R. VANDEVENTER

235 W. MAPLE AVENUE • SANTA MONICA, CALIFORNIA 90401 • (213) 451-2402

Mr. Mike Warner
IDS Financial Services, Inc.
500 IDS Tower
Minneapolis, Minnesota 55402

October 22, 19—

Dear Mr. Warner:

Please consider me for a career with IDA as a Personal Financial Planner. I feel that I meet the requirements of your ad in <u>The Wall Street Journal</u>, as briefly outlined below:

1. <u>Independent</u>—I have relied on my own work and research to come up with solutions and strategies used in my personal and financial decisions. I look before I leap.

2. <u>Self-motivated</u>—I achieved an M.S. in Geology, and am pursuing an MBA in the evenings, emphasizing Finance.

3. <u>Strong desire for achievement</u>—In the last few months I've contacted 110 oil companies on three separate occasions in pursuit of career opportunities. This demonstrates commitment, persistence, and strong goal orientation.

As you can see, my background is geology. Due to a strong recession in the oil and gas industry, it will be difficult for me to continue in my trained profession. Therefore, I have decided to pursue financial planning as a career.

My MBA emphasizes Finance, particularly investments, and I've undergone my own personal financial planning. I'm familiar with the steps of financial planning (the need for adequate insurance, having three to six months cash or liquid reserve, etc.), so I'll be able to use my own experience to help others.

I manage my own investments, involving such diverse items as rental real estate, oil and gas limited partnerships, real estate limited partnerships, growth and tax-exempt mutual funds, stocks, and equipment leasing programs.

I'm interested in discussing financial planning opportunities with IDA, and I'm looking forward to talking with you soon.

With good wishes,

Bruce R. VanDeventer

PASQUALE SCARPELLA
1100 Milam Avenue, Apt. 340
Houston, TX 77002
(713) 651-1384

November 12, 19—

Post Office Box 1630
Palmer Lake, CO 80133

Dear Personnel Manager:

I was very excited to find your advertisement for a director of Video Engineering in last week's Gazette Telegraph. After 23 years in the Government Aerospace communications industry, I am looking for a new challenge with a small, growing company.

I can bring the following assets to your organization:

— BSEE degree and 23 years of hands-on hardware experience with communications equipment and systems. I know how it's designed, manufactured, installed, and fixed. A proven ability to troubleshoot systems in real time.

— Experience with both antenna-radiated and cable-connected equipment from baseband to microwave frequencies; satellite and ground-based segments.

— Project and functional management expertise including project scheduling and cost control.

— Strong customer orientation. My primary responsibility as Program Manager was to keep the customer happy. Satisfied customers bring future business.

— Willingness to meet the world. A good portion of my previous job was traveling to customers' facilities and making "high speed viewgraph" presentations.

— Computer literacy. Auto-CAD was the standard for my projects and my Test Engineering department. I use a similar program, Design-CAD, on my personal computer as well as WordPerfect, Lotus 1-2-3, and telecommunications programs.

The attached résumé summarizes my experience and demonstrates my successful advancement. It's time for a change now and I'd like to explore this possibility with you. If, however, you do not see a potential here, I would still like to talk with you about your industry. I'll call next week to set up a convenient meeting.

Yours truly,

Pasquale Scarpella

Ryan Tolbech
4532 Cahilloval
San Angelo, TX 76902
(915) 942-9313

December 2, 19—

BT&K
2000 18th Street
Suite 300
San Angelo, TX 76902

Attention: Senior Creative Director

I am sending you my résumé in response to your ad in the May issue of Advertising Age for a Production Artist. I believe I have the skills that your company is seeking, and would like to be considered for the position.

I have extensive layout and design experience and enjoy working on precise, detailed projects. My background in 4-color production, camera work, and desktop publishing systems would also be an asset to your company. Working under tight deadlines is the standard of the advertising industry that I come from, and is not a problem for me.

I look forward to meeting with you personally, and reviewing the needs of BT&K in greater detail. I can be reached at the above telephone number.

Let's talk soon,

Ryan Tolbech

William D. Zwanzig
222 Helen Avenue
St. Louis, Missouri 63105
Home: (314) 241-2999

June 10, 19—

Box 025
c/o The Chicago Tribune
Chicago, Illinois 60611

Dear Sir/Madam:

I am writing to you regarding your recent advertisement for a Plant Engineer.

In my last position, I was very good at "hands on" trouble-shooting and process development. I am also a "self starter" and am very mechanically inclined. I strive for simple, cost-effective, common sense solutions to technical problems, instead of elaborate schemes to re-invent the wheel. The position that you describe sounds exactly like the kind of job I am seeking.

To make myself more competitive with local applicants, I am willing to pay my own relocation expenses. Because I am currently renting a home, I can relocate without problems and I am available immediately.

I started with Dresser Industries in 19— at $21,500/yr. After 5-1/2 years and three promotions, my salary was $38,500 plus car. In 19— I received a superior Performance Award of $1,350. I was the only engineer out of approximately 15 other candidates to receive this award. I mention my salary history only to show that I am an achiever and have been recognized for my accomplishments. My salary requirement is negotiable.

I would appreciate your time in reviewing my enclosed resume and I would welcome an opportunity to meet with you for a personal interview.

With many thanks,

William D. Zwanzig

DANIEL J. GOIN
6120 South Elm Court
Littleton, Colorado 80121
(303) 773-3417

October 30, 19—

Compensation Merit Systems
P.O. Box 181
Denver, Colorado 80218-0899

Dear Sir or Madam:

Your advertisement for Human Resources Director describes a position that I believe is well suited to my skills, experience and desire to apply my generalist background in a challenging new environment.

I have 14 years of experience in human resource management, including the following key areas:

o Recruitment

o Personnel Policy Development

o Compensation/Performance-Based Pay

o Benefit Program Design and Administration

o Affirmative Action/EEO

o Employee Relations/Supervisory Counsel

o Training and Development

o Personnel Records Management

I would greatly appreciate the opportunity to discuss more specifically how I might apply my background to meet your organization's needs. My current salary is $43,000 per year. My minimum requirement is $40,000. My resume is enclosed for your review.

Thank you!

Daniel J. Goin

DJG/ckr
Enclosure

Maria D. Archuleta
9350 S. Dixie Highway
Miami, FL 33156
(305) 670-7264

April 13, 19—

Personnel Manager
DAILY CAMERA
P.O. Box 591
Boulder, Colorado 80306

Dear Personnel Manager:

I am responding to your advertisement for a nurse recruiter.

As a results-oriented professional, I have over 14 years' experience in various
hospital and HMO environments. I have skills, ability, knowledge and personality
to make a contribution to your organization in the minimum amount of time.

These highlights may interest you:

— Served as nursing liaison to regional recruitment and retention
committee for two years.

— Presented committee recommendations to top-level management for
approval.

— Conceived and wrote job description, then actively recruited an RN
for the first Nurse Recruiter position in a local major hospital.

— Upgraded quality of supervisory staff hired in local HMO by revising
recruitment and hiring practices.

— Actively recruited supervisory and key technical staff for 22 patient-
care and specialty departments.

— Affiliated with National Association of Nurse Recruiters.

— Successfully recruit volunteers for fundraising, social activities, and
church functions.

I believe in excellence and have always dedicated my talents and creative
abilities to assure the successful accomplishment of company goals.

The ability to work well with people, to have the drive and interest to accomplish
the work, and several years of stable work experience make me uniquely
qualified for this position.

I look forward to meeting with you personally to discuss the opportunity and
how I may contribute to the ongoing success of your organization.

Thank you, sincerely,

Maria D. Archuleta

Richard A. Polson
12 Greenway Plaza, Suite 1100 • Houston, TX 77046
(713) 961-4030 (o) • (713) 961-4113 (FAX)

July 23, 19—

Post Office Box DG-921
1233 Regal Row
Dallas, Texas 75247

Dear Hiring Manager:

Your ad for a Vice President of Operations overseas caught my attention. I've traveled extensively for the last 22 years. Recently, I spent four years in Venezuela, South America, and two years in Dubai, U.A.E. (Middle East). As a result, I adapt quickly to new environments, and I've managed many different personalities and nationalities. Here are some of my recent results:

— Opened and organized new division with responsibilities covering five states and 356 employees.

— Reduced sales force 62% while increasing market share from 14% to 23.5%.

— Turned an operation from a $100,000 annual loss into the third most profitable operation in the region in less than a year.

— Had the most profitable operation in the central region of the U.S.

— Negotiated one-year contract in Bombay, India, for the purchase of raw hydrochloric acid. The price negotiated was lower than the current level and was during a period of rising prices.

I'm 47 years old and in excellent health. I'm married and have two children (one recently graduated from college, the other a sophomore in college). I hold a BBA degree from Texas Tech University.

I'm seeking a new challenge—one where my innovative and management talents can be applied. Your company seems to offer such a challenge, and my credentials match your requirements. I look forward to talking with you.

Sincerely,

Richard A. Polson

RODNEY B. RICHMOND

8447 W. 74th Place
Arvada, Colorado 80005   (303) 421-3444

April 29, 19—

Ms. Sandra L. Susilovich
Lexmark International, Inc.
425 Market Street, 6th Floor
San Francisco, CA 94105

Dear Ms. Susilovich:

I am answering your ad for a salesperson in the April 19 <u>Rocky Mountain News.</u> I am very interested in a technical sales position, and your product line sounds particularly appealing. As my résumé shows, I have 12 years experience in the computer field and I have used, repaired, and recommended the purchase of laser printers and support products. I am familiar with the Lexmark printer marketed under the IBM name.

Although my recent sales experience is limited, my interest and ambition is not. Through my own initiative, I enrolled in an intensive nine-month sales training course. Although I was working full time, I graduated number one in my class.

<u>To attest to my people skills and work ethic, I have included comments from letters written about my work.</u>

> *"We would like to take this opportunity to express our appreciation for your excellent work during the Barcode Technology Project"* . . . *"Your dedication and hard work were an integral part of the project's success."* COVIA, Field Service Support Manager

> *"Congratulations on being selected as the most productive computer technician at United Airlines for the first quarter of 19—. You have earned this award through your excellent efforts . . ."* United Airlines, Field Services Support Manager

> *"Martin Marietta Corporation would like to take this opportunity to commend the fine job performed by Rod Richmond, at our Open House, held July 15, 19—. Rod was most helpful in every way . . ."* Martin Marietta Aerospace, Food/Vending Services Manager

I would be delighted to talk with you about this position, and look forward to hearing from you soon. I can be reached at (303) 421-3444. Please leave a message if I am not there to personally receive your call.

With great interest,

Rodney B. Richmond

Douglas Gragg
10631 West Downing
Denver, Colorado 80236
(303) 835-6511

April 24, 19—

Search Committee
Colorado Historical Society
1300 Broadway
Denver, Colorado 80203

Dear Committee Members:

The position of Regional Property Administrator is an excellent match with my long-term intense interest in Colorado and Denver history, which culminated last winter in my receiving a master's degree in history.

At one point, my goals included teaching history, and I completed over 24 hours of course work in education.

As my resume indicates, I have spent many years in business, coupled with seven terms of course work at Barnes Business College, where I focused on business and financial management.

My extensive political involvement has honed not only my knowledge of volunteers and their needs, but also my abilities to organize and manage information. For a number of years, I have been in charge of our local political caucus, which includes prominent local politicians and business people. I have been active in more than fifty political campaigns, raised funds, and organized and managed "paper trails" for many elections. In last fall's national elections, I assisted in recruiting, training, and organizing more than 3,000 employees.

As a Denver native and third generation Coloradan, I would be excited and proud to be an employee of the Colorado Historical Society. The position advertised provides me an ideal opportunity to use my professional training in history and my long experience in business management. I look forward to talking with you.

Very truly yours,

Douglas Gragg

Kenneth W. Grove
1335 Olympian Circle
Lafayette, Colorado 80026
U.S.A.

May 8, 19—

Personnel Manager
International Education Services
Shi Taiso Building
10-7 Dogenzada 2-chome
Shibuya-ku
Tokyo, Japan 150

Dear Sir/Madam:

I am interested in applying for a position as English teacher for Japanese businessmen as described in your recent job announcement bulletin. I am a scientist by training and profession. Enclosed is a copy of my resume listing my academic training and professional experience.

My wife and I have very close ties to Japan and would very much like to live there for a few years. My sister, Linda Grove, is a professor of Asian studies at Sophia University in Tokyo. Her husband, Hideme Kondo, is a Japanese citizen and a curator at an art museum in Tokyo as well. My wife and I spent two weeks in Japan with my sister and her family in May of 19—. In the course of our stay, we thoroughly enjoyed visiting with the various Japanese relatives and felt very comfortable and at ease in the Japanese culture.

I hope that the above information will give you an understanding of our interest in spending more time in Japan and in teaching English to Japanese people.

We do not have a fluent understanding of the Japanese language. However, we have studied the language briefly for preparation for our trip in 19—. We also intend to continue to study Japanese as we have Japanese relatives whom we visit periodically.

I look forward to talking soon, and I'll call in the next few weeks if I don't hear from you.

With good wishes,

Kenneth W. Grove

Enclosure

Janet Bukowski
255 Omega Way
Colorado Springs, Colorado 80917
(719) 555-2323 Office
(719) 555-1929 Residence

August 2, 19—

Continental Airlines
Employment Department
P.O. Box 4330
Houston, TX 77210-4330

Dear Personnel Manager:

As a longtime resident of Colorado Springs, I am well aware of the outstanding reputation of Continental Airlines, which leads me to express my interest in this dynamic company. I am submitting my resume for your review for the position of Ticket Agent. I feel I have the necessary qualifications for your consideration and would appreciate the opportunity to demonstrate this in a personal meeting.

Although my experience in the airline business is limited, I am very interested and enthusiastic about learning. I am an outgoing, friendly individual who would enjoy developing personal relationships with customers. My strong communication and organizational skills would serve me well in responding to the needs of your company. My drive, determination and leadership ability are evident in my resume.

I am a hard worker who is noted for accuracy and timeliness. My performance evaluations have consistently been at the "above average" and "outstanding" levels, and I can furnish excellent references should you need them.

A recent staff reduction at KDI Electronics due to lack of work, has resulted in the elimination of my position as Senior Manufacturing Controller. Because of this mass layoff, I am eligible to participate in an On-The-Job Training Program which will reimburse you 50% of my wages during a negotiated training period. Enclosed is more information on this subject.

I feel that your airline would benefit from my contribution as a Ticket Agent. Should you have a position available on your staff, you may contact me at (719) 555-2323.

Thank you, sincerely,

Janet Bukowski

BRUCE D. ROBERTSON, CPA

3182 South Holly Street
Denver, Colorado 80222

(303) 756-7434 (H)
(303) 779-1417 (W)

June 20, 19—

Williams International
P.O. Box 500
F.D.R. Station
New York, New York 10150

Dear Employment Manager:

The overseas position you describe in your recent advertisement in the "National Business Employment Weekly" is exactly the type of position I am seeking! With my diversified international management, finance, treasury, taxes, planning, and consolidations experience, I know I can be an asset to many of your clients. In addition, I speak and read French. From 19— to 19— I also studied Business French through classes at Storage Technology Corporation.

Some highlights of my international, finance, and administration experience, which might interest you, are as follows:

— Number two man in Storage Technology's European operations in which annual subsidiary revenues grew in two years from $5MM to $55MM; in addition, we had OEM revenues of $25MM per year.

— Prepared worldwide budgets, plans, and consolidations.

— Established international consulting firm.

— Seventeen years' experience in management and financial controls.

This is only a brief summary of my abilities—there is more to share. As your Vice President of Finance Assistant, I know I can help your company achieve its worldwide goals and objectives in this fast-paced, high-tech environment.

I am looking forward to meeting with you to discuss this exciting, challenging position in more detail.

Sincerely,

Bruce D. Robertson, CPA
BDR:pr

Arnold C. Neuschwanger
1200 Midtown Tower
Rochester, New York 14604

May 22, 19—

Box T-300
The Wall Street Journal
30 Broad Street
New York, New York 10017

Dear Personnel Manager:

I'm responding to your May 19th advertisement in <u>The Wall Street Journal</u> for a President of your Kitchen and Housewares Division. The following comments show how my qualifications match your stated requirements:

<u>YOUR REQUIREMENTS</u>	<u>MY QUALIFICATIONS</u>
1. Dynamic professional with top-level management experience.	1. Former President of $100MM division of corporate giant. Member operations committee of two companies. Board Chairman of two subsidiaries.
2. Proven record.	2. Built sales from $25 to $100MM in three years by internal growth and acquisition. Top profits in corporation.
3. Experience in financial administration.	3. Total P&L responsibility for 4 enterprises comprising the division.
4. Sales Management.	4. Former V.P. Marketing for $400MM Corporation.
5. Consumer hardgoods.	5. Major housewares.
6. Product Development.	6. Brought out new food product for consumer market.
7. MBA.	7. Stanford University.

There are other accomplishments in my background which may be of interest to you, and I look forward to talking with you further to discuss this exciting opportunity.

Very truly yours,

Arnold C. Neuschwanger

February 5, 19—

Mr. Richard A. Rathbun
MSF 134
Data General Corporation
4400 Computer Drive
Westboro, Massachusetts 01580

Dear Mr. Rathbun:

This letter is in response to your advertisement in the Denver Post of February 3, 19—. Your ad outlined requirements for Graphic Designers within your marketing department. This position is very appealing to me since your needs match a great deal of my background. Specifically:

> Project Management—From large collateral print projects for Datagraphix, University Computing Company and Dravo Corporation, Denver, to corporate identity projects for Bank of Oklahoma and Old National Bank of Washington. Combined approximate project costs in excess of $500K with cost savings to each client.

> Public Relations—As the Communications Director for Arapahoe/Douglas Area Vocational Schools, I developed new communications tools for 20 individual programs, designed a multimedia slide/video production which was shown throughout five school districts in the Denver area, and thus assisted in a 20% enrollment growth for the Area School.

> Additionally, I was able to acquire approximately $300K worth of free air time on local radio and television for Area School promotion. Both the Executive Director and I appeared on two of the programs for a total of 1-1/2 half hours of air time.

> Print Production—For the past eight years I trained 250 secondary and post-secondary vocational students in graphic print production. In a recent five-year study done on my program through the State Board, my placement record topped 84%.

From 19— to the present I've been involved in vocational education. During this time I successfully took an "arts and crafts" fine art program into state-of-the-art graphic communications education. I've proposed and implemented a program which was originally budgeted at $3K per school year

Mr. Richard A. Rathbun
February 5, 19—
Page Two

to a current $21K per year. With this money, I brought the computer into the classroom six years ago. Currently, I've proposed the first CAD system and hope to incorporate this into the curriculum.

While teaching full time I've also continued to keep my design talents current with several projects a year through my private practice. At present, I have had over 27 years of experience in design. I have attached a resume which will outline my past employment history. I would be delighted to review my salary history with you on a more personal basis when we get together.

In closing, I look forward to meeting you when you come to Denver so we can discuss your needs in greater detail.

With great enthusiasm,

T. Craig Lincoln

TCL/

Enclosure

Sally W. Larson
2500 East Colorado Boulevard
Pasadena, California 91107

April 1, 19—

Box ME-16
National Business Employment Weekly
c/o The Wall Street Journal
400 Alexis R. Shuman Boulevard
Naperville, Illinois 60566

Re: Real Estate Attorney

Ladies/Gentlemen:

I would like to express my interest in the position of real estate attorney with your company. I believe my background in acquisitions and in securities would compliment the goals established by your company.

My experience in land acquisitions and securities is the result of my tenures with Amoco Petroleum Company, Texaco Oil Company, and in private practice. The areas, in which I have had substantial experience and responsibility, include:

* team participation in the acquisition of companies valued respectively at $18 million and $40 million dollars

* drafting of purchase and sales agreements for properties valued at $500 thousand dollars to $1 million dollars

* title examination and curative

* negotiation and drafting of contracts pertaining to lease acquisition, including farmins, options, pooling agreements and seismic exchange agreements, many involving wells costing between $1 million and $4 million

* drafting of limited partnerships and compliance with the Blue Sky requirements of numerous states

* team participation in briefing contracts which provided substantial basis for two joint ventures requiring minimum expenditures of $40 million and $100 million each

This list is not inclusive of all areas of authority, but does provide a fair overview of my responsibilities.

I have, for my own account, acquired real estate properties in the Pasadena metropolitan area valued at approximately three hundred thousand dollars. Two of the properties are rental units for which I handled the leasing. These investments are a reflection of my interest in a career in real estate investment.

My resume, detailing my background, is enclosed for your review. I would welcome the opportunity to meet and discuss my experience with you. Correspondence may be directed to me at the letterhead address. However, please feel free to contact me by telephone at (213) 681-3973.

Very truly yours,

Sally W. Larson

SWL/kb
Enclosure

Richard C. Kleczewski
420 Rowland Park Circle
Littleton, CO 80125
(303) 555-0020

May 14, 19—

Mr. Michael M. Morrison
Personnel Officer
San Marin County
Personnel Division
27 East Ocean Avenue
San Francisco, California 94105

Dear Mr. Morrison and the Selection Committee:

Your job announcement listed nine requirements for the position of Theater Auditorium Manager and I would like to discuss my experience in light of these requirements:

1. <u>Qualified</u>.

   — Twenty-one years' experience in the meeting and convention management business in such facilities as: The Denver Auditorium Theater, Red Rocks Amphitheater, Currigan Exhibition Hall and the Denver Auditorium Arena.

   — Consultant to Architects and Planning Staff on Major Convention Centers in Calgary, Oklahoma City, Kansas City, Toledo, Colorado and San Francisco.

   — Managed a wide spectrum of events including ballet, opera, symphony, trade and exhibit shows, auto shows, union meetings and other sit-down conventions, banquets, fashion shows, live theater, concerts, medical meetings, church conventions and associated spin-off meetings.

   — Coordinated meetings involving 10 to 30,000 people.

   — Coordinated banquets involving 10 to 5,500 people.

2. <u>Motivated</u>.

   I have an attitude of excitement and enthusiasm for "show business." During performances I stay on the premises and make myself available. I don't leave problems for subordinates to handle. You will find that I am "right at your elbow if you need me . . ."

3. <u>Thorough Knowledge of Performing Arts Facility Operation</u>.

   I have learned the performing arts business from the ground up. I started
   in Denver as an usher; then moved to head usher; then to stagehand . . . to
   assistant manager . . . to manager.

   This has given me expertise in all the different levels of operation.

4. <u>Ability to Manage Small Staff</u>.

   I understand how to choose appropriate personnel and make sure they are
   well-trained, well-disciplined, and have a *professional attitude*. I did all the
   hiring for the Denver Convention Complex for four years (janitorial and
   ushering personnel) and supervised as many as 150 people at Currigan Hall.

5. <u>Ability to Work with Performers</u>.

   I'm relaxed with performers. They look to me for personal assistance and
   security. I have always gotten along well with them and have worked with
   Johnny Mathis, Roger Williams, Al Hirt, Debbie Reynolds, Arthur Fiedler,
   Eddie Arnold, Liberace, Leonard Nimoy, and many others.

6. <u>Ability to Work with the General Public</u>.

   I love working with the public, as these comments suggest:

   *"We found Mr. Emerson to be the most congenial and helpful building manager
   we have worked with anywhere in the Nation. As a direct result of his ability and
   job thoroughness, we have scheduled our 19— Convention in Denver once again."*

      Bill Ackerman, Executive Director
      Western Apparel Manufacturers Association

   *"You've undoubtedly been one of the most cooperative men that it has been my
   pleasure to work with in planning for conventions."*

      Michael T. Scott, Financial Planning Secretary
      Southern Baptist Convention

"Your courtesies and kindness were most appreciated, and I do not think we could have had such a successful kick-off if it had not been for you and your personal thoughtfulness and that of the members of your crew."

    Robert E. Noonan, Executive Director
    Mile-Hi United Fund

"Once again, thank you so much for taking time out of your busy schedule to review many of the problems confronting convention and conference bookings."

    Robert B. Sullivan, President and General Manager
    Pueblo Chamber of Commerce

"Not only does Denver have one of the best designed facilities in the United States, but also appears to have one of the most knowledgeable and effective managers."

    Jack C. Thomas, Assistant Executive Director
    San Francisco Redevelopment Agency

"I can only hope that our future conferences will have a Richard Emerson in them. I look forward to working with you again."

    Robert B. Donner, Assistant Director
    Public Affairs Section
    International Association of Chiefs of Police

7. <u>Knowledge of Fiscal Aspects of Operation</u>.

I originated the annual budget of $400,000 for Currigan Hall and handled all the ordering and inventory control.

8. <u>Knowledge of Technical Aspects of Operation</u>.

I have complete working knowledge of: (1) heating, (2) air conditioning, (3) fire and safety regulations, (4) building codes, (5) crowd control techniques, (6) first aid, (7) security, (8) catering, (9) lighting, (10) seating and stage arrangements, (11) sound systems, (12) lead-in and lead-out time and, (13) union contracts.

9. <u>Strong PR Skills</u>.

I am experienced in sales. I know the way to book buildings and keep accurate records to prevent double bookings.

I can coordinate the activities of the performers, exhibitors, working personnel and management, and I can keep it all running smoothly.

"Thank you for taking the time to show me some of your convention center. You're the kind of person we like to deal with, because you don't try to hand out a lot of false information—you know what you're talking about."

    Jack Barker, C.L.U.
    Million Dollar Round Table

The last, and perhaps the most important requirement for this job is enthusiasm— and I'm excited and enthusiastic about discussing this unique job opportunity with you in person.

In the meantime, anything I can do to help you would be my pleasure. Best wishes for a successful venture.

Cordially,

Richard C. Kleczewski

BRUCE D. ROBERTSON, CPA

3182 South Holly Street
Denver, Colorado 80222

(303) 756-7434 (H)
(303) 779-1417 (W)

January 18, 29—

Ms. Jean W. Kingston
Vice President Human Resources
Bank of America
230 California Street
San Francisco, California 94111

Ms. Kingston:

I just received your letter of December 20th, and I am puzzled at not being
invited for an interview. My experience and your requirements looked like a
perfect "fit."

I understand that you are constantly reviewing resumes and that oversights
can occur. Please review the enclosed want ad and my resume and reconsider
me for a position in your company.

With many thanks,

Bruce Robertson, CPA

BDR:bl

Keith M. Bennett
16728 E. Prentice Cir.
Aurora, Colorado 80015
(303) 623-1239

May 19, 19—

Dear Hiring Manager:

I hope the difficult process of final selection for your Sales Manager is progressing well. I'm sure you've received many responses from highly qualified candidates, and due to the number of responses haven't been able to write each applicant.

Because of my enthusiastic interest in your firm, I'm writing to determine your level of interest in my background. I've enclosed a return envelope and brief response form for your convenience.

I appreciate the opportunity to be considered for this position and to become a member of your team. If I may provide any additional information, please do not hesitate to call.

Very truly yours,

Keith M. Bennett

To: Keith M. Bennett

From: Company Name

☐ Your background is of particular interest to us, and we will be in touch to schedule an interview.

☐ At this time, we are still evaluating the résumés and will be scheduling interviews in the future.

☐ We have made our selection, but will keep your résumé on file for future reference.

☐ We have narrowed our selection and found candidates that have a background that more closely matches our requirements.

References

Few hiring managers trust their own judgment when making hiring decisions, especially at higher levels. That's why companies seek outside opinions. Pay attention to what others say, because nothing can hurt you worse than a lukewarm reference.

In seeking testimonials, don't limit yourself to former bosses. Anyone who knows your work can speak on your behalf. That includes peers, subordinates, suppliers, vendors, consultants, even customers. In short, those who've been above you, below you, and all around you.

Don't leave matters to chance, hoping your references will say the right thing. They may be taken off guard, or they may actually contradict you. The best way to proceed is to draft a statement for your reference person to sign or revise. Giving them the raw material simplifies their task. Remember, few busy managers like to write. It's time consuming, and they've often got urgent matters to handle. If you don't provide them with a written draft, your request for a reference letter may be delayed for weeks.

A well-written reference letter should address these issues: 1) job title and dates of employment, 2) relationship of the writer, 3) key promotions, 4) duties and responsibilities, 5) work and/or management style, 6) areas of major strength, 7) special training, 8) global contributions, 9) specific results and achievements, and 10) warm personal endorsement, if appropriate. As always, emphasize results and achievements. That's what sells.

SNAFU reprinted with permission of NEA, Inc.

Alberto B. Diaz
124 East Bay Street
Miami, Florida 33131
(305) 342-8789

January 14, 19—

Mr. Peter W. Lincoln
334 Houston Tower, Suite 2300
Houston, Texas 77079

Dear Pete,

As a friend, I'd like to enlist your assistance in my search for a new career. I have put together a current resume to begin marketing myself for what should be a new and exciting career.

I'm open to an industry change since the oilfield is depressed. I'm looking for a job in Management or Marketing of technical products and services. I hope to draw on both my management experience and engineering background. Relocation is not a problem as Wendy and I find the prospect of moving exciting.

With your permission, I would like you to be a personal reference for me. I will keep you posted when I have used you as a reference so you will know who might call and won't be caught blind. Please let me know what you think.

If you are aware of any business associates or friends who may be in the market for new, bold and innovative thinking, I'd really appreciate your giving them a copy of my resume or giving me their names to contact personally.

I welcome any assistance or advice you can give me. Thanks for your support now and in the past.

Your friend,

Alberto B. Diaz

ABD:ak
Enclosure

MEMORANDUM

TO: Roger W. Van Dyke
FROM: Richard T. Baird
DATE: June 23, 19—
SUBJECT: Draft of reference statement. Roger, as we discussed,
I've put together an outline for a letter of reference from you.
Please review it, and let's discuss.

Mr. Baird was employed by Environmental Services, Inc. from August, 19—
through December, 19— reporting to me. In January, 19— he was promoted to
a controllership position in the Exploration Division. In addition he retained
the financial management responsibilities for the Environmental Division during 19— and continued his real estate management responsibilities until his
separation in June 19—.

Mr. Baird's position at Environmental Services was Financial Manager, a position that encompassed a broad range of financial and administrative responsibilities. He successfully designed and implemented accounting, administrative
and data processing systems and made a significant contribution to the management of the division.

His accomplishments include: a) implementation of an environmental review
of capital and operating plans; b) development of an environmental cost
analysis system; and c) nondisclosure negotiations with government agencies.

In addition, he profitably disposed of assets and played a significant role in
the consolidation of accounting and administrative services—resulting in
reduced costs and improved service.

Mr. Baird is an effective manager with an open communication style. He
established a good rapport with subordinates, peers, and superiors at the divi-
sional and corporate level. I found him to be a good team player and a reliable
professional.

As a result of departmental reorganization and consolidation, a process in
which he took an active and positive role, Mr. Baird decided, and I agreed,
that the organization's requirements and his career objectives were no longer
parallel and his goals could be better achieved in an organization that would
more fully utilize his expertise.

Charles D. White
2121 Eastern Ocean Avenue
San Ramon, California 75944
(415) 363-8630

November 12, 19—

Mr. Timothy Henning
California Home Health Care
24 Sandpiper Road West, Suite 1400
San Ramon, California 75944

Dear Tim:

Thank you for your offer to act as a reference for me. I believe it is important for me to be able to provide a reference from my last job. As I mentioned, most prospective employers prefer to speak personally to the reference rather than being provided a written document. Should the occasion arise, I would like to request that you be willing to speak personally to a prospective employer.

I am following the recommended procedure by contacting each of my references and sharing with them a brief outline I have developed for each job. Having such an outline available serves as a convenient tool to jog the memory and organize thoughts when a call is received. The outlines cover the following key factors:

o My strengths as an employee and manager.

o Significant accomplishments achieved during my tenure.

o The reason for leaving the job.

Of course, I want to ensure that the appraisal is honest and one with which you are in agreement. At the same time negative comments should normally be avoided.

Please review the attached outline for my job with CHHC. It parallels what I am communicating in my written materials (resumes, marketing letters) as well as what I say in interviews. I'll call in a few days after you've had a chance to review the material.

Sincerely,

Charles D. White

Charles D. White
General Business Manager
July 19— - October 19—

Charles was hired through a search conducted by a national retained search firm, interviews with senior company finance and operations personnel and a review by Rohrer, Hibler & Replogle, Inc—a national executive appraisal firm.

SIGNIFICANT ACCOMPLISHMENTS

1. Brought the accounting organization from chaos to a high level of professionalism.
   - handled consolidation into new center
   - released poor performers
   - upgraded staff, recruited nine new people
   - coordinated successful implementation of several new systems (accounts payable, payroll, fixed assets)
   - set up internal controls and procedures

2. Improved quality of accounting records and reports.
   - accurate and timely closings
   - clean FY19— audit (per Arthur Andersen)
   - created reports by subunits (board reports, statements)

3. Excellent job of handling the yearly budgeting project
   (19— & 19— fiscal years).
   - provided historical data and tools for assisting managers
   - one of only a few zones to completely fulfill requirements for content and timing

4. Significantly improved the yearly physical inventory project.
   - wrote detailed instructions for field staff
   - sent accountants into the field to observe and assist the count
   - provided instructions and oversight for the reconciliation by accounting staff

5. Spearheaded purchase and training of staff on PC's, maximized use of PC's for routine or repetitive tasks.

Charles D. White
Page Two

6. Improved human resources support for zone.
   - hired excellent personnel specialist to support zone in hiring and compensation/ benefits matters
   - encouraged improvement in hiring practices to reduce turnover
   - cleaned up personnel records and fulfilled corporate data requirements for new retirement plan, 401K plan, and payroll system

STRENGTHS AS A MANAGER

1. Organizational skills.
   - thinks through a task
   - gathers and allocates resources
   - follows up to ensure completion as planned

2. Recruitment skills.
   - a good judge of people
   - careful to do the background and reference checks
   - trusts his judgement, willing to present people with new challenges

3. Innovative.
   - likes challenges
   - enjoys bringing order from chaos and improving techniques

4. Positive attitude to technology.
   - tries to maximize use of personal computers and other office automation equipment

5. Keeps lines of communication open with subordinates.
   - highly regarded by his staff

STRENGTHS AS AN EMPLOYEE

1. Good business sense developed through broad experience in several industries.

2. An excellent analyst.
   - researches questions in a logical manner
   - digs into details, good at manipulating data

3. Does not make hasty or politically motivated decisions.

4. Good personal work habits.
   - focuses on organizing the task
   - meets deadlines

5. A good communicator.
    - expresses thoughts clearly
    - equally comfortable preparing written or oral material

REASON FOR LEAVING

Charles was hired to be the general business manager of the whole Tustin processing center, supervising accounting, accounts receivable, data processing and personnel. I initially limited his scope to supervision of the accounting group because this was the area where we had the greatest deficiencies which needed attention.

Subsequently, the home office revised the organization model to be used in each of the regional processing centers. The General Business Manager position was eliminated. Supervision of the center was split between as existing manager of receivables and a zone controller. Job specifications for the zone controller—education, experience and salary grade—were below those possessed by Charles. Consequently he was released.

PERSONAL CHARACTERISTICS

1. High level of dedication to his work.

2. Strong personal values of honesty and integrity.

3. A stable family life—a wife with a professional career and two young children.

4. Excellent education.

5. Professional appearance and manner.

6. Even tempered—handles stress well.

DOWELL SCHLUMBERGER
P.O. Box 3899
2899 E. Villard Avenue
Dickinson, North Dakota   58601

May 27, 19—

To Whom It May Concern:

It is with great pleasure that I recommend Jim Precup to you in
his search for employment. While employed with Dowell Schlumberger,
Jim was a very hard worker. Not only did he willingly and effectively execute the responsibilities of his position, but many times performed duties beyond what was required of him.

Jim's vast technical knowledge has been basically self-learned; however, I can speak for his technical skills with a great deal of confidence. Jim has been employed with DS for eight years, the last
five years in sales. He has performed above our expectations. While
employed with our company, Jim has not let health or personal problems ever conflict with his job.

Jim has maintained high morale while working in a depressed market,
and while doing so has displayed leadership to his fellow workers.

I was forced to lay Jim off due to lack of work in our area; however,
I highly recommend Jim for employment with you and am confident he
will be an asset to your business from the first day he is employed.

Please feel free to call me at (701) 225-4477 if you have further
questions or concerns.

Yours truly,

Robert C. Carpenter
Station Manager

Jane E. Buck
1315 Mountain Street, #A6
Lakewood, Colorado 80215
232-3485

September 29, 19—

Ms. Evelyn Brust
President
Great Western Association Management, Inc.
10200 East Girard, Suite 304C
Denver, Colorado 80237

Dear Evelyn:

Thank you for meeting with me last Thursday. I enjoyed our visit and lunch very much.
I hope your office move went smoothly and that you are pleased with the change.

I am most interested in a position with your firm and I believe many facets of my
present work and outside activities are applicable to your business operations, as we
discussed. The administrative work and project coordination are areas I am most
interested in pursuing!

Enclosed are my references which you may contact at any time. Again, I would
like to thank you for your time and interest, and I will look forward to meeting with
you again.

With good wishes,

Jane E. Buck

Enclosure

5000 North Franklin Street   (609) 555-2919 (o)
Cherry Hill, NJ 08003   (609) 555-1839 (h)

PROFESSIONAL REFERENCES

Gerald C. Anderson
Manager, Transportation Programs
City of San Diego
3990 Main Street
San Diego, CA 92101
(619) 555-6400

Mr. Anderson is the former Assistant General Manager of the Cherry Hill Transportation District. He was my direct supervisor for approximately two years when I was Project Manager for a light rail demonstration project. Mr. Anderson can provide insight on my skills in developing and managing complex, controversial projects. He is familiar with my skills in managing consultant contracts, supervising staff, delivering public presentations, and preparing written reports.

Richard M. Birnbaum
Senior Vice President
CH2M Hill
475 Fifth Avenue
New York, NY 10017
(212) 555-3893

Mr. Birnbaum is the former General Manager of the New York City Transportation District. He was a supervisor and mentor for over five years. Mr. Birnbaum can attest to my capabilities in project management, community relations, supervision, written and verbal communications, and problem solving at all levels, both internal and external to the organization.

Marcia K. Traynor
Consultant
4355 East Beach Street
Long Beach, NY 11561
(516) 555-6225 (h) — (516) 555-3999 (pager)

Ms. Traynor is the contract lobbyist for the City of Long Beach. As the City's legislative liaison, I worked closely with Marcia during the last three sessions. Our efforts included initiation and successful passage of two bills. Ms. Traynor is familiar with my capabilities in communications, organization, development of legislative strategies, and perseverance in pursuing and resolving difficult issues.

Sales Letters

Use sales letters after you have sent letters to personal friends, business acquaintances, and recruiters.

The letter to friends is like the grand opening for a store. It's the first step in your marketing campaign. It announces your candidacy to the world and launches your job search.

Write to recruiters second, because they are in the employment business. Although they don't work for you, and they fill a relatively small number of positions, they match candidates with employment opportunities all day long. There just might be a fit.

If you skip the friendship and recruiter letters and start with direct mail to companies, you're skipping two important building blocks in a campaign, and you may lengthen your job search unnecessarily.

There are some exceptions to this, of course. If you were an Executive Vice President for MicroSoft, and if you know Bill Gates personally, for example, most other software companies would probably want to talk to you immediately.

Sales letters are letters of self-introduction. They make "cold calls" for you and open doors that appear closed. Use them to scan the market to see who might be interested in talking further. Save yourself from being beaten up on the telephone (although you must follow most letters with a call). Calling to follow up on a well-written letter is much easier than calling cold.

"Hi, Jack's the name, sales is my game, check it out...Hi, Jack's the name, sales is my game, check it out...Hi, Jack's the name..."

Meet Janet O'Connell
FULL CHARGE BOOKKEEPER

Janet is -
    Honest
    Eager to Work
    Punctual and Organized
    Thorough (She never skips over problems—she asks questions.)

Qualified . . . strong background in the following areas:
    (1)   accounts payable,
    (2)   accounts receivable,
    (3)   payroll,
    (4)   payroll taxes and reports,
    (5)   cost control,
    (6)   taxes,
    (7)   bank reconciliation,
    (8)   cash dispersements and receipts,
    (9)   profit and loss statements,
    (10)   public contact in collections.

Janet is Machine-Oriented
    She can operate, care for and service the following machines:
    (1) CRT and IBM computers, (2) typewriters, (3) 10-key by touch
        adding machines, (4) bookkeeping machines like: L5000
        (Mag Card), NCR, Burroughs, Olivetti, Underwood and others.

A graduate of Colorado University in 19— with studies in Business
Administration, English, Music, Christian Education and Sports.

Why Bookkeeping?

    "I like responsibility . . . I like detail. I can put things in order."

YOUR COMPANY WILL GAIN

— An employee eager to prove herself ("I want to get the job done.")
— Someone used to digging in and solving problems.
— A lower turnover rate—I'm career-oriented.

One former employer said this . . .

    "If you are looking for a person who is always on the job,
    reliable, efficient, cheerful and mature, you will be pleased
    with your decision to hire her."

        Jack Moore, Division Manager
        Microtek Corporation

INVEST IN YOUR COMPANY'S FUTURE TODAY!
Call 893-2541 and ask for Janet O'Connell

MEET LINDA!

"A SALESMAN IF I EVER MET ONE!"
(Said by her former employer with over
25 years in sales who now manages a
large insurance company.)

LINDA IS:

    DYNAMIC
    CREATIVE
    INTELLIGENT
    RESOURCEFUL
    PERSISTENT
    HONEST
    DIRECT
    POSITIVE
    QUICK TO LEARN
    A RISK TAKER

QUALIFIED . . . STRONG PEOPLE BACKGROUND AND PEOPLE SKILLS IN:

    Handling Complaints
    Problem Solving
    Motivating Others
    Knowing When to Listen
    Knowing When and How to Ask Questions

A graduate of the University of Illinois in 19— with a bachelors in psychology and a minor in math and social work.

WHY DIRECT SALES?

$——AN OPPORTUNITY AT AN OPEN ENDED INCOME
FREEDOM——TO WORK MORE THAN 40 HOURS A WEEK
CHALLENGE——TO TAKE OPEN ENDED SITUATIONS AND MAKE THEM HAPPEN
ADVENTURE——TAMING THE UNKNOWN

YOUR COMPANY WILL GAIN

A person with a high drive to make money.
An enhanced reputation in the business world.
A lower turnover rate—I'm career oriented.

ABLE TO TRAVEL; EXCELLENT HEALTH

The potential is there waiting to be unleashed and molded into one of your company's top producers! Whatever it takes I can and WILL do—truly a diamond in the rough!

INVEST IN YOUR COMPANY'S FUTURE TODAY!

CALL: 832-3374 and ask for Linda Turnbaugh
830 Sherman Street, Denver, Colorado   80203

NANCY L. BOUCHARD
5757 West Century
Los Angeles, CA 90045
(310) 215-0641

May 17, 19—

Mr. Robert Rawson
Vice President & Controller
1st National Bank of Oakland
P. O. Box 5808
Oakland, California 94612

Dear Mr. Rawson:

Do you need a hardworking, creative and conscientious individual for your accounting or finance areas? If so, I can help you.

* Started my career on the audit staff of a "Big 8" public accounting firm. Have broad industry exposure.

* Became a CPA in 19—.

* Deal well with people. Good communication skills.

* Heavy exposure in development of cash management programs and accounting systems development and automation.

* Have good supervisory experience.

* Special interest in financial accounting, cash management and finance and systems development.

I would like to meet with you to discuss the contribution that I could make to **1st National Bank of Oakland**.

If you need someone who is highly motivated, eager to learn, and willing to work hard/smart to succeed, please contact me at 839-5600 before 8:00 a.m. or after 5:00 p.m.

All the best to you,

Nancy L. Bouchard

NLB/

Mr. Brandon Broga
7555 Tanbark Drive, NE
Bremerton, Washington 98310
(206) 692-2626

March 14, 19—

Mr. John Steele,
Owner
Architectural Drafting Services
2123 South Broadway
Seattle, Washington 98133

Dear Mr. Steele:

Do you need help with . . .

- — cleanup
- — running errands
- — filing
- — bookkeeping
- — drafting
- — typing
- — small jobs

If you need help, I think we should talk. I'm a high school senior. I learn
easily and am capable of doing any kind of entry-level work.

Qualifications

- — 4 years Drafting
- — 1-1/2 years Computer Drafting
- — 2 years Commercial Art
- — Business Math
- — Typing 60 wpm

If you need reliable part-time or full-time help, call me now at 692-2626.

Let's talk today,

Brandon Broga

<u>LOOKING FOR A HEALTH CARE MARKETER</u>?

<u>ONE WITH A HIGHLY SUCCESSFUL TRACK RECORD</u>?

If you are, please take a look at me . . .

o Sixteen years experience . . .
   from clinical care in rehabilitation . . .
   to director of marketing for a national medical center.

o A proven track record in getting patient referrals. . .
   in just five years achieved 42 percent increase in
   inpatients and a 386 percent increase in outpatients.

o Innovative and creative . . . developed and managed
   LUNG LINE, the first professionally answered, Q&A
   national telephone service . . . it has answered more
   than 130,000 calls at an average rate of 250 calls per
   day.

o A skilled manager . . . managed a 24-person marketing
   department with a budget of $800,000+ (excluding
   advertising).

o Ideas that work . . . with documented results to show
   that successful marketing is more than advertising.

o An accomplished diplomat . . . highly effective with
   both administrative and medical personnel.

o An established reputation . . . known for being a
   highly motivated achiever of even the most difficult
   marketing and management tasks.

I'm looking for a position at the level of vice president or national
director of marketing and planning in a medical setting committed to
market-driven, consumer-focused treatment.

For a resume please call or write:

CHRISTINE R. KLOTZ

7409 Mt. Meeker Road / Longmont, Colorado 80501 / 303-530-5426

Judy K. Ramirez
2828 North Mobile
Chicago, Illinois 60634
(555) 552-6572

January 29, 19—

Eric Erickson
Plant Manager
Baxter Pharmaseal
11060 Irma Drive
Chicago, Illinois 60630

Dear Mr. Erickson:

GOING, GOING, GONE!!

The last time I went to bat, I hit a home run! Let me have the opportunity to join your successful team, and I can hit a home run for you.

Here are just a few batting statistics for you to consider:

— Developed, packaged, documented, advertised, and spearheaded marketing and sales effort for new computer software product that attained "premier" status in the Cardiology Marketplace.

— Developed advertising and promotional pieces that led to 175 sales leads in a 12-month period.

— Conducted field sales presentations/seminars to an audience of physicians, nurses, clinicians, and hospital administrative personnel. Achieved 100% close ratio.

Want to hear more? I would appreciate the opportunity to further discuss not only my portfolio, but also how I can be a successful member of your team.

Let's go to the World Series! Please call me at 232-9087. Thanks for your time and consideration.

Sincerely,

Judy K. Ramirez

NEED HELP?

I love to repair, remodel, restore and reno-
vate. Freelance craftsman does quality
work at an excellent price. If you need help
from someone who's hard working, depend-
able and who cares, call me. (Will consider
barter or swapping for services.) For free
estimate or advice, call Scott at 771-4343.

NEED HELP?

Since 1967 I've helped hundreds of business owners and
managers achieve their objectives with:

- Telemarketing and direct mail
- Advertising and public relations
- Market research
- Acquisition Analysis
- New product development
- Recruiting and hiring
- Sales and management training

It may be that I can help you. To find out send me your
business card, or call Sunday (today) from 1-5 p.m.

Ralph Lauren, MBA - Consultant
5437 Cimarron Road, Oklahoma City, OK 73162
(405) 848-7136

203 EAST EXPOSITION AVENUE
DENVER, COLORADO 80209
(303) 342-4638

3 August 19—

Mr. Marv Rockford
News Director
KCNC TV, Channel 4
1044 Lincoln Street
Denver, Colorado 80203

Dear Mr. Rockford,

First, fast and accurate are a sharp reporter's trademark. Like your own
staff, I can promise those qualities, and MORE, to KCNC.

Over 25 times, my scoops have been replayed by a host of Denver media. A
more tenacious, ambitious and enthusiastic reporter you won't find. And I'm
ready to put my assets to work for you.

Let's talk. I've enclosed a few clips for your inspection. I'll call in a few days
to arrange a time to meet.

Sincerely yours,

Brad C. Bawmann

BCB/s
Enclosures

Susan J. Ottinger
7242 South Tamarac Street
Englewood, Colorado   80112
(303) 771-8108

July 14, 19—

Mr. Robert Davidson
Regional Sales Manager
Medical Pharmaceuticals
2000 E. Marketplace Road
Denver, Colorado   80210

Dear Mr. Davidson:

Are you searching for a salesperson in the Denver area who is outgoing . . . confident . . . loyal to a company and product she believes in?

<u>If so, then I am the person you are looking for</u>.

I am presently employed—with five years as Retail Sales Manager for a home oxygen and medical equipment company—but now plan to intensify my sales career.

My background as a Registered Nurse fits beautifully with pharmaceuticals. Because of my teaching background, talking to your customers or to large groups is easy.

I want to meet you to learn more about Medical Pharmaceuticals. Please contact me at your earliest convenience.

Enthusiastically,

Susan J. Ottinger

SJO/ao

WILLIAM E. POWELL
34 Cypress Point
Abilene, Texas 79606
(916) 692-2408

October 23, 19—

Mr. E. A. Breitenbach, Chairman
Scientific Software-Intercomp, Inc.
1801 California Street, Suite 295
Denver, CO 80202

Dear Mr. Breitenbach:

Few people understand the role of sales in a technical industry. Technical competence, while necessary for repeat business, is not enough to ensure growth. If you produce quality, but find your sales disappointing, chances are you're lacking an effective technical sales force.

No matter how excellent your product, there are certain things you need to do to realize your market potential. First, you must identify your market. This means finding out who needs and wants what you provide and has the funds and authority to buy. Second, you must establish rapport and credibility with the prospect, so that he trusts your motives and respects your technical competence. Next, you must communicate what your services can do for him in terms of specific benefits that he can relate to his own business and personal needs. Then, after you make the sale, you must deliver excellent service to the client, as perceived by him. Finally, you need to follow up after the job to support the benefits of your service and uncover additional needs that can lead to future sales. This, in a nutshell, is the role of technical sales.

I have battle-proven capabilities in technical sales management, line management, and technical sales, plus a strong background in science, mathematics, and liberal arts. I can develop a professional sales team that will ensure that your business meets its sales objectives. I would welcome the opportunity to meet and discuss your needs.

Sincerely,

W. E. Powell

E. J. Carr
17741 East Berry Place
Aurora, Colorado   80015
(303) 693-7436

September 27, 19—

Michael J. Levy
Vice President Operations
Sears
189 Wells Avenue
Newton, Massachusetts   02159

Dear Mr. Levy,

LOOKING FOR A SALESMAN OR GENERAL MANAGER?
        —ONE WITH A HIGHLY SUCCESSFUL TRACK RECORD?

        If you are, please take a look at me . . .

I've spent the last 19 years selling and servicing clients
with outstanding results for both the customer and my
company.

                    For example:

— Sold company services exceeding $900,000 in 19— (134% of
   quota) and $1,950,000 in 19— (110% of yearly quota in
   only nine months).

— Managed laboratories providing services to 15 states with
   80 employees generating in excess of $300,000 in monthly
   revenue.

I know I can bring the same positive results to your company—
or to some other growing company.

I will contact you in the next 10 to 14 days. I would like
to hear your thoughts about where you think someone with my
skills and abilities might be needed.

Sincerely,

E. J. Carr

P.S. I will not be asking you for a position in your firm,
      but would like five minutes of your time . . . and
      the benefit of your experience.

Bien Thi Nguyen
400 South Fourth Street
Clear Lake, Iowa 50428
(515) 420-7271 (w)
(515) 307-2977 (h)

August 30, 19—

Mr. Melvin G. Birky
Vice President, Human Resources
Lutheran Medical Center
8300 West 38th Avenue
Wheat Ridge, CO 80033

Dear Mr. Birky:

— Do you face increasing demands for training?

— Do you want more efficient, cost-effective ways to develop your staff?

— Would you like to increase revenue by offering continuing education for healthcare professionals?

<u>If so, I could be the "new blood" you need to put innovative projects into operation.</u>

I am currently implementing a Regional Health Education Center—the first of its kind in Iowa.

Last year I planned and directed the design of a mandatory Nurses' Education Day which increased attendance from 60% to 90%.

Because of my efforts, Saint Mary's Hospital is recognized as "the" resource for health education in northern Iowa.

I would like the opportunity to talk with you. I will call in the next week or so to talk briefly about your ideas regarding education and training in healthcare today.

With best regards,

Bien Thi Nguyen

**I KNOW OF NO BETTER
TYPIST THAN
ME**

<u>HOW CAN I HELP YOU?</u>

- I type 90 WORDS PER MINUTE.

- I believe a typewritten page should be a WORK OF ART.

- I'm a painstaking PROOFREADER.

- I finish all work ON TIME.

- I don't miss any DETAILS.

- I charge very REASONABLE RATES.

SO,

- If you have a manuscript (any length) or an article that
  needs to be typed,

CALL ME.

- If you have a term paper to be typed,

CALL ME.

- If you have anything to be typed,

CALL ME.

Bobbi Winston
<u>MY NUMBER IS: 232-5999</u>

YOU CAN REACH ME BETWEEN 8:00-10:00 a.m.

MONDAY THROUGH FRIDAY

10

"Miss Nettles, send in the young man who had enough gall to fax in his resume."

Cold Calls

Even if you have an extensive personal network, you may eventually need to introduce yourself to strangers. If you write a good letter—and all these qualify—most businesspeople will be courteous enough to talk to you on the phone, even if only briefly. Usually, a short conversation is enough.

The trick is to write a good letter. It must appeal to the audience. You'll notice that the letters in this section are full of benefits for the reader. Some sell past accomplishments. Others appeal to the reader's ego with compliments. Still others trade on industry knowledge. The last in the series is a blitz: three different letters to the same company. Not a bad idea, since most job hunters get discouraged and quit after one try.

Three things usually don't work: force, arrogance, and humor. Force and arrogance put people off. Employers laugh at humor; they may even pass your funny letter around at staff meetings. Everyone may be howling, but that usually won't get you interviewed—unless the field is PR, advertising, or marketing. In those fields where creativity reigns, almost anything goes.

Try several different approaches. Don't get stuck doing one thing. Repetition can kill you. You'll be bored with your campaign, and so will your readers!

But if you find one letter that always makes the phone ring, don't change a word of it. Send it out by the bushel.

RONALD L. KREJCHA
375 Park Avenue, Suite 3201
New York, NY 10152
(212) 688-8585 (o)
(212) 889-1543 (h)

June 29, 19—

Mr. R.L. Blackburn
Technical Sales, Inc.
1212 Woodland Place
Arlington Heights, IL 60004

Dear Mr. Blackburn:

I am writing to you because your company may be in need of someone with my financial and business experience. Here are some of the things I've recently accomplished:

— As Chief Financial Officer of a major, regional wholesale distribution company, I reduced excess inventory by $2.5M. However, customer service was improved to 96% and turnover to 8.0 turns for stock goods. This inventory disposition reduced interest expense by $350K over a five-year period.

— Implemented freight cost analysis to identify negative impact of absorbed costs on profitability. The company is now realizing annual savings of $240K.

— Solicited, negotiated and managed insurance risk programs to reduce annual expense by $40K. Loss control programs improved worker's compensation experience ratio from 1.61 to 1.00 in five years.

— Reduced personnel within my areas of responsibility while expanding both capabilities and productivity. Absorbed functions from other departments during this period.

— Improved quality of receivables, decreased bad debt expense and added new techniques for collection and protecting monies owed. Restaffed department. Reduced DSO by nine days, stabilized monthly collection percentage at 67%-68% level, and improved past due balances to less than 10% of receivables.

If you feel that your company is in need of someone with my background, I would enjoy talking with you about opportunities.

Please call me today,

Ronald L. Krejcha

Robert K. Hochstetter
2001 Ross Avenue
Dallas, TX 75201
(214) 220-3022 (o)
(214) 749-3428 (h)

May 22, 19—

Diane B. Holmes
Vice President
Financial Search Group
7825 Washington Avenue, Suite 550
Minneapolis, Minnesota 55435

Dear Ms. Holmes:

I am currently seeking an executive position in the Thrift/Mortgage Banking industry and have taken this opportunity to enclose a brief synopsis of my experience for your review and consideration.

I am a thoroughly seasoned executive with extensive experience/expertise in all areas of mortgage banking. Specific areas of expertise include:

1. Turnaround situations where my management experience can be used to identify and then effect necessary operating efficiencies.

2. Establishing a complete turnkey operation to include organizational setup, getting all required approvals, developing and training a staff, establishing credit lines, setting up all departments including the design, development and automation of all key functions, creating necessary forms and manuals, and installing necessary operating procedures and controls.

3. Well-developed oral and written communication skills including the ability to reduce complex issues to basic understandable action plans.

4. Sharply developed negotiating skills.

5. Common sense approach to problematic situations.

Finally, I have taken pride over the last 15 years in the fact that during each year of employment I have generated substantiated income to my employer many times the amount of my annual compensation.

Please contact me at your earliest convenience so that we may discuss the possibilities in detail.

Sincerely,

Robert K. Hochstetter

Richard R. Estes
6372 South Birch Court
Littleton, Colorado 80121
Office (303) 635-0987
Home (303) 635-0785

<u>PERSONAL AND CONFIDENTIAL</u>

November 8, 19—

Mr. Robert Dillon
Dillon Laboratories
2111 Northwest Maple Street
Denver, Colorado 80215

Dear Mr. Dillon:

My accomplishments and experience in eight years of corporate finance and ten years of public accounting should be of interest to you if you need a seasoned financial executive to help guide your organization.

I am a CPA with extensive experience in finance, management, accounting, and tax. I am Vice President and Controller of a subsidiary of Allegis Corporation, the Fortune 500 Company. I have also been controller of other companies and have broad expertise gained through experience with a wide range of clients and industries in public accounting.

At Allegis I participate in policy-making with senior executives and make and implement financial policy. I direct all accounting, consolidations, budgeting and profit planning for the subsidiary and its profit centers and work closely with the company's tax, treasury, and legal staffs on related matters. I participate in negotiations with outside contractors, financiers, and customers and provide liaison for internal and independent auditors. I report to the subsidiary president and its board of directors and am directly responsible for the quality and timeliness of work of a finance staff of approximately 25 people.

In public accounting, I was an audit supervisor with Mills & Company, the national CPA firm. I successfully managed several of the largest engagements of the Colorado Springs and Tucson offices, including construction, hospitals, auto dealers, direct mail sales, and manufacturing clients, among others. Coupled with experience in a large local CPA firm, my audit and tax work at Mills provided a broad base of expertise in finance and accounting.

Mr. Robert Dillon
November 8, 19—
Page Two

<u>My accomplishments include</u>:

- Successfully operated multi-million dollar distressed income property
  pending its sale, enforcing stringent cash expenditure restrictions which
  saved $25,000. Negotiated increased sale price and terms at closing
  table to save $5.6 million sale.

- Confronted contractor operating in conflict of interest. Took control
  of records, negotiated release of files and recovered $12 million of the
  subsidiary's notes receivable.

- Prepared, evaluated and negotiated financing proposals for construction
  and permanent loans, working capital and equipment loans, and bond
  issues.

- Reorganized several headquarters and division finance staffs, including
  personnel decisions, which enhanced expertise, upgraded performance,
  and eliminated unnecessary work.

- As an audit supervisor in public accounting, discovered a major error
  by client in use of LIFO which allowed 50% increase in client's income.

I'm seeking a Vice President, Finance or Chief Financial Officer position
which is responsible for treasury, accounting, budgeting, profit planning,
and tax, in which there is significant opportunity to contribute to achieving
company goals.

I'd appreciate the opportunity to discuss how my qualifications and
accomplishments may meet the needs of your company. Please phone me
at my office (303) 241-7868 to schedule a meeting.

Let's talk today,

Richard R. Estes

William R. Davidson
334 Ocean Front Boulevard
Panama City Beach, Florida 32407
(904) 343-4876

November 22, 19—

William S. Frank
President
CareerLab
9085 E. Mineral Circle, Suite 330
Englewood, Colorado 80112

Dear Mr. Frank:

I recently joined CHRA and perused your article entitled "SHRM Is The
Winning Edge." I liked what you said regarding professional activities giving candidates an edge in the job market. I also read your
article in the "National Business Employment Weekly" entitled "Get to
Know Your Product."

I like your aggressive business style and would like to have lunch
with you to discuss business philosophies. When I plan my next trip
through Denver, I will call you several days in advance to schedule a
luncheon meeting.

I look forward to meeting you.

Respectfully,

William R. Davidson

WRD/jd

Timothy P. Wood
5950 Berkshire Lane
Apt. 1600
Dallas, TX 75225
(214) 691-4966

November 20, 19—

Mr. William Frank
President
CareerLab
9085 E. Mineral Circle, Suite 330
Englewood, Colorado 80112

Dear Mr. Frank:

CareerLab's reputation has reached Scottsdale. Several associates have mentioned your firm, and you specifically. I understand you are well-connected with senior corporate executives and do quality work. We should certainly talk soon—It's very likely we can help each other. Here's a bit of my background:

> After becoming President and CEO of Realty Corporation, I led our 52-person, entrepreneurial, full-service, commercial real estate development team into 2 new markets—Phoenix and Denver—much to the dismay of our competition. Land sales volume set new records topping $40 million in one year. I understand the relationship between leadership and profitability.

> Our major joint ventures and key lender relationships have been more than a little surprised at our ability to make them money even in a tough market. I have streamlined the administrative staff, refocused the marketing efforts and fashioned various new and significant debt and equity financial structures. Overhead has been reduced 50% and building sales have doubled.

My multi-disciplined expansion of the company's businesses no longer fits Realty's long-term strategy; our chairman and owner recently announced his return from statewide political involvement and desire to actively liquidate the company's present inventory to accomplish his personal estate planning goals. I have been offered opportunities to acquire portions of the company's operations, but declined because of my desire to work in a more substantial organization which optimizes my contributions.

The timing is perfect to consider new opportunities. We should talk soon. Please call me at your convenience next week (week of 11/27). I have alerted my secretary that you will be calling— she'll put your call right through.

Sincerely,

Timothy P. Wood

Kenneth M. Evans
2133 Kipling Street
Wheat Ridge, Colorado 80033
(303) 889-0098

August 26, 19—

Mr. William S. Frank
President
CareerLab
9085 East Mineral Circle, STE 330
Englewood, Colorado 80112

Dear Mr. Frank:

I would like to thank you for your informative and helpful column which appeared in <u>The Rocky Mountain News</u> on Tuesday, August 24. If it is not too much trouble I would appreciate hearing your thoughts on a problem I have been having in implementing one of your suggestions. Specifically, suggestion number 30 is difficult for me in that no particularly helpful answer presents itself to the most predictable and relevant question that I hear in interviews.

To briefly fill you in on my situation: I have been admitted to the Bar in Colorado for approximately one year. I also have a Bachelor of Science in accounting. This is a double threat which should make me very employable given the conventional wisdom. The problem is that in today's tight job market I find myself competing for entry-level positions against attorneys and accountants who have three to five years experience. The question which is always present, spoken or unspoken is: "Why should we hire a person with limited experience whom we will have to train, when for the same money, we can hire a fully-trained experienced professional?"

Being a rational, economic man I can see their point. It is difficult to justify not hiring an experienced person, especially if they are to be paid an entry-level salary. Many of my friends are facing the same sort of problem. We are very interested in how to run the race when the starting gate won't open.

I fully realize that there may not be any adequate answer to the experience gap question. In any case I would be interested to hear your thoughts on this issue. If you don't have time to write, please feel free to call me at 889-0098.

Very truly yours,

Kenneth M. Evans

KATHY THOMAS
702 Skyway Tower • Southland Center • Dallas, TX 75201
(214) 748-9833 (o) • (214) 748-9800 (FAX) • (214) 748-9814 ext. 8344 (voicemail)

September 20, 19—

William S. Frank
President
CareerLab
9085 E. Mineral Circle, Suite 330
Englewood, Colorado 80112

Dear Mr. Frank:

On Tuesday, August 24, I read your article in the Rocky Mountain News, "Fear Checklist Calms Job-Hunting Nerves." At the time, I was not looking for a job, but had plans to do so soon. So, I decided to clip your article and post it on my refrigerator.

Now that I am actively seeking employment, I have many times referred to your list of helpful hints in overcoming job-hunting fears. And, sure enough, they work! Thank you for sharing your valuable ideas with me and the countless others in my situation.

As you may have guessed, your article made quite an impression on me. Not only were your suggestions helpful, your writing revealed admirable qualities about your organization. After reading your work, I determined that you probably must run a company that recognizes the needs of its employees.

Anyone who can suggest:
    "Don't withdraw. Don't hide. Stay active."
    "Laugh more often. Cry more often. Get angry."
    "Share your feelings."
                        and
    "Develop an emotional support group."
must surely have keen discernment of human nature and needs. And, this is the type of organization I want to work for!

For this reason, I am enclosing my personal data "flyer" and my resume. I would appreciate your perusing these two items, in hopes you would consider me for employment.

In the meantime, I shall try to heed your suggestion, "Don't put all your eggs in one basket."

I would be delighted to hear from you soon!

Respectfully submitted,

Kathy Thomas

MICHAEL TREASURE, JR.

9200 S. DADELAND BLVD., SUITE 516 • MIAMI, FL 33156 • (305) 661-5468 (O) • (305) 371-9672 (H)

January 3, 19—

Mr. William S. Frank
CareerLab
9085 E. Mineral Circle, Suite 330
Englewood, Colorado 80112

Dear Mr. Frank:

You are recognized to be a proven expert in the Colorado career market. Perhaps we can combine forces to our mutual benefit.

At 40, I am a seasoned business professional with a rich and varied management background. My 12-year career at NyTek Oil Corporation has encompassed accounting, finance, budgeting and planning, financial analysis, project management, corporate communications, and policies/procedures.

My education includes an MBA and many years of experience working closely with senior management at NyTek, a 70-year-old, $500 million (assets) public corporation headquartered in Denver. I am a proven team leader and team player.

I have successfully planned and directed multi-million dollar, multi-departmental projects. I managed the dissolution and liquidation of $60 million of public limited partnerships and have directed asset sales in excess of $40 million. I completed the selection and installation of a corporate local area network of personal computers.

As Vice President of Investor Relations and Administration for NyTek Exploration, Inc., 10,000 limited partners have looked to me as their primary information link with the corporation. I provide investment status, drilling results, financial statements, tax projections, ownership and estate questions, and general hand-holding. An ongoing reduction in partnership activity by NyTek, however, leaves me underutilized and unchallenged.

I value my oil and gas experience, but being a business generalist, am not tied to a single industry. An updated resume is available at your request. Feel free to call me at home or at my direct office number, 697-5743. I would very much like a chance to chat with you about today's job market and, of course, my prospects in particular.

Very truly yours,

Michael Treasure, Jr.

Phillip T. Wright
1931 S. Cherry Street
Green Bay, Wisconsin 54301
(414) 432-2357

June 12, 19—

Nancy Rodriguez
Senior Vice President
IBM
2000 Monument Avenue
Dayton, Ohio 45402

Dear Ms. Rodriguez:

Could IBM, or one of your divisions, benefit from a strong financial officer?

Having been repeatedly recognized for my financial and management contributions,
I have a succession of rapid promotions from Plant Controller to Division Controller
to Vice President Finance/Administration and Treasurer, including operational experience and responsibility, in companies whose sales ranged from $40 million to $700
million. On one occasion, I was considered for the presidency of the company.

Although nonquantitative in nature, I am proudest of my proficiency in managerial
and leadership skills to build a highly-respected and credible financial organization
whose resources were sought by members of the management team at all levels of
the corporate organization.

Opportunity and challenge in a growing company are my prime considerations, but
you should know that in recent years my total compensation has been in the range
of $75,000 to $90,000.

If you have a need, I could make a valuable management contribution. Thank you.

Sincerely,

Phillip T. Wright

Katherine M. Arnold
2324 Van Buren Street
El Cerrito, California 94530
(415) 473-3729

March 2, 19—

Mr. Lawrence K. Hill
Dean of Faculty
University of California
601 University Avenue
Sacramento, California 95814

Dear Mr. Hill:

This is perhaps the most unlikely letter seeking employment that you have ever received. Why? Because I am very happy in my present position. It offers the responsibility and challenges I need. I have discretion and authority, plus an opportunity to travel, to take on new projects and to be innovative.

Why, then, am I sending you the attached resume? Simply because the qualities that make me an effective employee require continuing opportunity to grow and develop. I have gone as far as I can developing the office that I head. I realistically acknowledge the fact of future budget cutbacks for local government in general and non-violent activities by law enforcement agencies. Good sense and an awareness of what motivates me tell me to explore the possibilities of a new work experience.

I hope you will take time to glance through my resume. My background and experience are varied and lend themselves to a wide range of possible applications.

I will call to see if we may discuss how I can be of value to your organization.

With best wishes,

Katherine M. Arnold

Enclosure

BRAD C. BAWMANN

203 EAST EXPOSITION AVENUE
DENVER, COLORADO 80209
(303) 342-4638

June 15, 19—

Mr. Lawrence Paddock
Managing Editor
The Boulder Daily Camera
1048 Pearl Street
Boulder, Colorado 80302

Dear Mr. Paddock,

I'm not going to pretend I've learned it all as a reporter for a Denver weekly newspaper. But I've learned an awful lot and I'm ready to help The Camera become the paper it aspires to be.

A more tenacious, aggressive reporter you won't find. Your own Entertainment Editor can attest to my drive, energy and enthusiasm—which are more than any three people might enjoy. I'm a go-getter, never satisfied with mediocrity.

Mr. Paddock, let's talk. I'm anxious to put my assets to work for you. I've enclosed a few clips. You may notice that many of the stories are scoops, which triggered other attention by Denver's electronic and print media.

I'll call in a few days to arrange a time to get together.

Looking forward to meeting you soon.

Sincerely yours,

Brad C. Bawmann

Enclosures

Patrick Kellogg
1420 Tenth Avenue
Portland, Maine 04110
(207) 385-4758

December 2, 19—

Ms. Kimberly Clark
Division Supervisor
Neenah Paper
Neenah, Wisconsin 54956

Dear Ms. Clark:

Can you use a person who has:

* An imaginative way of handling problems?

* Verbal skills, and the ability to deliver messages with impact?

* Personal confidence, especially in face-to-face contact?

* An extraordinary sensitivity to others?

* Organizing and planning ability?

I have these talents as illustrated in the enclosed resume. I would like to put them to work for Neenah Paper as a financial public relations specialist.

Although it may seem unlikely that Neenah Paper has a need for an individual with these skills, I would like to share a few ideas I have that could benefit Neenah Paper and your investors.

I will call Monday or Tuesday of next week to determine when a brief meeting would be appropriate.

Wishing you great success,

Patrick Kellogg

Enclosure

T. CRAIG LINCOLN

4720 West 49th Street
Denver, CO 80018
(303) 555-7114 (o) • (303) 555-1682 (h)

April 16, 19—

Mr. William T. Randolph
Executive Vice President Sales
Caterpillar Tractor Company
100 Northeast Adams
Peoria, Illinois 61629

Dear Mr. Randolph:

I've always been fascinated with the "Big Yellow" Caterpillar image. As a child, I received a toy Caterpillar tractor, and the gift has lasted as long as my fascination with Caterpillar.

In 1972 in Fresno, California, a Caterpillar representative brought your corporate story alive. The movie which told your story was incredible. It showed your approach to industrial education, international marketing (with special interest being given to the up-and-coming Third World Nations) and an overview of Caterpillar philosophies.

At a basic level, I was sold. If I hadn't been working on contract, I would have approached you the next day.

<u>I could very well imagine myself working in corporate design somewhere within the Caterpillar Organization.</u>

My background is sufficiently varied to lend you many avenues of expertise through good sound communications design at all levels within Caterpillar.

—From corporate image to international education.

—From advertising to product marketing.

—From film to video design.

Caterpillar still maintains the strongest image in design, engineering and manufacturing of heavy equipment in the world. Your name is synonymous with building. And I want to be a part of your team.

In the next few weeks I will be in touch with you to see if you want to discuss this further.

Wishing you the very best,

T. Craig Lincoln

Norman L. Steele
339 South Broadway
Redondo Beach, California   90277
(213) 540-2545 (o)
(213) 454-8383 (h)

May 22, 19—

Mr. Thomas K. Allison
MTK Incorporated
33015 Paramount Boulevard
Downey, California   90241

Dear Mr. Allison:

I am searching for a young, aggressive company that has the desire to become a national and then international leader in their field.   If your objective is to increase your stock price and sell to a large conglomerate, then our goals are not compatible.

I have followed your fine company for the last three years and invested in it as a result.   Now that the financial community has recognized your potential, as evidenced by the $18 share price, I hope you view this as the beginning and not the end.   Our country needs entrepreneurs with vision and dreams who are willing to invest in the future.

I am a very knowledgeable individual, but more importantly, I am creative, imaginative, and wish to share in someone's dream. As you can see from my resume, I have been responsible for the accounting, finance, and leasing areas, as well as substantial involvement in the tax, employee benefits, and corporate secretary functions.   You may not yet realize you need a person like me, but I believe you have reached a stage where my experience can be of great value as you continue to grow.

Please contact me at your earliest convenience.

The timing is perfect!

Norman L. Steele

Wesley T. Markowitz
123 Moss Hill Lane
Laguna Hills, California 92653
(714) 586-2998

January 6, 19—

William S. Frank
President
CareerLab
9085 E. Mineral Circle, Suite 330
Englewood, Colorado 80112

Dear Mr. Frank:

In light of the phenomenal 600% growth in outplacement since 19—, there is a strong probability that your plans for CareerLab call for continued growth and expansion for 19— and beyond.

If so, then perhaps my enclosed resume will be of interest. In it, you will find the highlights of a progressive career in outplacement services. My background encompasses all aspects of building and managing an outplacement firm from start-up through national expansion.

As a follow up to this letter, I hope to contact you directly by phone to learn your reaction to my background and determine whether setting up an exploratory meeting is indicated.

I have enjoyed bringing my background to your attention and look forward to speaking with you soon.

Call me today!

Wesley T. Markowitz

WTM:bh
Enclosure

November 18, 19—

Mr. William Robertson
Executive Vice President
Ogilvy & Mather, Inc.
Two West 45th Street
New York, New York 10036

Dear Mr. Robertson,

Advertising agencies are different in New York than here in Denver. Much bigger. More professional. Better people who are paid better. That's why I'm coming to New York to look for work.

I'm intending to send this note to the executive who does the hiring for the Creative Department. From your title I think that's you. But I'm not sure. So if I'm talking to the wrong person please send this in the right direction.

I was thinking about the difference between advertising and public relations the other day. One difference, it seems to me, is that in advertising there is an emphasis on ads as products. More so than in public relations where the concern seems to be more on a total image.

The emphasis on ads as things which perform a function explains in part my love for advertising. Craftsmanship becomes very important. Making better and better ads provides a satisfaction and sense of accomplishment.

I've always liked making things, but ever since I started making ads I haven't enjoyed making anything as much. My goal is to see if I can find a job doing the thing I enjoy most.

My interests are primarily in the area of copywriting, but I also do layouts. I've put together a portfolio of my best work. I'd like to show it to you.

I'll be in New York Monday, Tuesday, Wednesday and Thursday. November 27, 28, 29, and 30.

I'd really like to meet with you some time during those four days. I'll call you as soon as I arrive to see if we can arrange to meet at a time that is convenient for you.

Sincerely,

Jim Brodie

1050 14TH STREET / BOULDER, COLORADO 80302 / (303) 440-8477

August 26, 19—

Red Gates, Creative Director
Tallant-Yates Advertising
502 Fifth Avenue
New York, New York 10036

Dear Mr. Gates:

When I got my first ad agency copywriting job I thought all copywriters were pretty much the same.

I soon found I was very mistaken. Some writers were specialists. Others, generalists. Some used humor whenever they could. Others did the same with music.

For myself, I discovered I had a preference for technical products. I like the challenge of having to find out how a complex product worked before I could write about it. I much preferred working on industrial accounts to writing about candy bars or ice cream. And I discovered I was good at it.

Over the years I've written copy for agricultural chemicals, oil drilling equipment, building materials, dairy farming equipment, electronic sensing devices, mining equipment and cable-stringing trucks.

A year ago I came back to school to complete a master's in journalism, a project I had been working on and off for several years. Freelance jobs helped carry me through the year. Now I'm starting to shake the bushes for another full-time copywriting job.

I thought I'd contact you first because your client list looks pretty technical. And that excites me.

I'd like to meet with you, at your convenience, and show you my book.

I'll call in a few days to see if we can arrange a time to meet.

Sincerely,

Jim Brodie

1050 14th Street   /   Boulder, Colorado 80302   /   (303) 440-8477

February 16, 19—

Mr. Rick Olson
Creative Director
Campbell-Mithun Inc.
210 Park Avenue
New York, New York 10021

Dear Mr. Olson,

As a Creative Director you know how difficult it is to get a first job as a copywriter.

Agencies hire copywriters when they get new business. They need experienced writers who can handle the new business. Not beginners.

Training programs have been trimmed or cut entirely in an effort to streamline agency costs.

So there's a gap in the skill level of graduating students and the level required on the job.

I've been studying advertising for some time. As I'm approaching the time when I'll be seeking a full-time copywriting job I've become aware of the gap between school and work.

I feel an internship is a possible way to bridge this gap.

I'm in the process now of arranging an internship with an agency in the Twin Cities. Ed Richardson at Martin-Williams gave me your name as a person to contact at Campbell-Mithun.

I wonder if you'd have some time to meet with me and discuss the possibility of arranging an internship at your agency?

I'll call in a few days to see if we can arrange a time to meet.

Sincerely,

Jim Brodie

Jack P. Fallon
783 Whister Drive
Houston, Texas 77027
(713) 617-3893

Mr. William D. Cooke
Regional Manager
Amoco Production Company
1717 East 71st Street
Tulsa, Oklahoma 74136

Dear Mr. Cooke:

I am writing to you regarding employment opportunities that you may have for a Drilling Engineer or Cementing Specialist.

Due to current economic conditions, Halliburton has found it necessary to terminate my employment. For the past few years I have enjoyed a very good working relationship with Amoco and I would like you to consider me for employment. I think my background in cementing [oil wells] would be an asset to Amoco, especially in today's market.

Let me give you a brief summary of my qualifications:

- Five years field experience in cement slurry design and placement procedures for deep wells in Utah/Wyoming Overthrust Belt.
- Four years experience in supervision and operation of cement test equipment (high pressure consistometer, fluid loss, autoclave, etc.).
- Made major contributions to development of Halliburton's Slurry Placement Analysis program (cement job simulator).
- Contributed to development of annulus return rate monitoring system to measure U-tube effect during cement placement.

I would appreciate your taking the time to review my resume. (I have also included a list of personal references whom I think would give me a favorable recommendation.)

Thanks for considering me. After you've had a chance to review my background, I'll call to hear your reactions.

Best wishes,

Jack P. Fallon

BRAD C. BAWMANN

203 EAST EXPOSITION AVENUE
DENVER, COLORADO 80209
(303) 342-4638

June 15, 19—

Mr. Bill Baxter
Program Manager Scoopline Services
Mountain Bell
1005 Seventeenth Street
Denver, Colorado 80202

Dear Mr. Baxter:

If there's one thing I've learned in doing several stories involving Mountain Bell, it's that your company is a vibrant and growing force in our community.

The limits of Mountain Bell are only determined by the limits of its employees. And I'd like to help Mountain Bell set its limits even higher.

Mr. Baxter, as you know I am an aggressive, tenacious reporter with an eye for detail. My drive, energy, and enthusiasm are enough for any three people. I'm not easily satisfied with mediocrity—nor is Mountain Bell.

Let's talk. I'd like to put my assets to work for your company. I've enclosed some clips and a resume for your inspection.

I'll call soon to arrange an appointment to get together.

Thanks for your time and consideration.

Sincerely yours,

Brad C. Bawmann

Enclosures

CHARLES D. BRIDGEPORT

2493 CENTRAL AVENUE • WOODLAND HILLS, CALIFORNIA 91367 • (818) 788-3873

August 8, 19—

Mr. William S. Frank
Principal
CareerLab
9085 E. Mineral Circle, Suite 330
Englewood, Colorado 80112

Dear Mr. Frank:

I am writing you because of my interest in joining your firm in the outplacement industry.

My strengths include a broad knowledge of industries, organizations and jobs, an intense curiosity about people and careers, and a desire to help displaced employees find career satisfaction.

During my business career of 22 years, I have held various positions including my current position as a Human Resources Consultant for a New York-based financial services firm of 20,000 employees.

As Regional Marketing Manager:

Marketed employee communication services and had profit and loss responsibility for eight offices in the Southwest.

As Corporate Personnel Director:

Installed a company-wide performance evaluation system and developed corporate human resources policies.

As a Senior Benefit Consultant:

Sold, designed, and implemented employee welfare programs and trained employees for Southwest clients.

My consulting clients have included Motorola, Crown Zellerbach, Arizona Public Service, Alcan Aluminum, San Francisco State University, and Reliance Insurance Company.

If your firm has any expansion plans in the Southwest, I would welcome the opportunity to discuss them in a brief meeting.

Very truly yours,

Charles D. Bridgeport

CHARLES D. BRIDGEPORT

2493 CENTRAL AVENUE • WOODLAND HILLS, CALIFORNIA 91367 • (818) 788-3873

August 18, 19—

William S. Frank
Principal
CareerLab
9085 E. Mineral Circle, Suite 330
Englewood, Colorado 80112

Dear Mr. Frank:

This is a follow up to my letter of August 8, 19— regarding my interest in joining your firm in the outplacement industry.

Attached is my resume outlining more details on my work and education background.

As I mentioned in my previous letter, I empathize with displaced managers and believe in career guidance to assist individuals to find career satisfaction.

If your organization plans to expand in the Southwest, I would like to discuss my background in more detail with you.

Very truly yours,

Charles D. Bridgeport

CDB:bh
Enclosure

CHARLES D. BRIDGEPORT

2493 CENTRAL AVENUE • WOODLAND HILLS, CALIFORNIA 91367 • (818) 788-3873

November 28, 19—

William S. Frank
Principal
CareerLab
9085 E. Mineral Circle, Suite 330
Englewood, Colorado 80112

Dear Mr Frank:

This is a second letter to my initial inquiry in August about entering the outplacement field.

I have attached a resume summarizing my human resources experience and indicating my desire to enter the outplacement business on a full-time basis.

I solicit your comments and suggestions on how I can effectively make this transition into the outplacement industry in 19—.

Very truly yours,

Charles D. Bridgeport

CDB:ml
Enclosure

Response Forms

Problem: you mail job search letters and no one answers. You feel frustrated, hot under the collar, maybe even depressed. You wonder if anyone actually received your mail, or if it went into a black hole.

Solution: the response form—a nifty little trick that makes it easy, almost mandatory, for readers to answer.

Here's how it works. You enclose a response card or letter and a self-addressed return envelope with your mailing. It helps to pre-stamp the return envelope. The recipient answers you by checking a few boxes or by answering one or two questions. It's quick and easy for them; that's why it works.

The trick is to keep it simple. Design something the reader can handle in 10-15 seconds. If it's lengthy or hard to understand, they're likely to ignore it.

You can use response forms with virtually any letter to any audience: friends, recruiters, employers, venture capitalists— you name it. Experiment. Be creative. Watch your mailbox!

*"No, really, this time he **is** out."*

Jon B. Bartoshek
593 South Cole Street
Morrison, Colorado 80465
(303) 463-8326

March 15, 19—

Mr. Lawrence A. Wilson
President
HCB Contractors
4600 National Bank Building
Dallas, Texas 75202

Dear Mr. Wilson:

I am moving my family to Houston in the very near future and am seeking a entry-level construction management job.

The enclosed material helps to explain <u>what I can do for you and shows why you might want to hire me</u>.

To answer, please return the enclosed response letter (postage is paid) or call me in the evenings at the above number.

Sincerely,

Jon B. Bartoshek

Enclosures

FROM:
Jon B. Bartoshek
593 South Cole Street
Morrison, Colorado 80465

TO:
Mr. Lawrence A. Wilson
President
HCB Contractors
4600 National Bank Building
Dallas, Texas 75202

REPLY LETTER

_____ Please call me for an appointment.

Our telephone number is:_____

_____ Please call. I'd be willing to give advice.

_____ We're not hiring right now, but expect to be hiring on

_____ (Date).

_____ You're talking to the wrong person. You should contact:

Name: _____

Title: _____

Company: _____

Address: _____

City, State, Zip: _____

Comments:_____

_____

_____

_____

RWJ ROBERT W. JONES
6393 SOUTH MONACO COURT • ENGLEWOOD, CO 80111 • (303) 220-7826

March 4, 19—

Mr. James D. McMurphy
Senior Vice President
Bank Western
1675 Broadway, Suite 800
Denver, CO 80202

Dear Jim,

Wouldn't it be great to hire a part-time HR professional when you're short-handed...or have an emergency project you needed yesterday?

With more than 20 years hands-on human resources management experience in...

— classification
— employee relations
— interviewing
— HRIS and system design
— policy formulation
— terminations
— performance appraisals

I can help you quickly.

I've recently been doing contract work in...

compensation surveys
salary structure application
exit surveys
turnover analyses
special employee surveys
new-hire orientation program design
report preparation

and I'm looking for additional part time or special projects
work. My job is to make your job easier.

Please call me at 220-7826...or return the enclosed postage-paid response
form and I will call you quickly.

With best wishes,

Robert W. Jones

P.S. My IBM-compatible PC with WordPerfect and Lotus 3.1 can handle
sophisticated analysis and reporting. (I'm an expert in Lotus!)

RWJ ROBERT W. JONES
6393 SOUTH MONACO COURT • ENGLEWOOD, CO 80111 • (303) 220-7826

From: Mr. James D. McMurphy
          Bank Western

Dear Bob,

_____ I'd like to meet with you.

_____ Please call this number for an appointment:_____

_____ Let's talk on the phone—call me at (number)_____

_____ I don't have anything now, but call me in _____ days

_____ I don't anticipate any requirement for your services, but you might
try the manager listed below:

Name _____

Title _____

Company _____

Street Address _____

Telephone _____

Kenneth L. Hargrove
2475 S. Oakland Circle
Aurora, Colorado 80014
(303) 696-6754

September 24, 19—

Mr. Clifford Allen
Control Software, Inc.
777 S. 6th Street
Louisville, CO 80027

Dear Mr. Allen:

I am interested in joining your firm in the development of its exploration workstation.

My strengths include a broad knowledge of petroleum exploration techniques, a strong interest in exploration workstation development, and a demonstrated ability to manage a profitable business.

During my ten years in the petroleum industry, I have held both geological and geophysical positions, have conducted research in the use of geophysical workstations, and have been a principal in a geophysical services firm.

As Senior Geologist
Researched seismostratigraphic exploration needs and assisted the development of a geophysical computer-aided workstation for a major oil company.

As Geophysicist
Developed seismostratigraphic expression of subtle traps and managed a $4.4 million program to exploit the results with a large integrated petroleum firm.

As Principal
Guided start-up geophysical services firm to $5 million in annual sales while managing its geophysical research and data processing efforts.

I am interested in integrating my knowledge and interest in seismic stratigraphy with your computer-aided workstation. I have several concepts that integrate seismic attributes with the expression of stratigraphy that would be ideal on a workstation.

As your firm may be developing such capabilities, I would welcome the opportunity to discuss them with you.

Let's talk today,

Kenneth L. Hargrove

From:

Mr. Clifford Allen
Control Software, Inc.
777 S. 6th Street
Louisville, CO 80027

Dear Ken,

I'm returning the questionnaire that was included in your letter of September 24, 19—.

_____ Please call me to discuss your concepts and abilities.

_____ Please call to set up a meeting.

_____ This letter reached the wrong person. You should contact:

Name _____

Title _____

Phone _____

_____ We have no plans to develop such capabilities at this time. However you might contact:

Name _____

Title _____

Company _____

Comments:

_____

_____

_____

_____

Bill Frank & Associates

February 3, 19—

Dr. Charles D. Crane
American Geriatric Society
1503 Downing Street
Denver, Colorado 80218

Dear Dr. Crane:

Are you a good candidate for PR?

    — On the cutting edge of your profession?

    — Doing something new and different that the public
      needs to know?

    — Enthusiastic about what you're doing?

    — Already successful, desiring more success?

Are you concerned about increased competition in your field?

    ** In 1970 there were 310,000 doctors; in the year 2000
       there are likely to be 643,000.

    ** Private Practice magazine says that "doctors must
       realize that no matter where they went to medical
       school or how 'board certifiable' they are, they are
       not guaranteed a successful practice." (July 19—)

    ** "Physicians feel they are under siege," says
       Dr. Richard Wilbur, Executive Vice President of the
       Council of Medical Specialty Societies.

Public relations (PR) can help you specialize or increase the size of
your practice without advertising.

(Last year one of our clients received free radio, television and
newspaper interviews worth $28,824.50. Another doctor added 250
patients to his practice.)

If the topic of "practice-building" interests you, I'd like to visit
your office to show you what we do and explain the results others
have gotten.

Please return the enclosed response letter, or call (303) 771-4357.

Warm personal regards,

William S. Frank

BUSINESS REPLY LETTER

FROM:
Dr. Charles D. Crane
American Geriatric Society
1503 Downing Street
Denver, Colorado 80218

TO:
Mr. Bill Frank
Bill Frank & Associates
Denver Corporate Center
7800 East Union Avenue, Suite 420
Denver, Colorado 80237

Dear Bill:

1. _____ Please call me for an appointment.

2. _____ Send your brochure and written materials.

3. _____ I don't need your services right now, but I would
like to find out more about what you do.

4. _____ Send articles on marketing for physicians.

5. _____ Let's discuss a marketing seminar for our group.

6. _____ Please keep me on your mailing list.

_____
Signature

JAMES J. PRECUP
1969 East 116th Avenue
Northglenn, Colorado 80233
(303) 450-9587

September 25, 19—

Mrs. Beverly Richard, President
Intrawest Bank of Northglenn
10701 Melody Drive
Northglenn, Colorado 80234

Dear Ms. Richard:

Most people can't sell!

They're doing a job they don't wish to do.

It isn't natural for them.

For me, sales is natural.

> I'm a trained professional.
> I'll hit the ground running.
> No downtime.
> Quick start-up!

I'll start producing sales for you immediately—tomorrow.

If you'd like to learn how you can improve sales TOMORROW, please telephone
me at your earliest convenience, or return the enclosed postage-paid questionnaire.

Cordially,

Jim Precup

JJP:pr
Enclosure

From: _____

_____

Dear Jim:

_____ I'd like to meet you. Please call (number)_____
for an appointment.

_____ I'd be willing to talk with you on the telephone to
trade ideas. Call me at (number)_____

_____ You're talking to the wrong person. You should contact:

_____

    Name   Title   Phone

_____ We're not hiring now. Re-contact me after_____

_____ We're not hiring now. Try this company:

_____

    Name   Title

_____

    Company

_____

    Street Address

_____

    Telephone

_____ You have my name and title wrong. It should read:

_____

    Name   Title

_____

    Comments

_____

_____

_____

_____

BRUCE D. ROBERTSON, CPA

3182 South Holly Street
Denver, Colorado 80222

(303) 756-7434 (H)
(303) 779-1417 (W)

October 15, 19—

Robert B. Wood
Vice President and Treasurer
Sears Roebuck & Co.
10 Riverside Plaza
Chicago, Illinois 60606

Dear Mr. Wood:

As a fellow member of the Financial Executive's Institute, I want you to know
that I am seeking a permanent position in International Business as a Manager
of Administration and Finance. This decision is based upon a careful, in-depth
analysis of my abilities and experiences. Consequently, I have put together a
current resume in order to market myself for what I believe will be the most
productive and exciting years of my life.

A friend of mine from my STC days in London, John Dexter, works for
Burroughs in London. If you see him, give him my regards.

I am totally open to any industry with positions located almost anywhere in
the world.

Should you become aware of any of your friends, or business associates, who
may be in the market for new blood and innovative thinking, I would appreciate
your listing their names and phone number on the enclosed, postage-paid
questionnaire and returning it to me.

Also, any advice or assistance that you can give me would be greatly appreciated.

Many thanks,

Bruce D. Robertson

BDR:pr
Enclosures

April, 19—

FROM:
Robert B. Wood
Vice President and Treasurer
Sears Roebuck & Co.
10 Riverside Plaza
Chicago, Illinois   60606

Dear Bruce:

I'm returning your questionnaire. I have the following information for you.

_____ I'd be willing to talk with you to trade information and ideas.

Please call me at (number)_____

You could contact the following people:

Name _____

Title _____

Company _____

Telephone _____

Name _____

Title _____

Company _____

Telephone _____

Comments:_____

_____

_____

MICHAEL D. BURNS

TWO THOUSAND OAKS TOWERS • 2000 WEST FEDERAL STREET • BOSTON, MASSACHUSETTS 02110 • (617) 765-9898

January 18, 19—

Mr. William B. Nolan
Partner
Advanced Technology Ventures
1000 El Camino Real, Suite 210
Menlo Park, California 94025

Dear Bill:

Is your firm capitalizing companies in need of experienced managers? If so, I would like you
to be aware of my credentials. Enclosed is a resume and an excerpt from Fortune magazine which
summarizes my experience and highlights a few of my accomplishments.

Most of my career has been in management and the financial areas. With participation in two
turnarounds and one startup, my experience has been varied and I have built a consistently successful
track record. I am adaptable and learn fast as evidenced by my level of accomplishment in jobs that
varied greatly in content, and in three different industries. I have found that I greatly enjoy working
in smaller, more entrepreneurial businesses and that is what I am looking for now.

My job target is a position with a high management content, either in the operations or the financial
area. It would ideally be with a company that has an entrepreneurial outlook, perhaps be five to ten
years old and has sales of less than $100 million. I have no particular industry preference, having
worked in several, and am open to any situation that is challenging and will make good use of my skills.

I am flexible on immediate compensation if there is adequate potential for growth. An opportunity
to earn equity would be attractive. Although I am not seeking investment opportunities, I might
consider a limited investment in the right situation. Geographic location is not a major consideration.

Bill, this should cover the key points. I will be glad to provide any other information you may need
and can provide strong references when appropriate. Please call me today, or return the enclosed
postage-paid questionnaire.

Sincerely,

Michael D. Burns

RESPONSE LETTER

FROM:
Mr. William B. Nolan
Partner
Advanced Technology Ventures
1000 El Camino Real, Suite 210
Menlo Park, California 94025

TO:
Michael D. Burns

Dear Michael:

_____ Please give me a call for a telephone interview.

_____
Telephone Number

_____ I need more information. Please send _____

_____

_____ We do not invest in areas appropriate for your skills.

_____ I suggest you talk to the following people:

_____ Name

_____ Address

_____ Telephone

_____ Name

_____ Address

_____ Telephone

_____ I don't have any ideas for you right now, but contact me again
after _____ (date).

Comments: _____

_____

12

Hidden Jobs

When asked why Sony Corporation had been so successful, Chairman Akio Morita said, "We never follow. We do what others don't." That's the essence of marketing: going where others aren't!

Most job-hunters confine themselves to traditional approaches like answering want ads and working with recruiters. That's fine, but that's where your competition goes too.

Anyone who tries something new and different—but not idiotic—will have a big advantage. Few job hunters write to career consultants, conference attendees, media people, and venture capitalists. You might want to try it.

Listen to radio and watch newspapers and television for for items in your interest area. The media are in the information business. They are accustomed to trading ideas, so don't be afraid to approach them. Write to businesspeople featured in stories. Write to editors. Contact journalists who've written articles.

While outrageous tactics, like dressing like a clown or printing your resume on a T-shirt, seldom work, don't be afraid to "do what others don't."

Bien Hu Vong
1931 S. Cherry Street
Green Bay, Wisconsin 54301
(414) 432-2357

March 17, 19—

William S. Frank
President
CareerLab
9085 E. Mineral Circle, Suite 330
Englewood, Colorado 80112

Dear Bill:

As a career consultant, you must from time-to-time come across companies that are in need of a strong financial management team. I am a Chief Financial Officer in search of a challenging corporate position where my financial skills can be utilized in the development and growth of an organization.

I am a highly-motivated individual with excellent people and leadership skills, high business ethics, good management and business acumen, and a verifiable track record of many successful financial and business achievements. I am also willing to work long and arduous hours to accomplish the desired results.

My experience includes multi-location manufacturing and retail, real estate, IPOs, public stock and debt offerings, cash management, banking relations, loan negotiations, tax planning, budgeting and long-range planning, acquisitions and divestitures, SEC reporting, data processing, shareholder relations, and general office administration.

I have taken the liberty of enclosing a resume for your review. Any assistance or advice that you can give me will be greatly appreciated. If you have any questions, please do not hesitate to contact me at (414) 432-2357.

With warm thanks,

Bien Hu Vong

BHV/rj
Enclosure

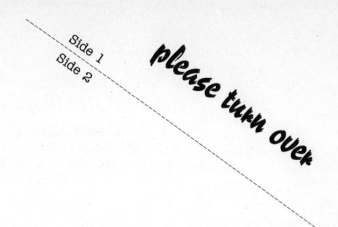

Side 1
Side 2

please turn over

March 18, 19—

I am seeking employment at the executive level of a small company. In particular, I am requiring a position with high visibility that has a significant impact on both the operating and strategic decisions of the company.

Specific management positions in which I have experience and for which I am qualified include Vice President of Finance, Vice President of Manufacturing, and Chief Operating Officer. In addition to Fortune 100 companies, I have experience with a start-up company that successfully acquired venture funding, bank financing, and a merger partner.

My education includes a BSEE and MBA.

I am only interested in opportunities in Boulder County.

If you have referrals that will help expand my job search network, please contact me at either number below.

Keith B. Kellogg

Home: 424-1300
Office: 449-2208

James B. Garrington
343 East Randolph Avenue
Chicago, IL   60601
(312) 782-6930

February 10, 19—

Bruce J. Howard
Director of Pilot Operations
United Airlines
O'Hare International Airport
Chicago, Illinois 60601

Dear Mr. Howard:

Your company's projected growth was highlighted in this month's *Professional Pilot* magazine. I enjoyed reading the article and am hopeful for the growth it projected.

As a professional pilot with six years experience, I thought my background might interest you, since you appear to have future jobs opening up.

My most recent experience was with Regional Carrier Operations, and I have listed some of my experience:

- Flew single-pilot IFR for Air Taxi/Air Cargo in the mountain states region.

- Maintained terminal operation for Air Cargo away from home base using C-210/C-310 equipment.

- Maintained consistent record of on-schedule operations in flying jobs.

At 26 years and unattached, I have a degree from Mesa College. Relocation and travel present no problem.

I will call you in a few days to introduce myself and learn more about your operation.

Very truly yours,

James B. Garrington

Richard H. Greene
891 West 23rd Avenue
Burlington, Vermont 05402
(802) 862-4277

December 2, 19—

Mr. Marshall Austin
President
Neenah Paper
Neenah, Wisconsin 54956

Dear Mr. Austin,

I recently noticed Neenah Paper's first quarter earnings. But despite this significant improvement, I also noted Neenah's common stock is selling far below book value on the NASD-OTC market.

I would like to share a few ideas I developed while working for Hill and Knowlton in financial relations. Many of our clients had a problem apparently similar to Neenah's. I think a brief meeting could benefit Neenah Paper and its investors.

I will call Monday or Tuesday of next week to determine when a brief meeting would be appropriate.

With best regards,

Richard H. Greene

Kenneth K. Yoshihara
1800 One Dallas Center
Dallas, Texas 75201
(214) 979-1200 (w)
(214) 979-4653 (h)

March 31, 19—

Mr. Steven A. Baldwin
The Dallas Venture Group
4500 LBJ Freeway
Dallas, Texas 75240

Dear Mr. Baldwin:

I have recently left Texas Instruments as Vice President of Operations and am looking to join a small to medium-sized manufacturing company in a chief executive or senior management role. My intentions would also include obtaining an equity position in the company.

I have been very successful and have been acknowledged for my accomplishments in startup operations in both domestic U.S. and international locations.

Most recently, I have been consulting with Toy Manufacturing, Inc. managing a major new product introduction. I have been coordinating the engineering pilot runs, sourcing, and manufacturing startup for TWI's main-line new product being introduced this fall. This product is now being shipped to customers per the original plan.

My annual salary and bonus compensation at TI totaled $140,000 annually. While I prefer remaining in the Dallas area, I will definitely consider relocation for the right opportunity.

I have enclosed a copy of my resume which details the record of my accomplishments over the past several years. I would appreciate that you take a few moments to look it over for a possible match with one of your start-up companies.

I will call you within the next week to discuss any possible opportunities of which you may be aware.

Thank you very much!

Kenneth K. Yoshihara

13

Les Moore™ by Phillip Jewell

1993 Phillip Jewell

NOTE WRITING EQUIPMENT

PENS $3.00

BOTTLES $5.00

CORKS $1.95

SCRAPS OF PAPER $1.00

Copyright © 1993 Phillip Jewell. Reprinted with permission.

Thank Yous

A job-search is a public relations campaign. The idea is to get others to like you so they will hire you directly or refer you to their friends. The sooner you build good relationships, the sooner you'll be hired, and the words "thank you" create good will.

The best marketing letter in the world is one that simply says "Thank you, I appreciate you." There's no more powerful appeal. No one grows tired of being thanked.

Any thank you is appreciated, but it's even more powerful to thank others unexpectedly. I often invite prospective customers to lunch—then send them a thank you for attending! That gets their attention. Sometimes I send books as sales gifts, and I always enclose some kind of thank you.

Use handwritten notes only for a few short sentences. Buy plain stationery, nothing fancy. Keep it businesslike. Cards that fold to $3\frac{1}{2}$" x 5" are ideal. Make sure your handwriting is easy-to-read. If it isn't, type the words so they're legible.

If your thoughts won't fit on a card, use a typewritten—not handwritten—letter. Letters must be professionally type-written or word processed—no exceptions. Long, rambling, hard-to-read thank you notes create more frustration than good will.

A thank-you letter is often a sales letter in disguise, so don't be afraid to put some "sell" into it. Send warm thanks to everyone who gives you any kind of help in the job search, however small. No exceptions. No excuses.

Nancy L. Navarez
49 Locust Street
Denver, Colorado 80222

June 22, 19—

Karen Bewley
Manager of Compensation and Benefits
National Jewish Hospital
1400 Jackson Street
Denver, Colorado 80206

Dear Karen:

Just a quick note to thank you for my interview on June 21. I find your
interviewing style very refreshing, and I appreciate your openness and
honesty.

I am very excited about the compensation and benefits assistant position and
the chance to work with such a great team. This position is exactly what I
have been looking for, and I sincerely hope I am the person you are looking
for as well. If you have any questions or concerns, please feel free to contact
me at 736-7374. Thank you once again, and I hope to hear from you soon.

With great interest,

Nancy L. Navarez

D A V I D   K .   S A W Y E R
1100 Louisiana
Houston, TX 77002
(713) 757-2511

July 21, 19—

Dr. William W. Anderson
Vice President, Technical Affairs
Motor Vehicle Manufacturers Association
300 New Center Building
Detroit, Michigan 48202

Dear Dr. Anderson:

Thank you very much for considering me for a position with MVMA. I enjoyed talking
to you and the senior staff. In your position, you enjoy a unique view of the automotive
industry. From my resume and our discussions, you have a pretty good idea of what I am
interested in and can do for the industry. I would appreciate it if you would pass on any
opportunities you see in the areas of program management or technology planning and
management.

Thanks again for your help.

Sincerely,

David K. Sawyer, Director
Industrial Business Development

DKS/jlg

STEVEN D. JORGENSEN
4482 South Argonne Court
Aurora, Colorado 80015
303/690-4459

February 13, 19—

Mr. Paul Gardner
Texas Oil Company
P.O. Box 269
Houston, Texas 77056

Dear Paul:

I wish to thank you and the other staff members at Texas Oil Company for taking the time out of your busy schedules to interview me last Thursday. I feel the day went extremely well and I appreciate the opportunity to talk to each of you.

During our conversations I gained an understanding of how your petrophysics group interacts with the geological and geophysical staff. I feel that with my geology background and open hole log interpretation skills, particularly with the Dipmeter, I could quickly make a significant and positive contribution to your company. I have developed a tentative plan to reach the goals that we had discussed.

If you decide to make this position available to me, I predict that Texas Oil Company and Steve Jorgensen could have a long and mutually rewarding association.

I look forward to talking again soon.

With kindest regards,

Steven D. Jorgensen

SDJ:bl
Attachment

October 27, 19—

Mr. Cole McClure
Bechtel
P. O. Box 3965
San Francisco, California 94119

Dear Cole:

Just a brief note to thank you for taking the time to meet with me last week—
especially on such short notice.

As you know, I spent the week talking with people in the hazardous materials industry
and these interviews confirmed my initial positive impression about its potential. I
want to become part of it and I appreciate your concrete suggestions. As you suggested,
I am writing letters to Edward S. Hall and Hugo Edwards. Please thank Suzanne for
sending me Mr. Hall's business address.

Once again, thank you for your help, and tell Art I also appreciated his comments.
I hope our paths will cross again soon.

Best regards,

Michael D. Burns

MB/fl

July 7th

Dear Lynn,

Thank You for a great lunch meeting. It was nice to learn more about your Company and about You personally. I felt inspired after we met.

Bill

Sent executive recruiter this note and two books as an expression of thanks.

July 15

Rich
Thanks for a wonderful lunch meeting. I know you're busy. It was nice of you to take time.

Bill

Enclosed article from *The National Business Employment Weekly.*

Tim,
It was nice to see you so happy at lunch. You're a very special person — don't ever forget that. Thanks to you I made contact with Mike Rand. We're off and running.

Bill

Followed lunch meeting to introduce one friend, a job hunter, to another friend, a potential employer.

Audrey Lake

677 85th Ave. Northeast
Bellvue, Washington 98010

April 29, 19—

Judith E. Martin
Senior Vice President
Merrill Lynch
1800 112th Avenue Northeast
Bellevue, Washington 98004

Dear Judy,

Thanks for taking the time to have lunch today. It was great seeing you again, and I admire you for the big challenge you have accepted.

I know you will do well in your new job, and I think you'll also love Bellevue once you finally get settled here.

Wishing you all the very best.

Sincerely,

Audrey Lake

AL/mf

BRUCE D. ROBERTSON, CPA

3182 South Holly Street
Denver, Colorado 80222

(303) 756-7434 (H)
(303) 779-1417 (W)

October 14, 19—

Dr. Peter A. Firmin
M+A International, Inc.
600 South Cherry Street, Suite 1125
Denver, Colorado 80222-1712

Dear Peter:

Thank you for the time you spent with me at lunch October 13. I am working on the many suggestions and ideas you raised during lunch. I will keep you posted on my progress in this job search.

I have put together the enclosed recap of my Administrative and Finance Capabilities in order to market myself for what I believe will be the most productive and exciting years of my life. Should you become aware of any of your business associates or friends who may be in the market for new blood and innovative thinking, I would appreciate your sending them a copy of my resume or capabilities recap.

Any additional advice that you can give me at this exciting time in my life would be greatly appreciated.

Also, I thought you might enjoy a couple of newspaper articles about M+A International, Inc. from the October 13, Denver Post.

With warmest thanks,

Bruce D. Robertson, CPA

BDR:bl
Enclosures

Pauline J. Garcia
18 West Princeton Place
Lakewood, Colorado 80227
(303) 745-1222

October 6, 19—

William S. Frank
President
CareerLab
9085 E. Mineral Circle, Suite 330
Englewood, Colorado 80112

Dear Bill:

Just a note of appreciation for the time you spent with me yesterday. Your insights into the Human Resources job market in Denver were helpful—not particularly encouraging, but certainly realistic and helpful. Per your suggestion, I have included three resumes—let me know if you need more!

I'll give you a follow-up call next week. Thanks again for your interest.

Sincerely,

Pauline J. Garcia

Enclosures

November 18, 19—

Robert Owens
Legal Department
Levi Strauss & Company
1222 Seventh Street
Santa Monica, California 90401

Dear Bob,

I am very grateful for our meeting last Friday. I appreciate
the information and your assistance in my career search. I also
appreciated the information about Levi Strauss, and I especially want
you to know that I am very impressed with, and interested in, Levi
Strauss. Your company has successfully made a transition into a very
competitive business environment. I believe that I could offer a
combination of experiences to you from my involvement with my own
firm.

Even if you do not currently have a position into which I could fit,
I thank you for your advice and help. I was particularly interested
in the similarities in our legal backgrounds and was very glad to
have the opportunity to talk to someone who seemed
to be able to relate to what I was saying.

Thank you very much.

Very truly yours,

Richard E. Hart

RH: jd

JOHN HAAG
2533 East 11th Avenue, #9
Denver, Colorado 80206
(303) 321-4688

February 22, 19—

Becky Garfield
Vice President Finance
United Technologies
Washington, D.C. 20380

Dear Becky:

I've just accepted a position with Jewish Family Services as a Career
Counselor/Job Developer. The position offers an opportunity to refine
my skills in doing workshops, individual and group counseling, job
development and job placement.

I'd like to share some thoughts with you about these past two years,
the completion of my career change, and the beginning of the next
stage of the journey. You played a part in making my career change a
success. You're part of an important network of people who provided
the advice, suggestions, referrals and support that helped bring to
life my career change.

To use the garden metaphor, you helped provide the necessary sunlight,
temperature, moisture, soil and nurturing. I provided the seed.
Together we did it! My new career has sprouted and, along with it,
an amazing feeling of satisfaction and fulfillment.

Thank you!

John Haag

Nancy M. Connors
820 South Madison Street
Kansas City, Missouri 64106

July 29, 19—

Ms. Janet Nelson
2001 Central Park Avenue
Kansas City, Missouri 64107

Dear Janet,

On August 8, I will start working as a research associate in the laboratory of Dr. Edward Bell. He is Chairman of the Department of Microbiology at the University of Missouri Medical School. His research interest is Herpes Simplex Virus, primarily Type 1 which causes fever blisters. Thirteen years ago, I was a postdoctoral fellow in that department and that probably helped. Also, the fact that I have a Ph.D. made me hireable as a research associate, a position outside the State Civil Service system.

Dr. Bell is a consultant for American Genetics International, whose president I interviewed in May. That interview was arranged by an employment agent who had called Forty Plus of Missouri. One of the members had given the agent my name and a summary of my background.

So, association with Forty Plus, a self-help group of unemployed executive, administrative and professional people, ultimately resulted in finding a job.

I am looking forward to the challenges of working and to learning about glycoprotein isolations, recombinant DNA techniques, and immunology as related to Herpes simplex.

Karen will be in the fifth grade in September. She and Todd are not really looking forward to the adjustments which will have to be made in our lives, but all of us will do just fine, eventually.

Thanks for your encouragement, advice and help during the past ten months while I was looking for a job.

Your employed friend,

Nancy M. Connors

November 18, 19—

Mr. Frank Holland
Vice President Marketing
Bank of America
3939 South Broadway
Redondo Beach, California   90277

Dear Frank,

Thank you for taking time out of your busy day to discuss some ideas
regarding my job search. Your input and information has been of
tremendous help.

You were the first person I talked to on this journey, and I think I
was both fortunate and lucky to have contacted you first. I felt a
tremendous amount of support from you and I cannot begin to tell you
how important that has been. I have talked to Sandy, who put me in
touch with Bill Ralston, the head legal counsel for United Banks of
California. I had lunch with Bill, who also turned out
to be very helpful. U.B.C. did not have any openings, but Bill gave
me the name of another person. I will be meeting with that person in
the next few days.

I have been involved in this process long enough that I am beginning
to be able to determine who the key players are in this city with
respect to corporate practice. I have also met numerous persons, and
have been astounded at how helpful almost everyone has been.

At this time, I have not really been in touch with many people who
are in a position to offer me a job; however, I am narrowing in on
some of them. This is a time-consuming process, but I believe I am
beginning to see how it all works. Since you were the first person I
talked to, I am particularly grateful for your encouragement.
I will let you know when something more definite develops.

Thank you very much.

Very truly yours,

Richard E. Hart

John H. Norris
2694 S. Lima Street
Aurora, Colorado 80014
(303) 755-6680

June 13, 19—

Mr. Peter K. Reiter
720 South 33rd Street
Federal Way, Washington 98003

Dear Peter,

I sincerely appreciate the assistance and support you provided me during my search for new employment. I'm pleased to let you know that I've accepted a position with Fireman's Fund Insurances in California. While leaving so many old friends here in Colorado will be difficult, we are looking forward to new friends, an excellent career opportunity, and the fabled California lifestyle. I find in Fireman's Fund many of the same positive qualities of young, progressive business leadership that I found at Colorado Banking.

Bill Frank, the outplacement consultant who guided my search efforts, told me that the process would be illuminating in terms of who my friends really are. He was right—it's been a powerful and positive experience. Bill also told me it was highly likely that my next job would come via a friend. My entree to Fireman's Fund was Virgil Pittman, a friend of eighteen years. Virgil is a very strong businessman who lives his beliefs every day. While I won't be working directly for him, I am looking forward to working with him and to renewing the relationship between my family and his.

Thanks again for your help and support. Please, let's make a mutual effort to stay in touch despite the miles between us.

Best regards,

John H. Norris

RICHARD T. BAIRD

102 STEWART STREET
SEATTLE, WASHINGTON 98101
(206) 441-4100

October 29, 19—

Mr. George Ochs
Urban Investment and Development Co.
1801 California Street, Suite 4600
Denver, Colorado 80202

Dear George:

I appreciate our meeting this morning and your insight into the real estate development and property management industries.

Property management is of particular interest as it provides the opportunity to manage assets as well as people. From your description, it's apparent that a large component of the job is client relations, an aspect which is most challenging and rewarding.

George, I am a resource manager with excellent interpersonal skills and a participatory management style. I thrive in an environment which is challenging and dynamic.

I look forward to speaking with you on Wednesday afternoon. Again, thank you for your time and consideration.

Wishing you further success,

Richard T. Baird

RTB/lac
cc: Mr. William Frank

RICHARD T. BAIRD

102 STEWART STREET
SEATTLE, WASHINGTON 98101
(2 0 6) 4 4 1 - 4 1 0 0

November 1, 19—

Mr. George Ochs
Urban Investment and Development Co.
1801 California Street Suite 4600
Denver, Colorado 80202

Dear George:

Many thanks for taking the time to provide the contact names. I plan on calling Mr. Becker and Mr. Hansen within the next week or so.

If I may ever be of assistance to you, please do not hesitate to contact me.

Very truly yours,

Richard T. Baird

RTB/lac
cc: Bill Frank

Herman Doering
2911 S. Downing Street
Englewood, Colorado 80110
(303) 772-6272

September 5, 19—

Brad Frank, M.D.
Chief of Medicine
Deputy Chief of Professional Services
Greater Bridgeport Community Mental Health Center
1635 Central Avenue
Bridgeport, Connecticut 06610

Dear Dr. Frank:

Thank you for the referral to the job opportunity at the Department of Mental Health in Hartford, Connecticut. I immediately followed up with a cover letter and resume to Ken Nicholson, the Director of the Information Systems Division. I hope to be hearing back from him in the near future thanks to your thoughtfulness.

Sincerely,

Herman Doering

November 14, 19—

Mr. Thomas Rollins
666 East 17th Street
Santa Ana, California   92701

Dear Tom,

Thank you for taking time out of your day to discuss some ideas
regarding my job search. Your input and information has been of
tremendous help. I have been gratified and deeply touched by all of
the help and support that I have received. The information, leads
and support which you gave me are truly appreciated.

I have tried to call both John and Sherry Bradbury, but have not yet
spoken to them. I am sure I will talk to them in the near future. I
have had a couple of meetings since our luncheon, and
I incorporated some of your suggestions into my discussions with the
persons I met with. Your comments were very helpful, and seemed to
make a favorable impression.

Again, thank you very much. If ever there is anything I can do
for you, please let me know.

Very truly yours,

Richard E. Hart

RH: jd

BRUCE D. ROBERTSON, CPA

3182 South Holly Street
Denver, Colorado 80222

(303) 756-7434 (H)
(303) 779-1417 (W)

October 14, 19—

Ms. Gail Adler
1444 Kingswood Court
Willowbrook, Illinois 60521

Dear Gail:

Thank you for agreeing to help me out in my job search by sending me the classified ads weekly from the Tuesday Wall Street Journal, Southern Edition. I hope it wasn't too much trouble. If for any reason you are unable to continue sending these ads, please feel free to stop.

I will keep you posted as to the progress of my job search and its forthcoming successful conclusion.

Your friend,

Bruce Robertson

BDR/bl

Bruce K. Ward
188 West Randolph Avenue
Oak Brook, Illinois 60521

January 30, 19—

Mr. Allen S. Sutton
President
TransCon, Inc.
5000 Medco Road
Birmingham, Alabama 35217

Dear Mr. Sutton:

Just a brief note to thank you for returning the response form I sent you earlier this month. Also, thank you for the Mike Bergmann suggestion. That is not exactly the type of work I am looking for, but I may contact him later after I see how this effort works out.

In my search I'm focusing on the management area rather than sales. I would not be adverse to combining the two in the appropriate position, and this might be possible in the financial services area. Please keep me in mind if you hear of any other situations that might be appropriate.

Thanks again for the note and interest.

Best regards,

Bruce K. Ward

BKW/dk

Follow-up

Sooner or later, every job search becomes mostly follow-up. It gets to a point where it's poor marketing to continue to initiate new contacts, because you spread yourself too thin. It's better to hammer two or three opportunities to conclusion than to begin in a dozen new directions. Aggressive follow-up often ends a job-hunt quickly, and there are literally hundreds of creative ways to follow up without pestering.

For example: clip pertinent magazine or journal articles and send them to your friends and prospects as a subtle reminder that you're still around. You need not mention your job situation. Attach a note that says, in effect, "Just thinking of you." Or "Thought this might help."

It's important to pick the right article for the audience. Don't send a technical scientific publication full of equations to general managers; and don't send *The Art of Leadership* to Ph.D. research scientists (unless the scientists are also managers).

Following up means not letting things slip through the cracks. A letter that arrives the day after an important event says, "I really care. This is important to me." I'm amazed that job hunters can wait days, sometimes weeks, to send important follow-up letters.

A letter that arrives late says either, "I don't care very much," or, "I'm slow." If that's the case, it might be better not to write at all.

"8½ by 11 bond paper, white with black printing. I sent out about a hundred last month and haven't heard a word since."

1128 2ND AVENUE SOUTH   EDMONDS, WASHINGTON 98020

October 25, 19—

Mr. Michael B. Dixon
Holland and Hart
P. O. Box 2147
Denver, Colorado 80302

Dear Mike,

I was interested to hear that your firm is considering ways to acquire more capability regarding international business transactions.

As you know, I have worked as an independent consultant these past two years dealing with the business, financial and governmental problems that accompany overseas investments. I have found, however, that companies large enough to have significant international exposure are bombarded by major league players such as:

    a) the large investment banking houses,

    b) major law firms,

    c) consulting firms such as McKinsey and Arthur D. Little,

    d) and, increasingly, by the consulting units operating
         within the major accounting firms.

It has become pretty clear that marketing my "Lone Ranger Act" in the face of this kind of competition is, at best, a difficult job. For the past few months I've been investigating ways to merge my talents into a better known and more broadly based entity. If you are looking for additional arrows to round out Holland and Hart's quiver of talent, then perhaps we should do some talking.

The many hi-tech firms in the Front Range area are beginning to push into the international arena, and you mentioned that you have already taken steps to strengthen your intellectual property team. These hi-tech groups often face significant trade issues in Washington as well as complex government and financial negotiations abroad.

Michael B. Dixon
October 25, 19—
Page Two

There are many other exporters in this area—such as the U.S. Meat Exporter Federation (composed of entities such as Monfort)—that are large enough to have real international needs as well.

Some of your "competition" has already mounted a campaign to try to serve these needs—see the attached flyer on "Going International."

The clipping from the Wall Street Journal of October 16, 19— shows what firms such as Stearns Roger and Morrison-Knudsen are up against internationally. I've marked the clipping to show how the things we did for Cuajone parallel what Bechtel is doing now.

The resume information attached after the clippings just mentioned is probably a bit on the over-kill side, but lawyers love to read and it does demonstrate the extent and depth of my international experience.

I expect to travel back east the 6th and 7th of November to talk to Price Waterhouse's new affiliate partnership that deals in "International Financing Consultancy Services," but will be here Monday, November 5.

Best regards,

Richard P. Ruby

RR:cr

BRUCE D. ROBERTSON, CPA

3182 South Holly Street
Denver, Colorado 80222

(303) 756-7434 (H)
(303) 779-1417 (W)

October 8, 19—

Mr. Robert C. Kingston
Corporate Controller
232 Main Street
Tiburon, California 94920
(415) 435-2000

Dear Bob:

It was great to meet you at the Financial Executive Institute's 55th International
Conference here in Denver. I thought it was a stimulating meeting and found
the sessions most interesting. One of the things I really enjoyed was the opportunity to meet you. I look forward to visiting with you at future conferences
and meetings. I trust you enjoyed your stay in Colorado.

I am seeking a permanent position in finance or international business. To
help market myself, I have put together the enclosed resume. I am open to
any industry with positions located almost anywhere in the world.

Should you be aware of any openings, which might be appropriate for me,
I would appreciate you informing me so that I may follow up. Thank you very
much for your assistance.

Sincerely,

Bruce D. Robertson, C.P.A.

BDR/bl
Enclosure

DOUGLAS P. ARNOLD, JR.

295 TREETOP LANE N.W. • FT. COLLINS, COLORADO 80521 • (303) 578-2929

December 22, 19—

Mr. Scott A. McLean
Vice President
The First National Bank of Columbus
5000 Royal Atlantic Avenue
Columbus, Ohio 43201

Dear Mr. McLean:

When I mentioned to Mr. Charles Hill that I would be leaving my position as Controller of Robertson Manufacturing at the end of this month, he suggested I contact you with regard to locating a new position.

During my tenure at Robertson, I had the opportunity to work closely with Mr. Hill and some of the financial analysts at the bank. The professional manner in which they dealt with a very difficult situation has shown me that The First National Bank of Columbus may be the kind of organization where I could find a good "fit," and fully utilize my abilities.

While I understand that there may not be a suitable position open at the bank at this time, you or the commercial lending officers may be aware of a bank customer who may be in need of my skills.

Enclosed are two copies of my current resume. Please feel free to share the information provided with any employer who may be interested in the skills and experience I can provide.

After the New Year, I will call you to arrange a time, at your convenience, when we could meet should you decide a meeting would be appropriate.

Thank you for your consideration.

Seasons Greetings!

Douglas P. Arnold, Jr.

DPA/
Enclosures

William T. Bujarski
7800 South High Street
Littleton, Colorado 80122
(303) 770-4344

April 15, 19—

Mr. Larry Forest
Health Care Centers of America
3570 Keith Street N.W.
P.O. Box 3480
Dallas, Texas 75237

Dear Mr. Forest

My interest in pursuing a position with Health Care Centers of America has increased following my interviews in Cleveland and follow up visits to several of your centers in Denver. I'm concerned that I have not had the opportunity to discuss this with you personally. I am aware that the resignation of Tom Patrick has put additional demands on your time, but please know that I would make myself available to meet with you whenever it is convenient.

My contact and conversations with your staff in Dallas and in Denver have really excited me about the challenges and opportunities that your organization offers.

I am sincerely interested in exploring how I can be a part of the continued success of Health Care Centers of America, given my interests and financial management background.

I'll look forward to your call.

With great enthusiasm,

William T. Bujarski

Samir Y. Naguib
7704 West Coal Mine Place
Littleton, Colorado   80123
(303) 973-3456

July 21, 19—

Jeffery D. Emerson
Arthur Andersen
501 Second Street
Sixth Floor
Rockford, Illinois   61110

Dear Jeff,

It was great meeting with you the last two days. I would like
to take this opportunity to let you know I enjoyed my visit to the
office and Rockford very much. I feel that things went beautifully
and that I got along well with everyone I met.

I especially liked the total client service attitude and the
professionalism the partners displayed. I also enjoyed my tour
of Rockford in the afternoon. I was even tempted to extend my visit
an extra day to get a chance to see more of the community.

Jeff, I feel that there is a good match between my background and
expertise and your needs. The office, and the firm in general, seem
to have many learning and professional growth opportunities for me.
I also feel that I have talents and expertise I can contribute to
you—especially in the area of research and consulting and the area of
advancing the automation of the tax and accounting functions.

I am very interested in pursuing a career with Arthur Andersen and I
am looking forward to talking to you again in the near future.

Very truly yours,

Samir Y. Naguib

T. Craig Lincoln

4720 West 49th Street
Denver, CO 80018
(303) 555-7114 (o) • (303) 555-1682 (h)

April 28, 19—

Mr. Norman S. Powers
Executive Vice President
Ogilvy & Mather
520 Fifth Avenue
New York, New York 10017

Dear Norm,

I don't know if our lunch last Friday could be considered a "power lunch," but if it was I did feel a definite boost in horsepower. And it wasn't the jambalaya.

Your ideas and your philosophies on the business of advertising are impressive. I'm sure that when your concepts are implemented, Ogilvy & Mather will not only be the oldest ad agency in New York . . . it will be the best!

Where and if I fit into your plan at present is still an unknown. But I do know this. On many levels, I totally agree with the way you do business. And I strongly identify with your frustrations regarding the creative profession.

Simply stated, I believe that advertising is really marketing and that creative design means as much to the "bottom line" as it does on the layout pad. I would very much enjoy learning from your business and marketing expertise. In return, I would bring to your organization . . . creative accountability. Together, we would be a formidable account team.

Let's meet again. Let's talk again. Let's see how I could help you keep your organization out in front of the competition.

Till then, thanks for a most enjoyable Friday.

Sincerely,

T. Craig Lincoln
Lincoln & Associates

RICHARD T. BAIRD

102 STEWART STREET
SEATTLE, WASHINGTON 98101
(206) 441-4100

December 14, 19—

Mr. Norman B. Ferris
Certified Financial Planner
Ferris & Associates, Ltd.
1020 East Joseph Street
Seattle, Washington 98102

Dear Norm:

I thoroughly enjoyed our discussion yesterday. I had almost forgotten how stimulating business luncheons are. I sincerely appreciated your time and interest.

Even though I had the opportunity to tell you a little about my background, the enclosed résumé will provide further detail. Briefly stated, I have 18 years' experience in financial management including controllership, treasury, planning and administrative responsibilities. I have worked with large and small organizations in automated and manual financial systems environments. My management responsibilities ranged from 2 to 20 people and I am equally effective in "hands on" or staff management roles.

I am looking to the "smaller" organizations which employ between 300 and 500 people. I believe these organizations offer the opportunity to make significant contributions and reward hard work with increased responsibility.

Norm, I would appreciate your reviewing the résumé and mentioning my qualifications to your business associates. You could also assist me by providing the names of two or three people to contact and discuss my career plans and objectives. I will call you within the next week to discuss this.

Again, thank you for your time and consideration. Best wishes for a Happy Holiday Season and Prosperous New Year.

Sincerely,

Richard T. Baird

BRAD C. BAWMANN

203 EAST EXPOSITION AVENUE
DENVER, COLORADO 80209
(303) 342-4638

9 July 19—

Mr. Randy R. Hanson
Manager of Public Information
St. Anthony Hospital Systems
4231 W. 16th Avenue
Denver, Colorado 80204

Dear Randy,

You're fantastic!

I can't tell you how much I enjoyed meeting you this morning and learning more about your hospital system. I was most impressed by your enthusiasm and attention to detail.

I know we could work well together. Like yourself, I am versatile, accepting of constructive criticism and deeply committed to doing a good job.

Let's get together again, soon. Perhaps we could meet for lunch—that's the least I could do to thank you for taking the time this morning.

Have a great today!

Warmest regards,

Brad C. Bawmann

BRAD C. BAWMANN

203 EAST EXPOSITION AVENUE
DENVER, COLORADO 80209
(303) 342-4638

15 September 19—

Mr. Dan Richards
Vice President Account Services
New York Advertising, Inc.
300 Cherry Creek North Drive
Suite 3000
Denver, Colorado 80209-3852

Dear Dan,

You're super!

Thanks so much for taking time to meet with me today.

Per our discussion I've enclosed a few clips of my stories for your inspection.
I'd appreciate any feedback you might have. Otherwise, I'm taking your
suggestions to heart and contacting other agencies.

I thank you again for your time.

Sincerely yours,

Brad C. Bawmann

Enclosure

Richard A. Petersen
212 Old Lake Road
Worthington, Ohio 43085

July 25, 19—

Dr. Milton Bennett
Vice President, Technical Resources
Service and Technology Department
TRW, Inc.
19 Bridgestone Road
Cleveland, Ohio 44124

Dear Dr. Bennett:

Ron Price discussed my interest in TRW with you recently. My nearly 20 years in contract research has involved the development of close working relationships with various levels of industrial management in the United States and Japan. From this experience, I bring certain strengths that I believe could be effectively utilized by TRW:

* Very broad technical interests and understanding;

* The ability to understand technology in strategic business terms; and,

* Excellent people management skills.

I am seeking a position in line management, program management or technology planning that allows me to use these strengths in a creative environment. An acceptable salary level would be contingent upon the nature of the job and the location. The Cleveland area is especially attractive right now because of my wife's employment situation. I will call you in a week or so and answer any questions that you might have.

I appreciate your efforts on my behalf.

Very truly yours,

Richard A. Petersen

RAP/sl

James T. Evergreen
117 N. Jefferson Street
Chicago, Illinois 60606

December 29, 19—

Mr. Raymond K. Martin
Personnel Manager
Digital Equipment Corporation
290 Shasta Boulevard
Rockford, Illinois 61107

Dear Mr. Martin:

Kathy Quinn told me you were looking for someone to fill the position of Finance and Information Systems Manager. She suggested that the position description matched my qualifications very closely, and that I should look into it.

She also gave you a draft copy of my resume. Enclosed is a finalized version. I do understand that the particular position mentioned above may not be a possibility at this time. Nevertheless, I would appreciate the opportunity to meet with you. Condensing a 17-year career into a two-page resume necessarily omits many significant achievements that may be of interest to you.

Everything I know about Digital leads me to believe that "DEC" is the kind of organization where I could fully utilize my skills, experience and education, and make a valuable contribution.

Please note that I am presently an MBA student, majoring in Management Information Systems. I will be awarded the degree in June, 19— and will take the CPA exam soon thereafter.

Thank you for looking this over. I want to meet at your convenience, and I will call you in the next week or two.

Let's talk further,

James T. Evergreen

Enclosure

John F. Ovecka
6122 Snow Mountain Road
Bakersfield, California 93309
(805) 424-7111

February 24, 19—

Mr. Bob Stevenson
EDS International
Devonshire House-4th Floor
London, WI, England

Dear Mr. Stevenson:

You were referred to me by Mike Sherman. He and I talked about your European Division when I was in Lansing last summer doing some EDS-related telephone work for Butler Telecommunications.

I am deeply interested in working for EDS and further, expressly interested in working for EDS in Europe.

I know that EDS has entered, and continues to aggressively penetrate, telephone markets worldwide. And since I have an extensive telephone design and engineering background, as well as some solid experience in other related areas, I believe I could be a genuine asset to your organization.

Enclosed is a recent resume for your perusal. I believe two of my greatest strengths—which do not appear on my resume—are a strong work ethic and an ability to learn rapidly. I will provide references, both business and personal, at your request.

Please let me hear from you.

Sincerely,

John F. Ovecka

Enclosure

David K. Swanson
6704 Stanford Street
Washington, Ohio 43085

July 23, 19—

Mr. Philip J. Robins, President
Research International, Inc.
Post Office Box 3253
Gorham, Maine 04038

Dear Mr. Robins:

Richard Thomas recently introduced me to your company and I have learned something of your activities from Richard and from your promotional literature.

After over 14 years of contract research and management at Battelle, I have decided to seek career opportunities in a smaller, more innovative company where I can have an impact. Research International is involved in many areas in which I have actively worked in my nearly 20 years in contract research and I would like you to consider me as a candidate for your senior staff.

My technical background is in the materials area—specifically tribology. In this area I functioned in both the principal investigator and program manager roles. In addition to laboratory-oriented R&D and hardware development, I also have engaged in techno-economic studies related to synthetic lubricants and led two classified trade impact studies in the areas of ball bearings and synthetic lubricants.

For the past several years, I have managed profit centers engaged in R&D and commercialization in the transportation (air and automotive), structures and energy areas for both industry and government. My organizations have been active in the conception and execution of multiclient programs and cooperative research programs. I am experienced and knowledgeable in intellectual property exploitation and innovation management.

Since I took over as Director of Industrial Business Development, our industrial sales have grown 20% and our profitability in industrial business has increased from losses in 19— to nearly 10% return on volume. This is due in large part to a focused marketing strategy that I was instrumental in planning and implementing. For the past year,

Mr. Philip J. Robins, President
July 23, 19—
Page Two

I have been actively involved in the Japanese marketplace. I have a good understanding of Japanese business practices and the transfer of technology both to and from Japan.

I understand the business from the lab bench to the marketplace, and I believe that I have a great deal to offer to Research International. I would like the opportunity to discuss my qualifications in greater detail and I will call you next week to see if we can meet.

Very truly yours,

David K. Swanson

DKS/sle

1128 2ND AVENUE SOUTH   EDMONDS, WASHINGTON 98020

October 23, 19—

Mr. John D. Macomber
Presidential Search Committee
The Americas Society, Inc.
1280 Park Avenue
New York, New York 10021

Dear Mr. Macomber:

Please include my name on your list of persons interested in succeeding
Russell Martin.

Last week in New York, Edward Page—who knows me well from my years
with ASARCO—indicated that you hope to attract a major figure from the U.S.
corporate world or a significant and highly-respected public official.

If you determine that the person you seek should function basically as:

o a staff leader, and as

o a facilitator/arranger of quiet dialogue between the heads of U.S.
   companies and top officials of both Latin and U.S. governments, rather
   than speaking in his own name,

then you should find my records interesting.

Having dedicated most of my working life to Latin America, including 15 years
of residence in four countries, the strengths I would bring to the Society are:

* Substantial experience and significant personal accomplishments in the
   development of U.S. investments in Latin America and the conduct of
   day-to-day business operations.

* An understanding of the economic development of Latin America over
   the last two decades—its strengths of success, and its many failures.

* Years of successful negotiations at the ministerial level and contact work at the presidential level.

* Thorough familiarity with the structure and functioning of the expatriate communities in Latin countries, and considerable accomplishment and recognition within same.

* The ability to understand, develop rapport with, and be meaningfully accepted by Latin businessmen and government officials.

* A consistently clean and honest record as the spokesman/defender of U.S. interests—both corporate and public.

* A love of the arts and a lifetime of participation (mostly amateur) in musical activities both here and in Latin America.

My participation in the activities of the Americas Society goes back to the early 70s, and I am well known to some of your senior staff. Also:

* I have become acquainted, through the good offices of his former general counsel, with Mr. William Davidson.

* Steve Baker is a friend of many years.

* Hans Steiner is a friend and working colleague.

* I am well known to St. Joe's people in Lima, Hal and Lisa Wright— especially Lisa because of our years of work together on the board of the American school in Peru.

Thank you for considering me. I expect to be in New York in early November if you wish to schedule a meeting.

I'll call you,

Richard P. Ruby

RPR:djs

Bruce K. Markowitz
188 West Randolph Avenue
Oak Brook, Illinois 60521

February 1, 19—

Norman B. Simpson
Management Advisory Services
5919 East Jean Avenue
Phoenix, Arizona 85018

Dear Norm:

Just a brief note to thank you for returning the response form I recently sent you.

You might find it interesting that the exercise of looking for a new position has one real positive side. It has brought me in contact with people that I wouldn't have known otherwise, such as yourself. I've enjoyed meeting you.

With regard to the search itself, I'm still actively looking and hope you will keep me in mind if you hear of a situation that might be appropriate.

I appreciate the help and encouragement.

Best regards,

Bruce K. Markowitz

BKM/dk

Stuart T. Jackson
27 Northeast 105th Street
Miami Shores, Florida 33138
(704) 342-9093

January 29, 19—

L. Robert Williams
CRS Sirrene Engineering Group
216 South Pleasantburg Drive
Greenville, South Carolina 29607

Dear Mr. Williams,

Thank you for returning the response form I sent you. I realize business conditions limit the opportunities to bring new people on board at this time. However, I am still interested in learning more about your company.

I would like to call you next week to talk about your organization. I won't take more than ten minutes of your time.

So that you know more about me, I have attached a resume outlining my professional career.

Looking forward to talking,

Stuart T. Jackson

STJ/ha

Attachment

Susan J. Ottinger
7242 S. Tamarac St.
Englewood, Colorado 80112
(303) 761-8229

August 3, 19—

Ms. Nancy K. Rawlins
Research Pharmaceuticals, Inc.
Department 578
211 Carnegie Center
Princeton, New Jersey 08540-6213

Dear Ms. Rawlins:

Thank you for acknowledging receipt of my resume. I am anxious
to hear from you concerning a time we can get together
and discuss my background and objectives further.

I am most impressed with the Research commitment and quality of
its products for the consumer. I have been marketing and retailing
the ostomy and urological products from your HealthTek Division for
the past five years. This is the kind of corporation I want to be
associated with and especially to represent in this area.

In my present management position, I have just completed developing a mail order catalog system, the first of its kind in our corporation, which is expected to generate an additional $1,800,000
annually to our present revenue locally. This has created a great
deal of excitement with our regional office and is expected to be
spread to our other 400 stores across the country.

The recent completion of my Certificate in Management from the
graduate school at the University of Denver gives me added confidence
to broaden my business administration responsibilities and become a
top-notch representative for Research Pharmaceuticals in the Denver
area.

I am certainly looking forward to hearing from you again soon!

Enthusiastically,

Susan J. Ottinger

DOUGLAS P. ARNOLD, JR.

295 TREETOP LANE N.W. • FT. COLLINS, COLORADO 80521 • (303) 578-2929

January 20, 19—

Mr. Glenn T. Gordon
Xerox Equipment Corporation
Human Resources Department
3000 Southern Boulevard
Ft. Collins, Colorado 80521

Dear Mr. Gordon:

Thank you for taking the time to speak with me on the telephone last week, regarding the status of the Finance and Information Systems Manager position at Xerox. I appreciate your candor and encouragement.

Since you indicated I would be considered for the position should the decision to "look outside" be made, I have enclosed a summary of my recent career accomplishments. This summary should indicate the range of my abilities, and the kinds of results I have achieved.

Please do not hesitate to telephone should you have any questions or wish additional information.

Best regards,

Douglas P. Arnold, Jr.

Enclosure

BRAD C. BAWMANN

203 EAST EXPOSITION AVENUE
DENVER, COLORADO 80209
(303) 342-4638

10 June 19—

Mr. Timothy Wilson
News Anchor
KUSA Channel 9
1089 Bannock Street
Denver, Colorado 80204

Dear Mr. Wilson,

The last time I spoke with you on the telephone you mentioned positions at your station are created. "Openings," you said, "don't just happen—they have to be made."

I'm intrigued by that notion. And I'd like to sit down with you to discuss it. Perhaps we could meet for coffee.

As you know, I'm anxious to learn more about the field of television journalism. I think you could provide some key insight into the industry.

I'll call in a few days to set up a time to meet.

Thanks for your time Mr. Wilson. I'm looking forward to meeting you soon.

Sincerely yours,

Brad C. Bawmann

Kenneth K. Delgado
1800 One Dallas Center
Dallas, Texas 75201
(214) 979-1200 (w)
(214) 979-4653 (h)

October 19, 19—

Mr. William Gill
Vice President, International Division
Medical Products, Inc.
5020 Technology Drive
Dallas, Texas 75202

Dear Bill:

Thank you for taking time to talk with me over the phone this past week. I have enclosed a copy of my resume which details my accomplishments over the past several years.

While Vice President of Operations for Texas Instruments, I was responsible for the development and implementation of Just-in-Time (JIT) throughout the entire manufacturing and distribution operations. The approach taken with JIT was to eliminate waste, whether it was wasted effort, time, space, inventories, machine setup, materials handling, or financial accounting practices.

The hard results produced through implementation of the various programs allowed TI to consolidate Denver manufacturing operations from three facilities to one with over 200,000 square feet of floor space savings. Inventories were reduced substantially, scrap was reduced, product quality was improved and materials were pulled through the manufacturing process in much less time.

JIT is an ongoing program as there are always opportunities to reduce waste in every area. I found that JIT was an attitude and was especially successful because of the commitment developed throughout the total organization.

Bill, I will call you early next week after you have had a chance to review my resume. I would like to meet with you personally to discuss my capabilities.

Thanks you for your interest!

Kenneth K. Delgado

MICHAEL D. BURNS

TWO THOUSAND OAKS TOWERS • 2000 WEST FEDERAL STREET • BOSTON, MASSACHUSETTS 02110 • (617) 765-9898

January 25, 19—

Mr. George W. Blake
Fortress Enterprises
7399 South Tuscon Way
Englewood, Colorado 80112

Dear George:

It was a pleasure talking to you this afternoon. I am enclosing a resume and an excerpt from *Fortune* magazine which summarizes my experience and highlights a few of my accomplishments.

My career has been in management with a strong finance background. During the last year I worked as a personal investment advisor. I was successful in this profession, designing and implementing a telemarketing approach that brought over 45 six- to seven-figure net-worth clients in less than five months. Prior to joining Intek, I was offered the position of Vice-President for Marketing at Canadian Coal, but the excitement of the oil business at that time was just too strong.

My ideal job target is with a company that has an entrepreneurial outlook, is perhaps five to ten years old, and has sales of less than $100 million. I am flexible on immediate compensation if there is adequate potential for growth. An opportunity to earn equity would be attractive. Although I am not seeking investment opportunities, I might consider a limited investment. Geographic location is not a major consideration. I am open to any situation that is challenging and will make good use of my abilities.

George, this should cover the key points. I will be glad to provide any other information you may need and can supply strong references when appropriate. I look forward to our next conversation.

With warmest regards,

Michael D. Burns

Enclosures

RONALD L. EVANS
375 Park Avenue, Suite 3201
New York, NY 10152
(212) 688-8585 (o)
(212) 889-1543 (h)

September 17, 19—

Mr. Michael Williams, President
L.L. Bean
2805 Liberty Boulevard
Dubois, Pennsylvania 15801

Dear Mike:

Needless to say, I was disappointed to learn that you have chosen someone else to fill your Controller's position. I felt that your company's needs and my background very closely paralleled, and that I possess the management experience to work with you in building the organization.

If something changes, please do not hesitate to call me. I know that I can meet the high standards which you are striving to achieve. I was very excited, and hopeful, that I would have the chance to work with you and your staff as a member of the team.

Please thank your managers for their time and consideration on my behalf. I know how difficult it is to make a decision such as you were all faced with.

Your organization is producing a high quality product. That was obvious from my observations during my tour of the facilities. I was very impressed with the company and its personnel. I truly enjoyed my visit in August.

My best regards,

Ronald L. Evans

RONALD L. EVANS
375 Park Avenue, Suite 3201
New York, NY 10152
(212) 688-8585 (o)
(212) 889-1543 (h)

September 20, 19—

Mr. Norman Dean, Vice President
L.L. Bean
2805 Liberty Boulevard
Dubois, Pennsylvania 15801

Dear Norm,

Needless to say, I was disappointed to learn that you have chosen someone else to fill your Controller's position. I felt that your company's needs and my background very closely paralleled, and that I have the management experience to work with you and Mike in building the company. The fact that I have worked in a variety of industries, including engineering and construction, would have provided the opportunity to use techniques from many different disciplines.

If something changes, please do not hesitate to call me. I know I can meet the high standards you are striving to achieve. I was very excited with the prospect of helping develop a growing organization.

Now, however, I would like to ask for your assistance. Should you be aware, or become aware of any business associates, friends, or others who may be looking for someone with my talents, please provide them with a copy of the attached resume, or give me their names to contact personally. Positions involved with general or financial management in the industries of manufacturing, distribution, engineering and construction, or equipment sales and service, are my primary targets. I am willing to relocate to further my career.

Any further advice or counsel that you can provide will be greatly appreciated. For instance, it would be very helpful for me to know your thoughts on my qualifications and whether I related well to your company needs. If possible, I would like to meet with you once more to obtain any counsel regarding my search. If lunch or breakfast would suit you, I would be happy to meet.

I want to wish you and the company much success in the future. I really enjoyed meeting you and Mike. Thank you for your time and effort during your consideration of my candidacy.

My best regards,

Ronald L. Evans

W I L L I A M   A.   K A U F M A N
2323 Dunwoody Crossing
Atlanta, GA   30338
(404) 454-7216

April 8, 19—

Dr. Robert Bond
The Cardiology Corporation
1960 Main Street
Belleview, Washington   98004

Dear Dr. Bond:

Our talk last Thursday left me with the impression you felt
my experience in getting clinical cardiovascular devices to a
successful product launch was exactly what you need. Hence, my difficulty understanding the note I received yesterday from Cindy Black,
indicating my application is not under current consideration.

I do understand the potential difficulty you mentioned regarding the
new person who will be assuming control soon and his possible desire
to select his own people for the function. That may be a risk, as
you suggested, and it is a calculated one.

Unless you have new information since we talked, my judgment is that
the risk is counterbalanced by the opportunity to demonstrate my
unusual combination of technical, clinical, and marketing skills.
They are precisely those skills your group now needs during clinical
trials, to assure the excimer angioplasty laser is the successful
product it should be when you receive commercial approval.

If you've already selected the person you want in that slot, I'd
still like to talk to you about your alternate suggestion—working
with you on a temporary or consulting basis. As you said, the highlighted points in my cover letter corresponded exactly with what you
feel the company needs.

Right now, The Cardiology Corporation is a small company with a few
people and a big job to do. You need good people with as many of the
right talents as possible, who understand what is needed to develop
the products and the company to its potential, and who will do the
job to make sure it happens. I have that diverse background and a
drive to make those contributions. Let's get together and discuss
what we could do and how to do it. Please give me a call—
days or evenings are fine.

My best regards,

William A. Kaufman

BRAD C. BAWMANN

203 EAST EXPOSITION AVENUE
DENVER, COLORADO 80209
(303) 342-4638

29 June 19—

Ms. Penny Harcourt
Vice President Public Affairs and Education
Colorado Hospital Association
2140 South Holly
Denver, Colorado 80222

Dear Ms. Harcourt:

You're fantastic!

Thank you for your time on the telephone last week. Enclosed is a sampling of my work at "The Creek."

As a reporter for a weekly newspaper, I've been fortunate to sink my teeth into a wide range of subjects. However, none are ever more enjoyable than a story about the medical profession.

My contacts in the industry are numerous, and they can speak to the credibility of my work. A more tenacious, aggressive reporter you won't find.

Some say my energy and enthusiasm are enough for any three people. And my drive, desire and determination make me an ideal candidate for a top-notch organization in the medical field.

Moreover, my educational background drew heavily on the natural and social sciences, as I once contemplated attending medical school.

Ms. Harcourt, if there is anything more I can share with you please let me know.

I will be in touch to make sure you have received my materials.

Once again, thanks for your time and consideration. Any suggestions or referrals you could make would be most appreciated.

Sincerely yours,

Brad C. Bawmann

BRAD C. BAWMANN

203 EAST EXPOSITION AVENUE
DENVER, COLORADO 80209
(303) 342-4638

8 July 19—

Ms. Barbara Barrow
Public Relations Director
University of Colorado Health Sciences Center
Box A092
4200 East 9th Avenue
Denver, Colorado 80262

Dear Ms. Barrow,

Per our phone conversation earlier in the week I've enclosed a few clips of pertinent stories.

Being a journalist I watch the medical profession intensely for new developments whether good or bad. But my reporting style is always unbiased and sensitive to the needs of the public.

When Florida's trauma network fell on hard times I investigated Denver's trauma system, only to find it doing quite well. And when the Taiwan flu threatened the area I was the first to alert both the public and the rest of Denver's media to the potential hazards.

A more tenacious, aggressive reporter you won't find. And my communication skills—both oral and written—are honed razor sharp. In addition, my energy is limitless; my enthusiasm unequaled; my attention to detail unparalleled.

Let's at least talk. I know I can help the Health Sciences Center become the hospital it aspires to be.

I'll call in a few days to arrange a time to meet.

Sincerely yours,

Brad C. Bawmann

MICHAEL TREASURE, JR.

9200 S. DADELAND BLVD., SUITE 516 • MIAMI, FL 33156 • (305) 661-5468 (O) • (305) 371-9672 (H)

October 13, 19—

Rebecca S. Gardner
Sr. Vice President Human Resources
AT&T
2900 Camp Hill Road
Fort Washington, PA 19034

Dear Rebecca:

I enjoyed our phone conversation today and look forward to meeting you for breakfast on the 27th. I will see you at the Hyatt Regency restaurant at 7:00 a.m. By the way, so you have no trouble finding me, I am 6'4" with a brown mustache.

My resume is enclosed.

Very truly yours,

Michael J. Treasure, Jr.

MJT/s

Enclosure: resume

DOUGLAS P. ARNOLD, JR.

295 TREETOP LANE N.W. • FT. COLLINS, COLORADO 80521 • (303) 578-2929

January 15, 19—

Ms. Deanna Randall
Chief Financial Officer
Metropolitan Systems Incorporated
1600 West Center Street
Salt Lake City, Utah 84047

Dear Ms. Randall,

Thank you for selecting me as a candidate for a position at Metropolitan Systems. I appreciate the opportunity to meet with you, and look forward to learning more about your company.

So that our meeting can be most productive, I have enclosed a list of my significant career accomplishments for your examination. I believe this summary shows the way in which I approach my work and the kind of results I have achieved.

I will be pleased to provide any additional information you require when we meet on Tuesday the 19th.

Enthusiastically,

Douglas P. Arnold, Jr.

DPA/

Enclosures

October 23, 19—

Mr. Larry L. Johnston
President
Petroleum Waste, Inc
2701 Patton Way
Bakersfield, California 93308

Dear Larry:

The following, plus the attachment, sets out a brief summary of my experience and qualifications:

1. Worked over 20 years with Amoco and Exxon before joining InTek in 19—. Have a BS
   in Geology from Colorado University and an MBA from Stanford.

2. At Exxon, as a geologist, discovered the South Eola field in Garvin County, Oklahoma
   (30-40 million barrels).

3. At Amoco, progressed through a series of jobs in operations and in headquarters where I was
   associated with, or a member of the management groups directing the exploration, production
   and financial activities of Amoco's various natural resources activities, both in the U.S. and
   overseas.

4. As President of InTek, turned the company around and then led it to the most successful
   exploration program in its history, participating in the drilling of 125 prospects in midcontinent,
   Gulf Coast and Rockies, with a success ratio of 44%. Success ratio for follow-up drilling was
   85% and InTek's reserves were nearly doubled.

I look forward to talking with you next week and will be glad to provide any additional information.

Best regards,

Michael D. Burns

Attachment

THOMAS K. JACOB
8118 South Garfield Way
Littleton, Colorado 80122
(303) 694-2412

April 6, 19—

Mr. Frank Murphy
N L Baroid
P.O. Box 60070
Houston, Texas 77205

Dear Frank:

I really enjoyed our phone conversation concerning your plans to market Ml79 soil sealant. Your comments reminded me of many similarities between my past experiences with Dowell and what you are looking for in your new venture.

— Selling to industry and government
— Developing new markets for existing products
— Solving client technical problems
— Designing solutions with the aid of laboratory data
— Melding various groups to achieve the desired goal

I've included an example of a problem I faced with Dowell that is very similar to problems you might face. In fact, this project used a crosslinked, dry powder form of polyacrylamide; similar to the Ml79 system.

After you've had a chance to look this over, I'll give you a call to get your reactions. Or you call me.

Sincerely,

Tom Jacob

TJ/bl
Attachment

PROBLEM

I had the opportunity to perform the first enhanced oil recovery project on the North Slope of Alaska. Dowell's normal products and equipment would not do the job due to the severe weather and environmental concerns of the client. In addition, the client's technical and operation people disliked each other.

STRATEGY

I arranged for our chemical specialist and our equipment specialist to meet with me and the customer's engineers and operation personnel, then led an eight-hour meeting to design a new system (chemistry and equipment) to perform to the customer's requirements.

RESULTS

I moved men, materials and equipment to the North Slope, then assembled the equipment and began operations on time with outstanding technical results. This pilot project generated additional revenue of $300,000 for Alaska operations in a two-month period.

THOMAS K. JACOB
8118 South Garfield Way
Littleton, Colorado 80122
(303) 694-2412

April 22, 19—

Mr. Craig D. Sutton
1343 Wilshire Boulevard
Beverly Hills, California 90212

Dear Craig,

I'm writing to remind you that I am still in the job market.

I'm seeking a job that involves modifying technical products and equipment in
the field to meet customer specifications.

This job could be called something like:

    — Field Engineer
    — Sales Engineer
    — Service Sales Engineer
    — Field Applications Engineer, or
    — Product Troubleshooter

The chemical, industrial controls and instrumentation, water treatment, hazardous
waste, machinery and manufacturing, sales/marketing, construction and
materials handling industries would appeal to me.

I have created a non-oilfield resume that focuses on sales and marketing. Please
review it and pass it along to anyone who might be looking for someone with
my talents.

Any help you can give me will be greatly appreciated.

Your friend,

Tom Jacob

TKJ/bl
Enclosure

Jack Mooney
5711 E. Crestline Ave.
Englewood, Colorado 80111
(303) 771-0987 (W)
(303) 987-8654 (H)

February 27, 19—

Mr. Conrad W. Andersen
Transportation Engineering, Inc.
1250 Broadway
New York, New York 10001

Dear Conrad,

I have taken a temporary job in financial research but I am still very interested in working with your firm.

I have recently updated my resume to include some important accomplishments missing in the earlier version. I think it represents me more accurately.

Please review it and I'll call you in a couple days for your comments.

With warm thanks,

Jack Mooney

JM:kar
Enclosure

Samir Y. Naguib
7704 West Coal Mine Place
Littleton, Colorado 80123
(303) 973-3456

July 21, 19—

Kent Sullivan
US West Financial Services
8200 South Quebec Street, Suite 330
Englewood, Colorado 80111

Dear Kent,

In our last conversation you asked me to call you on or about
July 7th. I am not having much luck calling you while you are available. Therefore, I thought I'd drop this note in the mail
to let you know that I am still interested in pursuing a position
with U.S. West.

Kent, I recently revised my resume and I am enclosing a copy for your
review.

I am looking forward to hearing from you in the near future.
I may be reached at 897-0987.

Very truly yours,

Samir Y. Naguib

Enclosure

BRAD C. BAWMANN

203 EAST EXPOSITION AVENUE
DENVER, COLORADO 80209
(303) 342-4638

September 16, 19—

Mr. Butch Montoya
News Director
KUSA-Channel 9
1089 Bannock Sreet
Denver, Colorado 80204

Dear Mr. Montoya,

Thank you for your letter dated August 28, 19—.

Even though there are no openings currently at KUSA, I want you to know I'm still interested.

I'm a "content" man, able to squeeze every drop out of a story. And my drive, enthusiasm and energy, most agree, are astounding.

My tenacity in getting the most out of a story is made manifest by my recent revelation that actress Shirley MacLaine plans to open the first of her spiritual centers here in Colorado. I fought long and hard for that story and I broke it first.

Let's at least meet for a cup of coffee. I want to show you how my assets are too valuable to forego.

I'll call in a few days to arrange a time to meet.

Sincerely yours,

Brad C. Bawmann

203 EAST EXPOSITION AVENUE
DENVER, COLORADO 80209
(303) 342-4638

June 17, 19—

Mr. Scott Wade
Editor
The Denver Post
650 - 15th Street
Denver, Colorado 80201

Dear Mr. Wade,

A no simply won't do. I can help make <u>The Denver Post</u> the newspaper it aspires to be.

My news sense is made manifest by your paper frequently replaying my scoops. A more tenacious, aggressive reporter you won't find.

My drive, energy and enthusiasm are enough for three people. I will work for you like no other.

Let's talk.

Some say times are tough at <u>The Post</u>. I prefer to think you're rebuilding for the future.

I'm ready to be with the best. Are you ready to have the best?

I'll call in a few days to set up a time to meet.

Sincerely yours,

Brad C. Bawmann

Enclosure

RONALD L. EVANS
375 Park Avenue, Suite 3201
New York, NY 10152
(212) 688-8585 (o)
(212) 889-1543 (h)

July 27, 19—

Mr. John Hill, Vice President
Materials Equipment Company
2 Pennsylvania Plaza
New York, New York 10001

Dear Mr. Hill

I want to thank you for the assistance you have so kindly provided me. As I told you yesterday, I have contacted Mr. Morris and forwarded him my resume. I appreciate your suggesting that Mr. Sloan and Mr. Rice be contacted since they have good business contacts and can probably offer suggestions.

I was disappointed that you decided not to add a financial management position for the company, because I'm certain I could make a significant contribution with service work order controls, parts inventory management, computer system opportunities, reliable financial reporting, personnel productivity measurements, and assisting with your efforts for enhanced service to customers. As you know from our conversation, I am a proponent of the importance of excellent customer service.

I was very impressed with you as a concerned manager and with the pleasant environment I observed in your facility. That atmosphere, friendly and yet productive, represents the kind of situation I am seeking.

I hope you will reconsider your decision. I would be glad to meet with you and the owners further to explore the benefits of adding a financial management position.

I don't want to belabor the subject; however, because I believe there is very good potential, agree with your stated ideals and goals, and like the attitude of the organization, I know I would enjoy being a member of your management team.

Again, I want to express my appreciation for the help that you are providing. I will keep you informed about any developments or changes in status.

Wishing you great success,

Ronald L. Evans

1128 2ND AVENUE SOUTH   EDMONDS, WASHINGTON 98020

January 24, 19—

Dr. Richard C. Taylor
Scientific Software, Inc.
1801 California
Denver, Colorado 80202-2799

Dear Dr. Taylor

Some months ago Jim Stovall suggested that I make a second effort to see you.

Recently Mike Hildebrand of Federal Express indicated that early February might be a good time.

Most of my life has been spent working through or around the many obstacles that third world governments love to put in the way of the continuing relationship that SSI must want to have with the overseas oil agencies. I've also participated in the development and day-to-day functioning of several significant international partnerships—which is an option that SSI might want to begin exploring.

Could we schedule a meeting to see if SSI is encountering enough third world roadblocks to warrant making use of my experience? We could consider employee status or an outside attorney relationship, as I'm well into conversations regarding joining one of Seattle's major law firms, and could serve SSI equally well from that base.

Yours truly,

Richard P. Ruby

cc: Jim Stovall
     Price Waterhouse

TWO THOUSAND OAKS TOWERS • 2000 WEST FEDERAL STREET • BOSTON, MASSACHUSETTS 02110 • (617) 765-9898

March 22, 19—

Mr. Allen E. Tufts
President
Tufts Technical Services
660 Kirkville Road
East Syracuse, New York 13057

Dear Allen:

It was good to talk with you last week, but I am disappointed to see that our discussions are proceeding so slowly.

From my side, I am eager to get to work and, as you might suspect, I have been pursuing a very active search. This search has developed several possibilities, but I keep thinking about your situation, which is such a good fit with what I do best, and I am reluctant to see it possibly closed off by a coincidence of timing rather than actual decision.

It is my understanding that you are looking for someone who could provide strong assistance with day-to-day management responsibilities so that you could concentrate more on the longer-term issues. You feel you have assembled a strong group of people, whose only deficiency is a lack of broad management experience. This will come with time, but you need someone to help you right now.

If this understanding is correct, I think I can provide you some real help. As you know, my management experience has been quite broad and varied, and at InTek I had a similar situation. Most of the department heads there were also in their early 30s and quite bright. It was a situation in which I served as both leader and teacher. I very much enjoyed doing this and along the way, we also built a very strong and aggressive organization.

Please give these comments some serious thought, and I will phone you in early April when you are back from your trip.

Best regards,

Michael D. Burns

1128 2ND AVENUE SOUTH   EDMONDS, WASHINGTON 98020

December 16, 19—

Mr. Kenneth D. Blackman
Corporate Counsel
Storage Technology Corporation
2270 South 88th Street
Louisville, Colorado 80027

Dear Kenneth,

You will recall that I visited you a few months ago at Bill Henry's arranging. Our discussion started with copper—which has been a large part of my life— and then moved to the role and responsibilities of a corporate counsel for a smaller hi-tech firm.

Since our talk, I have been interviewing in the east, and expect to be back there in the next week or so—but, as I mentioned to you, I would much prefer to stay in this area.

Your current state of work overload may well last for much longer than any- one suspects. I wonder if you might be feeling the need for some additional, battle-scarred strength in your office, to help you keep track of and deal with the many outside big-league players now buffeting STC.

A press release describing the financing we put together for the Peruvian copper mine in the '70s is enclosed—simply to give you an idea of the complexity of the undertaking. I had a lot to do with the entire effort, and would be glad to explain my work and accomplishments in detail if you should ever wish.

Chase Manhattan was the lead commercial bank on the financing. The Millbank Tweed lawyer who carried their load is now the senior outside legal counsel to Chase. He knows me well from that period, and he or his assistant (also a Millbank partner) could give you a reading on my contribution. ASARCO'S outside legal counsel was Covington and Burling, specifically Phil Rathbun and Dick West both of whom knew amd valued my work highly. Phil, after it was all over, commented that my ability to master a complex tangle of financial and commercial relationships, and to keep all the pieces lined up and moving in the desired direction, was crucial to the success of the legal side of the endeavor.

Please call me if you think there might be something to talk about in this suggestion.

Yours truly,

Richard P. Ruby

William B. Tyburski
1302 West 22nd Street
Willmington, Deleware 19810
(302) 475-4829

May 27, 19—

William S. Frank
President
CareerLab
9085 E. Mineral Circle, Suite 330
Englewood, Colorado 80112

Dear Mr. Frank:

A few months ago I wrote to you regarding the possibility
of doing some work with you. I am a consulting psychologist with 25
years background in a variety of different roles, and have had experience in career testing and counseling.

I am writing to you again to see what opportunities might
presently exist to do some part-time consulting work with you.

Since writing to you before, I have been doing some career management consultation work, part-time, with two other firms in the
Denver area. However, they use a marketing approach to career development exclusively, which I do not prefer and feel is not fully
appropriate for clients.

I think that a solid understanding of an individual's preferences
and capabilities, together with a keen awareness of his or her
emotional motivations, are needed to help a person implement their
career goals. I prefer more of a counseling approach to career
development, and as I explained in my previous letter, use a directive
approach in my counseling and work with clients.

If your firm has a need, I feel that I can provide assistance to
you in such ways as the following:

* Career counseling in helping clients learn to manage
   their own career development and job search campaign.

* Career testing and assessment of a person's
   preferences, attitudes, and values.

William S. Frank
May 27, 19—
Page Two

       * Consultation with more difficult clients who are
         experiencing motivational problems, or are even
         resisting the efforts of your program.

       * Assisting with the difficulties encountered when a
         client is going through an outplacement process.

I also understand that there appears to be somewhat of a declining market for career services with certain firms in the Denver area. If this has not affected your business, and there is a continuing call for your services, then you might have need for some additional assistance.

If I can be of help to you, and my qualifications are of interest, please contact me so that we might arrange a meeting.

With enthusiasm,

William B. Tyburski

MICHAEL D. BURNS

TWO THOUSAND OAKS TOWERS • 2000 WEST FEDERAL STREET • BOSTON, MASSACHUSETTS 02110 • (617) 765-9898

November 9, 19—

Mr. Larry Anderson
President
Petroleum Waste, Inc.
2701 Patton Way
Bakersfield, California 93308

Dear Larry:

Just a brief note to thank you and your group for the time you spent with me last Thursday and Friday. I appreciate the detail that was provided and candor that was evident. You have an excellent group of people in your operation and it would be a pleasure to work with you and them.

<u>Expanding a few points that we discussed:</u>

Yes, I am interested in the job of Site Manager. You are apparently concerned that this job does not have the scope of some of my previous positions, but I know that it has plenty of challenge and problems and it will give me a great deal of satisfaction to be allowed to handle them. You can see from my resume that once I take a job I stick with it. I have only worked for three companies; my shortest time with any one was more than four years, and I worked nearly 20 years for Amoco.

Another concern seemed to be whether I feel I can handle a job that requires "hands-on" management, and also an ability to cope with a frustrating corporate environment. My time spent managing start-up and turnaround situations has given me considerable OJT in both these areas. I enjoy "hands-on," and I have always been able to achieve efficiency regardless of the environment.

Larry, I would appreciate a shot at the job.

Best regards,

Michael D. Burns

MB/mb

Jonathan B. Field
1000 Louisiana Street
Houston, TX 77002
(713) 658-2887

February 13, 19—

Mr. Jerry D. Speer
Senior Vice President
International Environmental Services, Inc.
P.O. Box 609
Deer Park, Texas 77536-0609

Dear Mr. Speer,

This is in response to your request for additional information about me. I have enclosed a resume as well as completing your application.

I would like to point out what I feel are my areas of expertise:

o   Solid management experience in the operations of an organization.

o   Success in sales/marketing of technical products and services.

o   Consistent financial results through market penetration and cost control.

o   Firm dealings with personnel issues of discipline, compensation and employee development.

As I indicated in my original letter to you, the similarities between my background and your business would allow me to use my experience effectively.

I worked with Halliburton following graduation from Illinois Technological University in 19— until the end of 19—. My ending salary was $6,700 per month. I have been the recipient of several incentive stock options since 19—.

I will provide you with references, including the Vice President and General Manager I last reported to, assuming our discussions develop further.

I will call you next week after you have had an opportunity to review my resume.

Thank you for your interest,

Jonathan B. Field

BRUCE D. ROBERTSON, CPA

3182 South Holly Street
Denver, Colorado 80222

(303) 756-7434 (H)
(303) 779-1417 (W)

June 3, 19—

Michael J. Browning, Ph.D.
Vice President and Academic Dean
Roberts Wesleyan College
2301 Westside Drive
Rochester, New York 14624-1997

Dear Dr. Browning:

I am very interested in applying for your vacant faculty position in Accounting at Roberts Wesleyan College. Thank you for sending me the application forms, which I have completed and enclosed. I am looking forward to visiting you to discuss this exciting teaching opportunity in more detail.

Since your letter of May 20, I had an informative telephone conversation with Dr. Jim Baker. Dr. Baker filled me in concerning your school, new accounting programs, and teaching philosophy. This position is exactly the type of teaching opportunity that I am seeking—one in which I immerse myself.

Last night, I was talking with my choir partner, Bill Griffith, at our Colorado Chorale Concert. He mentioned that you two worked together at NCHEMS in Boulder.

If you have any questions, or need any additional information, please feel free to call me at 303-779-1417 (W) or 303-756-7434 (H).

Sincerely,

Bruce D. Robertson, CPA

BDR:pr
Attachments

cc: Dr. Jim Baker

MICHAEL D. BURNS

TWO THOUSAND OAKS TOWERS • 2000 WEST FEDERAL STREET • BOSTON, MASSACHUSETTS 02110 • (617) 765-9898

November 24, 19—

Mr. Robert T. Wagner
Ecology and Environment, Inc.
P. O. Box D
195 Holtz Road
Buffalo, New York 14225

Dear Mr. Wagner:

First of all, I want to thank you for the time you took to talk with me on the phone last week. Your comments make sense and your enthusiasm about the future of Ecology and Environment, Inc. is contagious. The company sounds like a very dynamic and progressive place to work.

As we discussed, I am looking for a position in general management, and I do have those "well-balanced, multi-discipline skills" necessary to make one effective in such a job. I began my career in a technical area as a geologist, and then broadened it through both education and job experience. I have worked in three different industries, in situations that have included both startups and difficult turnarounds. I am a true management professional and feel I have a lot to offer your company.

A summary of my credentials is enclosed and I will be glad to provide any additional information you might need. As we discussed, I am free to travel and open to relocation.

Once again, thank you for your help and I look forward to talking again in the near future.

With warm regards,

Michael D. Burns

Enclosure

BRUCE D. ROBERTSON, CPA

3182 South Holly Street
Denver, Colorado 80222

(303) 756-7434 (H)
(303) 779-1417 (W)

October 14, 19—

Mr. Donald B. Martin
Pendleton Resources
1899 Logan, Suite 250
Denver, Colorado 80203

Dear Donald:

Hope you have a great vacation! As you suggested I will call you after your
return the week of October 20th.

Just to jog your memory, I am the individual referred by Bill Black for the
international position which is on hold until late October while the new
President is traveling the world to see the company.

In addition, I have put together the enclosed recap of my Administrative
and Finance capabilities in order to market myself for what will be the most
productive years of my life. This is the same information as in my resume
I gave you, but in a different format that you may find useful.

I am looking forward to meeting with you to discuss the exciting, challenging
international position in more detail.

Sincerely,

Bruce Robertson

BDR/bl
Enclosure

BRUCE D. ROBERTSON, CPA

3182 South Holly Street
Denver, Colorado 80222

(303) 756-7434 (H)
(303) 779-1417 (W)

Consulting Capabilities, Specialties, and Experience

I. International Operations

    A. Was Managing Director of IMEC, Ltd. (International Management and Engineering Consultants, Ltd.).
    B. Lived and worked in Europe. Was number two man in European operation which grew in two years from $5 million to $55 million in sales.
    C. Planning and control. Developed international strategic plan and budgets.
    D. Communicate in French in business matters.
    E. Administrative, finance, organizational, and operational experience.

II. Strategic Planning and Budgeting

    A. Develop and implement plans.
    B. Feasibility studies.
    C. Cash flow planning.
    D. Budgets and forecasts.
    E. Develop budget control systems based on business flow.

III. Business Management

    A. Problem Solver.
    B. Operations management. Chief Operating Officer for 300-person operation.
    C. Management assessment and auditing.

IV. Management Development

    A. Strategic planning, international business, finance, and accounting systems.
    B. Motivate enthusiastic employees.
    C. Develop management personnel.
    D. Develop successful Management by Objective (MBO) systems.
    E. Help managers to use MBO as their own key personal management tool.

V. Accounting and Finance

    A. Accounting systems and operations. Design and solve operational problems.
    B. Establish foreign bank lines.
    C. Venture capital.

BRAD C. BAWMANN

203 EAST EXPOSITION AVENUE
DENVER, COLORADO 80209
(303) 342-4638

August 10, 19—

Mr. Jeff Rundles
Managing Editor
The Denver Business Journal
2401 - 15th Street, Suite 350
Denver, Colorado 80202

Dear Jeff,

Lunch was fabulous!

Your suggestions and insight concerning the media industry were most relevant and quite welcome.

I've enclosed samples of my work from both The Creek, a weekly newspaper, and UPI, where I interned in London.

I'll call in a few days. I'm anxious for your feedback.

Warmest regards,

Brad C. Bawmann

Enclosures

BRAD C. BAWMANN

203 EAST EXPOSITION AVENUE
DENVER, COLORADO 80209
(303) 342-4638

August 10, 19—

Ms. Janet Case
Publications Manager
The Children's Hospital
1800 Emerson Street
Denver, Colorado 80204

Dear Ms. Case,

It was great speaking with you over the telephone Friday. As promised, I've enclosed a few work samples.

Let me emphasize, however, I am much more than an aggressive reporter/ writer. Versatility, enthusiasm, and ceaseless energy are but a few of the assets I can promise you.

In addition, as my letters of recommendation indicate, I'm willing to go the extra five miles it sometimes takes to make a project sparkle and shine.

If there is more I can do in your decision-making process please feel free to call.

I'm anxious to show you how I am the best candidate for the position.

Thanks for your time.

Sincerely yours,

Brad C. Bawmann

Enclosure

15

Consultants or Consulting

My definition of a consultant is "someone who wakes up every morning unemployed." Good consultants tend to work themselves out of a job rather quickly. Because consultants move from job to job, from company to company, they are perpetual job-hunters. (Only they call it "business development.") You can often lean on them for marketing advice because a large part of their work is finding new clients. Finding new clients is no different than finding a full-time employer. The steps are exactly the same.

Most consultants know a lot of successful, influential people. (They must to stay in business.) If you know consultants, call them. If not, meet some through friends. Ask for their advice and ideas. If they like you—and why shouldn't they?—they will offer to share their contacts.

It's not uncommon for job-seekers to pursue consulting and a "real job" at the same time. Typically, what happens is that one direction emerges as the winner. Either you land a full-time job, or you nail down several consulting assignments. The decision about which direction to go tends to make itself. If a consulting lifestyle appeals to you, don't be afraid to let people know you could either consult or work full-time.

Berry's World

BERRY'S WORLD reprinted with permission of NEA, Inc.

"Maximize fees! Minimize work!"

GREGORY A. HATFIELD
RR#2 Box 237A
Terrance, Indiana 47390
(317) 584-7475

July 25, 19—

Nancy Blackwell
Management Consultant
The Leadership Group
7700 East Arapahoe Road, Suite 275
Englewood, Colorado 80112

Dear Ms. Blackwell:

I saw your listing in the Boulder County Manufacturers Directory. My fiance will be entering the University of Colorado in September, so I am seeking placement with firms in the Boulder area. I hope you can assist me.

I am currently living with my parents in Indiana. Their failing health required me to move there temporarily while attending to family business. Now that things are under control, I am beginning my job search.

I have enclosed a copy of my current resume. I would summarize my strengths as follows:

- Ten years' management consulting experience during which I developed superior business communication and presentation skills.

- A detailed, results-oriented consulting approach. Many consultant's primary product is a report with recommendations for action. My experience and inclination is to take the next step and assist clients in implementing necessary change to organizations, policies, procedures and systems.

- Strong functional experience in the areas of Strategic Planning, Accounting, MIS, and Manufacturing Operations.

- Extensive project management experience—in some cases managing projects entailing multi-million dollar budgets and employing scores of personnel.

- A solid business education focused on marketing.

Nancy Blackwell
July 25, 19—
Page Two

I am interested in pursuing one of the following positions:

o A product marketing or staff marketing position with a growth-oriented manufacturing concern.

o A consulting position with opportunity for attaining partnership within one or two years.

o A product marketing or sales support position with a software development concern.

I worked slightly less than nine months in 19— and my income was just over $75,000. I need your advice on salaries in the Boulder area. My gut feeling at this time is that $40,000 per year would be a minimum acceptable salary given my experience and background.

I am looking forward to discussing my situation with you. I will be calling in the next few days to get your input.

Thanks so much,

Gregory A. Hatfield

May 18, 19—

Ms. Marilyn Henry
1238 Oak Creek Drive
Littleton, Colorado 80121

Dear Marilyn,

While continuing the search for a full-time job, I wish to add some new consulting assignments. I hope that you can help me in that regard.

A partial list of things that I can do for clients is enclosed. Please take a few minutes and think about friends, or customers, or problems where my talents and intelligence would be useful.

I'll call next week to hear your ideas.

With many thanks,

Paul Gutknecht

PG/
Enclosure

Steven R. MacDonald
11285 Admiral Road
Albuquerque, New Mexico 87112
(505) 821-4420

February 3, 19—

Mr. Jeffrey D. O'Toole
Vice President
Deloitte, Haskins & Sells
2000 East Randolph Drive
Chicago, Illinois 60601

Dear Mr. O'Toole:

I know what it takes to make a profit in the consulting industry because I have been there—as a Managing Partner in a large consulting engineering firm (Dames & Moore), as President of a mid-size consulting firm, and as Founder and President of a multi-discipline firm.

I am interested in a firm that has growth and/or diversification goals and needs an executive manager who can assume both P&L and marketing responsibility and, eventually, an equity position.

I know the consulting industry. I know that it takes an innovative and unique marketing strategy to produce a top line, and it takes decisive management to meet chargeability goals—I can provide both.

In addition, I have the financial experience to manage and analyze accounting information and negotiate with bankers and other financial groups with respect to long- and short-term borrowing, letters of credit, payroll arrangements, etc.

I would like to meet to see if an association would be beneficial to both of us, and I'll call you early next week.

Very truly yours,

Steven R. MacDonald

SRM/btk
Enclosure: Fact Sheet

T. CRAIG LINCOLN

4720 West 49th Street
Denver, CO 80018
(303) 555-7114 (o) • (303) 555-1682 (h)

July 20, 19—

Ms. Margaret Keegan
Director of Communications
Mercedes-Benz of North America, Inc.
1000 Broadway
Fort Lee, New Jersey 07024

Dear Ms. Keegan:

Usually when you call in an artist, that's exactly what you get. An artist. Good art, but questionable business understanding.

When you hire me you get a "business artist." Someone who is a professional design artist. And someone who understands business.

— I am a one-person design team. Very small. Very personal.
— With over 25 years of experience in business art.
— I designed and implemented the corporate identity program for Old National Bank of Washington which saved them $7,500.
— I designed and produced a capabilities proposal for the Dravo Corporation. As a result, they were awarded a $35,000,000 engineering and construction project.

I could quickly achieve the same results for you.

<u>USE ME FOR</u> . . .

1. Corporate design of all printed materials.
2. Industrial and architectural graphics.
3. Interior space planning.
4. Industrial and vocational education design.
5. Corporate advertising and marketing communications.

Let's meet. Let's talk. Let's do some business that will put you out front and keep you out front in your market.

At your earliest convenience, please contact me if you would like to hear and see more. During the day you can reach me at 303-555-7114.

Sincerely,

T. Craig Lincoln

October 14, 19—

Mr. Mark O. Goodman
Texaco, Inc.
440 South Fox Street
Denver, Colorado 80223

Dear Mr. Goodman:

From time to time, your company may need well-written publicity or other business writing that you don't have the time or personnel to handle. How would you like to have a good business writer on call without adding to your permanent payroll?

Introducing Julie Normand Business Writing Services.

As a free-lance copywriter specializing in publicity and business writing for small companies, I have had experience with a wide variety of products and services. Attached is a partial client list.

My specialties are:

* Brochure and catalog copy

* Company and marketing newsletters

* Press releases

* Correspondence, form letters, direct mail letters

* Training manuals, employee handbooks

Because I'm not affiliated with any agency and my overhead is low, my rates are very reasonable. I also have word-processing equipment that enables me to provide quick turnaround on rewrites.

Whether you have an extensive project or simply a one-time "impossible" letter to write, I can help you. Please give me a call at your convenience.

Let's talk soon,

Julie Normand

COMPUTERIZING THE LAW OFFICE

February 8, 19—

Mr. Robert D. Bennett
200 Colorado State Bank Building
Denver, Colorado 80202

Dear Mr. Bennett:

I specialize in helping small law offices (1-15 attorneys) get the computer systems they need—be it a stand-alone microcomputer or a complete network; basic word-processing through legal billing and timekeeping; file sharing through Lexis research.

Because I do not sell either hardware or software, or represent any vendors whatsoever, I am not required to sell you a particular line of products. I recommend solutions that will work best for you, be it IBM PC and compatibles, or Macintosh hardware and software. I then negotiate with a variety of vendors to get you the best price, service contracts, installation and guarantees of performance available.

My services are straightforward:
- To help you analyze what you want to do, recommend the most cost-effective solutions, and the best providers of service. To help you negotiate the best prices I am only paid by my clients. I accept no fees or commissions from any vendors or companies.
- To supervise all purchases, delivery and installation, advising you when to "accept delivery."
- To help with attorney training.
- To help with staff training and conversion.

In short, I save you time and money by insuring that you get the quality, products and service you require quickly. During the 10 years I've been in the computer business I have never had a client who didn't save far more than the cost of my fee by avoiding jargon, frustration, wasted hours, inappropriate hardware and software choices and incomplete service contracts.

There is no charge for my first hour of consultation. During this hour you and I will be able to tell if my services are appropriate for your firm. I look forward to talking with you about how I can be of service. Give me a call today.

Sincerely,

Rory Donaldson, Owner

P.S. Phone 777-7068 to set up a free consultation. Ask for me personally.

Jay Levinson
900 Wilshire Blvd.
Apt. 900
Los Angeles, CA 90017
(213) 620-1490 (h)
(213) 386-5204 (o)

November 6, 19—

H. H. Thomas
Pacific Telephone & Telegraph
1313 53rd Street
Berkeley, CA 94705

Dear Mr. Thomas:

The dollar bill attached here symbolizes the thousands of dollars Pacific Telephone & Telegraph may be wasting by not utilizing the services of a prime quality free-lance writer.

During this year alone, I have accomplished writing projects for VISA, Crocker Bank, Pacific Plan, Gallo, Bank of America, the University of California, and the Public Broadcasting System. Although these companies do not ordinarily work with free-lancers, they did work with me.

In each case, the projects were completed successfully. In each case, I was given more assignments. There must be a reason why.

If you want to provide Pacific Telephone & Telegraph with the best free-lance writing available for any type of project—or if you have a seemingly impossible deadline—I hope you will give me a call.

I have enclosed a description of my background—just to inform you that I have won major writing awards in all the media and that I have served as a Vice-President and Creative Director at J. Walter Thompson, America's largest advertising agency. I guarantee you, however, that I am far more interested in winning sales than winning awards.

By your company settling for mere competent writing, or by having your writing assignments handled by traditional sources, you just might be wasting Pacific Telephone & Telegraph's money. A good number of the Fortune 500 companies have already figured that out.

Now, I look forward to hearing from you.

Very truly yours,

Jay Levinson

P.S. If you are not the person who assigns work to free-lancers, I would appreciate it if you would pass this letter (and this dollar) on to the person who does. Thank you very much.

THOMAS   WESTON   &   ASSOCIATES

One Financial Tower
1800 Broadway, Suite 3500
Denver, Colorado   80202 /303-692-2950

May 5, 19—

William S. Frank
President
CareerLab
9085 E. Mineral Circle, Suite 330
Englewood, Colorado   80112

Dear Mr. Frank:

Your clients face a variety of uncertainties: job, location,
longevity, and income. The counseling benefits you offer address
many of their concerns.

We would like to be a part of your network. We can offer a wide
range of personal, unbiased financial services—from individual
consultations to group workshops.

Enclosed is information to help you assess our firm's capabilities.
Please do look it over.

We will call you in a few days to ask if you would like to talk about
the possibility of a relationship with us.

We look forward to meeting you.

Cordially,

Thomas Weston, CPA

Certified Financial Planner
Admitted to The Registry of Financial Planning Practitioners

SIGMA GROUP INC.
717 Seventeenth Street
Suite 1440
Denver, Colorado 80202-3314
(303) 292-6720

July 9, 19—

Mr. William S. Frank
President
CareerLab
9085 E. Mineral Circle, Suite 330
Englewood, Colorado 80112

Dear Bill:

Thank you again for the opportunity to meet you and to discuss mutual business interests. I hope we have the opportunity to work together in the very near future.

When I refer potential clients to you, I will normally call you first to alert you to the fact that I have made a referral. Please do not feel obligated to assume a client relationship if it does not seem to make sense. Be assured, these referrals will only be senior people. At the same time, I would also appreciate the same courtesy.

Again, thanks for your time this week, as I appreciated the opportunity to become personally acquainted.

Best wishes,

George L. Reisinger
Managing Partner

Your Success
Is Our Only Business
SM

9085 East Mineral Circle

Suite 330

Englewood, Colorado 80112

303-790-0505

FAX 303-790-0606

May 27, 19—

Mr. Norman E. Weatherman
Sherman & Howard
2900 First Interstate Tower North
633 Seventeenth Street
Denver, Colorado 80202

Dear Norm,

Thank you for your referral to High Technology, Inc. I met with them today and we are mapping out a strategy for helping the eighteen supervisors who will be leaving the company.

I am recommending two days of workshops—a couple half days now, and one full day nearer the date of the plant closing. (By the time you get this letter, everything might have changed.)

I would also work individually by the hour with supervisors obviously needing extra help after the workshops are completed.

Thank you for this referral. It was kind of you to think of me. I will keep you posted on all new developments, and I will certainly return the favor to you at the earliest opportunity.

As I told you on the telephone, Tim Silva did a superb job in his presentation to my personnel friends. They were more than impressed, and knowing them, I'm certain you will be seeing some new work coming out of our joint marketing effort.

Call if you need me.

Sincerely yours,

William S. Frank

PAUL H. GUTKNECHT

11374 QUIVAS WAY • WESTMINSTER, COLORADO 80234 • (303) 465-1236

February 23, 19—

Robert C. Evans
Controller
Firestone
234 Union Avenue
Memphis, TN   38112

Dear Bob,

As you know, my consulting business has been fun and interesting. However, I prefer to have the responsibility and authority to make things happen. I want to move back into the corporate world and make another ten-year contribution to a company's success.

Management, financial and accounting skills are valuable to any industry, and some of my consulting has been outside the petroleum industry, but the oil business is still my first love. Similarly, Mary and I like Denver very much, but we would cheerfully relocate for the right opportunity.

Please take a few minutes to think about possible needs among your friends and associates for a man of my talents. You can either give them the enclosed copy of my resume, or give me their names so that I can follow through.

Any assistance or advice you can give me is greatly appreciated.

Thank you!

Paul H. Gutknecht

PHG:kam

Enclosure

PAI
3000 Youngfield Street, Suite 344
Lakewood, Colorado 80215
(303) 232-9313

July 9, 19—

Mr. William S. Frank
Outplacement Consultant
CareerLab
9085 E. Mineral Circle, Suite 330
Englewood, CO 80112

Dear Mr. Frank:

If you need to update your employee communications but lack the in-house
staff or time to get the job done, let me introduce you to PAI Communications.

We are a team of communications professionals with expertise in technical
and human resources communications. Our staff is experienced in researching,
planning, writing and producing employee handbooks, benefit books, newsletters,
employee orientation and recruiting materials for a variety of industries.

No matter what size the project, we'll help you balance the creative with the
practical. Our focus is on your business objectives, your deadlines and your
budget. We think you'll find that our services are among the most professional
and cost-effective in the area.

If you are interested, please complete the form below so we may send you
more information about our services.

Many thanks,

Pat Nichols
Managing Partner

CONTACT PERSON————————————— TELEPHONE —————————————

COMPANY NAME ————————————— ADDRESS —————————————

I AM INTERESTED IN RECEIVING MORE INFORMATION ABOUT
UPDATING/PRODUCING...

[ ] EMPLOYEE HANDBOOKS   [ ] BENEFIT BOOKS

[ ] SUMMARY PLAN DESCRIPTION   [ ] BENEFITS SUMMARY

[ ] RECRUITING MATERIALS   [ ] OTHER

16

Public Relations

One of my most successful job hunting clients explained his success this way: "I create relationships . . . the relationships create the jobs."

The hardest job search is the one that begins with no network or no personal good will. Job hunters who've neglected or damaged their personal relationships tend to stay unemployed longer.

How can you develop a strong support network? Congratulate friends in writing when they accomplish something noteworthy, take new jobs, or appear in the media. They'll appreciate and remember you for it.

When you see an article by or about someone you know, clip the item and send it to them along with a note of congratulations. Even if they've saved it themselves, they'll appreciate the extra copy to share.

From time to time, send small gifts to friends, recruiters, and business acquaintances to remind them you're still around. Inexpensive books work nicely. A newspaper, magazine, or journal article counts as a gift, and unexpected gifts are especially welcome. A warm letter sets the tone.

If you write or publish something, if you're featured in a news article, if you present a professional program or appear in the media, copy the articles and programs and mail them to your network, along with a note, "Thinking of you."

In marketing personal services (job-hunting), relationships are everything. Seek opportunities to build good will for yourself in the community. You'll never be sorry.

Copyright © 1993 Eli Stein. Reprinted with permission.

*"You can knock off that holier than thou attitude with me. I helped you find **your** last job, remember?"*

April 4

Dear Bill

Congratulations on the article
" Job Hunters Beware." Did you
place that ? You really do a
great job ! And I love the
artwork the newspaper provided
really eye — catching

Best Wishes. Talk to you soon

Sharon Remick

CAREERLAB

9085 East Mineral Circle

Suite 330

Englewood, Colorado 80112

303-790-0505

FAX 303-790-0606

August 25, 19—

Mr. Michael T. Simmons
Director of Administration
Prudential Real Estate Group
1800 Broadway, Suite 1800
Denver, Colorado 80202

Dear Mike,

I was extremely pleased to learn that you've gotten happily re-established in human resources and administration.

I'm also glad you stayed in Denver. I appreciate your friendship, and would have felt a loss had you left.

In addition, you're a great resource to the community.

Congratulations!

William S. Frank

The West Real Estate Company
Box 2002, Keystone, Colorado 80435
(303) 467-2011

January 18, 19—

Beverly M. Fairchild
5300 Bell Flower Way
Denver, Colorado 80236

Dear Beverly:

I am pleased and excited about your good news.

There was no question in my mind that it was just a matter of finding the right slot and correct niche for this thing to finally come together. When an individual possesses the talent and capabilities you have so clearly demonstrated and takes your approach to look for new opportunities, it was simply a matter of timing.

I hope your new position offers you a tremendous challenge and fulfillment in addressing those challenges. We look forward to a good 19— and hope you will continue to keep in touch and drop by anytime you are up in this area.

Very truly yours,

Todd L. Hansen
President

TLH/jd

Your Success
Is Our Only Business ℠

9085 East Mineral Circle

Suite 330

Englewood, Colorado 80112

303-790-0505

FAX 303-790-0606

August 18, 19—

Robert W. Englewood
Vice President Human Resources
Compaq Corporation
1200 Antrim Drive
Roseville, California 95678

Dear Bob,

Take a minute to review **The Customer Comes Second**. I think you'll be amazed.

I discovered it at an airport. The title jumped out as a little too cute. I thought it was some kind of gag, another empty management text—but once inside, I found the best reading I've seen in years.

On the plane I devoured the book cover-to-cover, highlighting nearly every page. It was full of great ideas.

Rosenbluth's message is simple: take care of your people first—keep them happy—then they'll take care of your customers. That drives profits. He ought to know. He built the world's largest, more profitable travel agency serving 1700 corporate clients worldwide. His management philosophies are so revolutionary he's had to start a new training company to handle requests for information.

I'm trying to define the corporate culture inside **CareerLab** as helping, people-caring, and personal growth. I've always wanted a strong collaborative, co-operative team. This book tells us HOW.

I think you'll find **The Customer Comes Second** fascinating, just as I did. Give it a look, and let me know what you think.

Wishing you success,

William S. Frank

CAREERLAB

9085 East Mineral Circle

Suite 330

Englewood, Colorado 80112

303-790-0505

FAX 303-790-0606

April 7, 19—

Mr. Richard D. North
Regional Employee Relations Manager
Connecticut Mutual
300 South Parker Road
Aurora, Colorado 80014

Dear Rich:

   <u>Denver Business</u> recently interviewed me about outplacement
and the nation's retirement epidemic.

   I thought the article was interesting and timely and wanted you
to have a copy.

   I would enjoy hearing your thoughts and ideas after you have had
a chance to look it over.

   Wishing you all the best.

Sincerely,

William S. Frank

WSF:kam
Attachment

BRUCE D. ROBERTSON, CPA

4325 Buffalo Road
N. Chili, New York 14514

(716) 594-2766

Kelly Weitz
Vice President
Georgia International
5500 Interstate N Parkway, Suite 500
Atlanta, GA 30328
(404) 952-4727 (o)
(404) 952-4814 (FAX)

Dear Kelly,

Many exciting things are happening in my life since I wrote you last spring.
First, I have become a facilitator for the Management Roundtable (TMR).

TMR, a national organization headquartered in Denver, Colorado, consists of
groups of 10-15 CEO's or Senior Level Managers. I like that TMR provides such
a great opportunity for these individuals to meet monthly for issue resolution,
management development, enrichment/education, and mutual support. I am
organizing TMR's first group in Rochester, New York. CEO's will start meeting
early next year.

I have just begun my second year of teaching at Roberts Wesleyan College.
My favorite courses last year included Strategic Planning, Managerial Accounting
and Motivation, Money and Banking, and Income Tax. This fall I initiated a
job-search workshop class for all business seniors. Each student develops and
manages his own MBO's for resume preparation, job network-building, and
practice interviewing.

This summer, I spent a month visiting Colorado and western New York. In
Colorado, I was again part of the Breckenridge Music Institute's choir workshop. We premiered a two-piano piece by Berger based upon Psalms 118 & 119.
Rafting down the Colorado River was my risk-excitement for the summer. In
New York, my sons and I visited many parks. We found the waterfalls in the
western New York area fantastic. Brian loved Niagara Falls. (Sorry Colorado,
nothing there comes close to these beauties.)

As to the future, the first meeting of The Management Roundtable in
Rochester will be held January 20th. In addition, my parents and I are
planning a business/pleasure trip to Europe, May & June. I will also be
offering a new course this spring entitled International Business. With my
special interest in international affairs, I am really excited about this new
offering.

May you all have a blessed and successful fall and winter.

Bruce D. Robertson

HUMAN GROWTH and DEVELOPMENT ASSOCIATES
6780 South Adams Way, Littleton, Colorado 80122-1802

YANCEY E. STOCKWELL, M.Ed., NCC, LPC
(303) 794-6811

MARY K. KOURI, Ph.D.
(303) 771-8424
FAX (303) 773-1264

December 2, 19—

Bill Frank
President
CareerLab
9085 E. Mineral Circle
Suite 330
Englewood, CO 80112

Dear Bill:

Thank you for the exquisite gift of the Sierra Club calendar.

It will lift my spirits each time I look at it through the coming year and I'll remember your thoughtfulness many times over.

Best wishes for laughter and peace to you and your family during the holidays and through 19—.

Cordially,

Mary K. Kouri

17

Copyright © 1993 Phillip Jewell. Reprinted with permission.

"Looking for a job has been tough...I've been branded as somewhat of a loner."

The Media

Job-seeking is much like running for political office. It's important to be seen in public. Employers can't hire you if they don't know you exist. Recruiters can't find you, either.

Use every avenue at your disposal to gain public visibility. Contribute time to volunteer organizations. Write a letter to the editor of your local paper or to *Forbes*, *Business Week*, or any appropriate technical or professional publication. Some of your letters won't be published, but many will. This tactic generally won't bring calls from strangers, but someone who knows you may suddenly be reminded to call you.

If you enjoy writing, contribute articles to newspapers, magazines, and professional journals. Some of these publications will actually pay you to write!

If you're a speaker, give talks. Teach at the local community college; you'll create an instant network. If you're asked to appear on radio or television, say yes. Too many job hunters work desperately to be noticed, but turn down free opportunities to be seen. Several contributors to this book didn't want their real names published. While I respect their privacy, I also wonder, "Why not? It's free publicity!" The next time you're in the job market—which could be any time—more people will know you.

Do whatever it takes to gain public visibility: write, speak, appear, volunteer. Make certain you are seen and noticed, and that will help you get hired.

CAREERLAB

9085 East Mineral Circle

Suite 330

Englewood, Colorado 80112

303-790-0505

FAX 303-790-0606

February 12, 19—

Ms. Jane Diehl
Managing Editor
Up The Creek
2038 South Pontiac Way
Denver, Colorado 80224

Dear Jane:

    Thanks for discussing my story idea on <u>the brighter side of unemployment</u>.

    Yes, Denver's economy is suffering, but there are some "tricks of the trade," some simple ways to be <u>creative and innovative in the job market</u>.

    Fifty-five-year-olds don't have to be unemployed for 6 to 12 months and they don't have to work delivering pizzas.

    Let's talk about it.

Sincerely,

William S. Frank

WSF/bk

**Your Success
Is Our Only Business** _{SM}

CAREERLAB

9085 East Mineral Circle
Suite 330
Englewood, Colorado 80112
303-790-0505
FAX 303-790-0606

July 28, 19—

Mr. David Black
General Manager and Vice President
KSTV Channel 8
2300 Broadway, Suite 5200
Denver, Colorado 80202

Dear David:

I have been watching the exciting things you are doing at
Channel 8.

You appear to be always reaching out, risking, looking for the
new angle—the new idea—the new gimmick to benefit your viewers (and
glue them to the set).

How would you feel about doing a brief weekly segment related to
jobs and career—a very timely, HOT topic these days!

You might show such things as:

1. The <u>excitement</u> in the career market (not the 3.6 percent
   that aren't employed, but the 96.4 percent that <u>are employed</u>—
   and specifically the very few that <u>love their work</u>. The
   success stories. How they got there. The challenges they faced.

   Their advice!
   Their ideas!
   Their enthusiasm!

2. Community resources and information.

3. The Denver market: Where it's HOT and where it's NOT.

4. How to choose the right job.

5. How to get a job fast—and so forth.

I would like to help you put these ideas together—and here's <u>why you would benefit</u>:

1. The public needs this information, wants this information—it's timely.

2. Companies are cutting from the top and no one is "secure" anymore. People are running scared.

3. The job market is in a turmoil, changing faster and faster, and that's not going to stop.

4. No one else is doing this.

I would be a good person to help you because I am a professional career planner—that's all I do. I have contacts and resources. I know the Denver job market inside out, <u>but most of all, I am</u> . . .

- Great at getting people excited.
- Great at getting people talking about themselves.
- Great at getting people <u>involved</u>.

Does this sound workable? I have lots of ideas—and I'm sure you do too! Let's get together and talk.

Enthusiastically,

William S. Frank
President

Enclosures

Your Success
Is Our Only Business ℠

9085 East Mineral Circle

Suite 330

Englewood, Colorado 80112

303-790-0505

FAX 303-790-0606

January 25, 19—

Ms. Dottie Wahl
News Reporter
KCWB Television
2000 Bellaire Drive
Los Angeles, California 90046

Dear Dottie:

I'm excited about getting to meet you. I think we will have fun together—and job-finding is a very timely topic. To help you prepare, I am going to tell you a little about myself and suggest some topics for discussion. OK? Please use this as a guideline and call me if you need to!

Highlights of My Training:

— M.A. in philosophy, 1969, Colorado State University.
— Studied psychology, 1965-1990.
— Studied psychotherapy with Warner A. Baker, M.D.,
  a Denver psychiatrist.
— Studied with Dick Bolles, the country's leading career
  expert, the author of What Color is Your Parachute?
— Was Vice President for the country's largest outplacement
  consulting firm.

Profile of the People I Work Best With:

— High level business executives and professionals.
— People going through a major life transition
  (such as divorce).
— Age groups 30 to 55.
— People in confusion about how it all "fits together"—
  especially, right-brain, creative, intuitive types that
  don't necessarily fit into a "slot" in our left brain,
  detail, fact, figures, and data-oriented culture.
— Professionals (dentist, lawyers, doctors) seeking to
  build successful practices.

Dottie Wahl
January 25, 19—
Page two

How I Work:

My special talent is to help people sort through confusion
quickly (sometimes in as little as one hour) and come to
a point of clarity about exactly who they are and exactly
where they're going. We try to resolve this at a deep
level—for the long-term, not just for "now."

My chief tool is to ask questions. Knowing which questions
to ask is one of the key things I do. (Someone once said
that the best therapist is one who can say "absolutely
nothing" at exactly the right moment.) And I think this
is what I do.

I also use written exercises, and standardized tests
when they are appropriate.

Suggested Topics for Discussion:

1. Why do people have trouble deciding which job they want?

2. The media is painting a very black picture of unemployment.
   What are some of the positive things happening in the world
   of work? (Well, for one thing, there's a revolution going
   on in job-finding.)

3. What can this unemployment now teach us? (For one thing, it
   is a preview of the future. "Job security," working 40 years
   for a company is practically a thing of the past. It is no
   longer possible to take a job and "forget about it." In the
   future people may change jobs four to five times in a lifetime. Therefore, we must be ready, plan, pack our parachutes,
   and be ready to jump.)

4. How has job-hunting changed?

5. Why is job-finding a sales job—and how do you do it?

6. What are some of the helpful community resources? (Like books,
   job networks, community college courses, and organizations.)

 I hope this helps, Dottie. See you soon!

Bill Frank

18

Termination

A poor performance evaluation, especially after many years of good ones, can mean that your company is setting you up for termination. If possible, stand up for yourself and get the poor evaluation off your record. Write a letter contesting any claims you feel are unfair. Substantiate your position with facts and figures. Ask for a meeting with your manager, and discuss the contested items line by line, but don't be hostile.

If you decide to leave, or if you are forced to leave, negotiate a fair severance package and get it in writing. If you do leave the corporation, leave on good terms. Don't burn bridges.

The few hours surrounding your departure could be the most important moments of your career, because they help define your reputation. Your behavior will be carefully watched, and you'll be remembered for years, either as a respected professional or as a troublemaker.

Keep in mind, you want this employer to serve as a reference in the future, and your next job offer(s) could hinge on what they say. You may be one of two finalists for your ideal job. If you leave "kicking and screaming," reference-checking could ruin your candidacy.

Future employers often check references as far back as ten years. Don't lose a valuable job offer because you once left a company on bad terms.

"I'm afraid we'll have to let you go, Stan... you're just not making enough noise."

DATE: January 15, 19—

TO: Michael Bond

CC: David Johansen
Kathy Richardson

FROM: Barbara Howard

SUBJECT: My contributions to Silicon Valley, Inc.

I have completed in-depth discussions with the people you recommended, and I would like to summarize what I've heard and realized, my beliefs about what I need to do, and evidence of constructive actions taken since my poor performance review. Please consider these factors in the decision whether outplacement is appropriate.

Issues for improvement noted by manufacturing managers:

1.   Excessive analysis or "perfecting," leading to low productivity.

2.   Errors in prioritizing goals and conflicting inputs.

3.   Inadequate communication with team members and supervisor.

My realizations and convictions following recent interviews:

In 19—, my contribution to Silicon Valley, Inc. was not acceptable either to me or to you. I need to:

1.   Take the initiative to identify changes which will make a tangible difference in the product line;

2.   Be tenacious in causing these effects to be realized in a minimal time period;

3.   Create closer linkage with our team and management to achieve a consensus about priorities and my agenda;

4.   Focus my 15 years of experience on judging the shortest path to effective results; and

5.   Avoid unnecessary diversions from the key commitments.

What I have addressed and changed since my last review:

1.   An example of productivity and avoiding "perfecting" is four completed Engineering Change Order releases of all KKD, Checkout, and Product Acceptance procedures of SEMI and T-Systems, as the products have evolved through trials, controlled release, and first production. These were on time, easier to use, and have credibility with

the Checkout Technicians because they were heavily involved in the development. There were few errors noted in recent audit.

2.   Toward improving communication and prioritizing, I initiated "On-Target" objective tracking, as well as weekly "defect resolution" meetings with Checkout and team engineers/designers. Defect diagnosis and elimination, training, and cooperation are the goals.

3.   In the area of responsiveness to varied inputs, my role as Product Engineer for review and classification of all SEMI-2 Engineering Change Orders has been executed with quick turn-around times and concise recommendations to originators.

There is no doubt of my error in failing to confront the issues of my review more widely. Whereas I consulted only Jim Thomas, Bill Randolph, and certain SEMI-2 team members, I would have done better to work with you and the managers recently interviewed. However, the issues have been addressed in earnest over the last six months and I feel that substantive corrections have already begun. Based on recent candid feedback from my teammates and manager, I feel comfortable in recommending their opinions to you as evidence of improved contribution.

<u>My ability to change certain behaviors</u>:

Some course corrections have occurred, Mike, but we both know that behavioral changes are evolutionary and progress slowly, if they happen at all. However, I'd like to offer some evidence of meaningful change which came unexpectedly in the recent interviews. In discussing some positive attributes, a number of managers used words like "personable," "well-liked," or "easy to get along with." This was good news to me because a key Area-For-Improvement in my early years at Silicon Valley, Inc. was "interpersonal skills." I'm suggesting that this behavior has been altered enough to be no longer an issue.

In summary, Mike, I believe that my level of contribution has improved visibly this year and that most members of my team would agree. I hope you will consider recent performance in your decision.

Wishing you well,

Barbara Howard
Project Engineer

TO: T. Randolph Edwards
FROM: Robert Wolfe
DATE: April 18, 19—
SUBJECT: Outplacement, Director of Finance

This memo is a follow-up to our meeting of April 12th in which we discussed the arrangements necessary for me to make a smooth transition from Worldwide Manufacturing to another company. Here are the 10 points we covered:

1. My employment as Director of Finance will continue at my current salary level through January 2nd, and I will be free, at my discretion, to take time off for personal business.

2. I will receive a lump sum severance payment amounting to 12 months' salary (based on my current rate of pay) the day I leave the company.

3. All my benefits (Medical and Dental Insurance, Matching Donations, Thrift Plan) will continue for one year after my departure.

4. All bonuses (gainsharing, executive incentive paid at target achievement level) will be paid for 12 months after my departure, as though I were a full-time employee. Bonuses to be paid when other employees receive their checks.

5. You will permanently remove my recent poor performance review from personnel file, and I will review and approve my personnel records before leaving.

6. Senior management will give my reason for leaving as "Position eliminated by corporate restructuring caused by sale of company."

7. Worldwide Manufacturing will provide me outplacement assistance of $16,500 (15% of annual compensation) within 30 days of joint approval of this agreement.

8. I will vest 100% in pension and 401K plans.

9. Existing stock options will take effect upon my departure.

10. I will be free to cease active employment at any time before January 2nd, if I accept a job offer.

Randy, I have enjoyed our work together, and am sorry to see it coming to an end. I am confident this package is fair to all of us, and that it represents a sound basis for a smooth transition.

INTER-OFFICE MEMORANDUM

TO   Mike Taggert   **DATE**   November 3, 19—

SUBJECT   Resignation   **FROM**   Dan Goin

This will confirm my resignation as Director of Personnel and Compensation at City Medical Hospital.

I have accepted the position of Human Resources Director at a growing operations management company in the Denver area. I am looking forward to my new position and the challenges that await me.

My last day of work will be December 31, 19—, which should provide sufficient time to complete existing projects and turn over management of the personnel, benefits and compensation areas. Please feel free to contact me at any time should you have any questions regarding my past work. I hope that the transition will go smoothly for everyone.

The past 15 years with CMH have been rewarding. I appreciate your trust and confidence in my abilities and your support. I am grateful for the opportunities and experience afforded me and for the many friends that I have made along the way. I wish you and the organization continued success.

Telectronics, Inc.
7400 South Tucson Way
Englewood, Colorado 80112
Telephone: (303) 790-8000
Telex: 454571
Facsimile: (303) 799-1241

   TO: Priscilla Matthews

FROM: Craig Lincoln

DATE: October 4, 19—

PRISCILLA,

It is with deep regret that I must tender my resignation to you, the Communications Department at **Telectronics** as of Thursday, October 18, 19—.

Over these last 14 months, I've grown very fond of **Telectronics**. In our day-to-day operations, I've become proud of being part of a company whose individuals and products are leaders in medical science and technology in the marketplace. This past year has been a very positive experience for me, and I will truly miss all of you.

But due in great part to my financial position, I must now move on in my career. I do hope, however, that we can continue our professional relationships and that I can be of assistance to you and **Telectronics** in the future.

Thank you, sincerely,

Craig Lincoln, Art Director

19

Reprinted with special permission of North America Syndicate.

Help Friends

If you're a job seeker:

When appropriate, encourage your close friends to write to their key contacts on your behalf. They should send both a letter and a resume, and they should follow up within a few days to check for leads. If they find interest, they can ask their friends to telephone you, saving you the pressure of making a cold call.

Let's take an example: Suppose you're goal is to be Controller for a large printing company, and one of your close friends sells for International Paper. Since you know the salesperson well, it makes sense to ask them to mail a letter and resume to introduce you to their contacts in printing companies. (Draft a sample letter to show them what to say.)

If you have an unemployed friend or relative:

It's difficult to know what to say or do when friends or family are unemployed, especially if they're having a difficult time in the job market. But sometimes you can help them more than they can help themselves. You may be able to open some doors for them.

Think carefully about your own personal contacts. Do you know someone who has information or influence? Someone who can help? Someone who might want to interview the candidate? Can you provide a personal introduction? If so, don't be afraid to volunteer assistance. Most job seekers welcome all the help they can get.

Your Success
Is Our Only Business
SM

		9085 East Mineral Circle
		Suite 330
		Englewood, Colorado 80112
		303-790-0505
		FAX 303-790-0606

December 15, 19—

Michael Kenner
Vice President Human Resources
IBM
1383 Fountainview, Suite 2300
Houston, Texas   77057

Dear Mike:

I seldom write a marketing letter for someone—in fact I never have—but this time I'm making an exception, because there's someone I think you should meet.

I have a personal friend who is still employed and successful. Mike is stable and not in danger of losing his job. But he is looking for another position in human resources, because he has outgrown his present company.

He's the kind of guy who tells it like it is and gets things done. In fact,
he is . . .

— Outspoken
— An action-taker
— Very results-oriented
— Also risk-oriented

In short, he's probably the kind of human resources professional you'd like to have around.

For nine years he's been an outstanding performer in the oil and gas and electronics industries—and his strengths are in O.D., Succession Planning, Compensation and Benefits, Training and Development, and Wage and Salary Administration.

I NEED YOUR HELP.

1. Call me if you have some ideas.
2. Call me if you know of suitable openings.
3. Call me if you'd like to learn more.
4. Call me if your friends might know something.

I can be reached at 303/771-4357 and would enjoy meeting you.

Sincerely yours,

William S. Frank

Daniel I. Stack
100 East Ninth Avenue
New York, New York 10038

August 2, 19—

<u>PERSONAL AND CONFIDENTIAL</u>

Mr. William S. Peterson
Office of the Chairman
Continental Illinois National Bank
231 S. La Salle Street
Chicago, Illinois 60693

Dear Bill:

My congratulations to the Continental directors and to you on your new assignment!
You will have a full measure of both challenge and opportunity—you and John
should make a great team.

On seeing the announcement, a former Asarco/Southern Peru lawyer-executive
sensed an opportunity and phoned me to ask that I introduce him to you. I asked
Mr. Ruby to send me a dossier. It arrived this morning and is enclosed.

The dossier fairly presents Mr. Ruby's experience as I know it. He worked directly
with me during the later stages of Asarco's Mexicanization exercise and subsequently
was a principal participant in handling the Southern Peru end of the extraordinarily
complex Southern Peru/Cuajone mine financing. He has had unusually solid hands-on
experience in "making things work" in Latin America.

Mr. Ruby is an intensely creative, smart, energetic, outspoken bilingual executive. He
thinks he would be useful to Continental in providing fresh insight, ideas, and follow
through in the area of structuring and negotiation work out of non-performing Latin
American loans. My experience with him suggests he would be a superior candidate
for just this sort of position.

If you or one of your associates would like to talk to me about any aspect of the enclosed,
I would be pleased to respond. I have a new phone number: (212) 520-3000.

All the best,

Daniel I. Stack

Enclosure

GEORGE L. OCHS
6031 West Rowland Place
Littleton, Colorado 80123
(303) 979-9294 (H)
(303) 629-4567 (B)

August 2, 19—

Mr. Bill Frank
CareerLab
9085 E. Mineral Circle, S-330
Englewood, Colorado 80112

Dear Bill:

Enclosed is a resume from a friend of mine, Russell Murray. His specialty is
corporate communications. He has often provided me with consulting advice
over the past few years in my work for Prudential in Aurora.

Should you come across any employers who have the need for someone with
Russell's background, I would appreciate your putting Russell in touch with
them.

As you well know, Russell is attempting to make effective use of the networking
technique. Therefore, please keep his resume on hand for a few months and
keep his corporate communications background in mind when going about
your business.

I've been very busy on a new assignment with Prudential and have not
been able to touch base with you. I apologize for that and hope to get back
in contact with you, perhaps the second half of August.

Warmly,

George L. Ochs

GLO/cb
Enclosure
cc: Russell Murray

December 12, 19—

Louis H. Goldman
Managing Partner
Data & Strategies Group
463 Worcester Road
Framingham, MA 01701

Dear Lou,

Recognizing your contacts with various companies and headhunters, I'm sending you a friend's résumé.

Julie has worked for our **Electronics Center** for 10 years. She is creative, self-starting, self-directing, cooperative, personable, well-organized and hard working. She is the unfortunate victim of heavy cost cutting pressures that have particularly targeted staff functions. Although she was laid off several months ago (head count control), **Major Technologies** has brought her back on contract at least through the end of the year.

At the **Electronics Center** she reported directly to Bill Adams, Vice President of Strategic Planning and Business Development. Bill's group was responsible for a variety of functions including traditional planning, program management of internal development projects and major customer programs, as well as market and competitive research, new product selection and planning, market planning and alliance arrangements. Julie was an important contributor to Bill's functions. I am sure he will also highly recommend her.

Julie could be a viable candidate for the position you mentioned in the Midwest. She understands how to research a marketplace, its competitors (direct and substitute products). She knows how to pull plans together, including getting the various VP's and line functions aligned, and she is financial planning literate.

Bill and I would appreciate any leads you could provide.

Best personal regards,

James F. Madden

STATE
NATIONAL
BANK
OF PARK RIDGE

R. William Collins
President

February 10, 19—

Mr. Thomas D. Becker
2028 South Strathmore Drive
Park Ridge, Illinois 60068

Dear Tom:

I have received your letter of February 8, and I wanted you to know that I will do anything possible to assist you in locating a suitable position. As you undoubtedly know, I have the highest personal respect for you, and in my conversations with other banks in Park Ridge, I will keep your availability in mind.

Tom, if there is any other way in which I can be of assistance to you, please let me know. By all means, use my name as a reference should you wish to do so. You did not indicate if you would be interested in a banking position outside of Illinois. If so, please let me know. I am acquainted with a large number of banks throughout the country, and I may be able to assist you in this regard.

Please express my warmest best wishes to your entire family.

Cordially,

R. William Collins

RWC/sjh

20

Get a Raise

Before asking for a raise, notice how well your department and company is doing. Is your manager complaining about cutbacks? Right timing is essential. Don't suggest a raise when business is down.

Prepare a statement of major accomplishments. List your results, achievements, and home runs. Give specific examples with percentages, numbers, facts, and figures. Make before-and-after comparisons. Write your goals for next quarter. Rather than explaining your need for a raise as a personal issue—for example, "My husband lost his job"— present it in a business framework. Explain how others with similar responsibilities are paid. Show industry research and show your accomplishments and goals.

Never present your request for a raise as a demand or threat. That makes you an adversary. Instead, take a questioning approach supported with written facts. You could say: "I've accomplished more than expected (show accomplishments), and I plan to do even more next quarter (show goals). How do you think the company would feel about paying me X-dollars per month (indicating the raise)? That's what others in similar positions are making these days (show market research).

Last of all, wait until your manager is on a personal high, and don't expect a decision overnight. Give the boss your ideas, then give him or her time to think. Chances are, if you've been producing more than expected, your manager can justify a raise.

*"You want a raise? But I thought **you** were my boss."*

CHICAGO
COMMUNICATIONS CORPORATION

To   Evin W. Laird
         Samuel Short, Personnel Director

From   Jean Creasy

Subject   Salary Adjustment

Date   April 15, 19—

It is never easy writing a letter such as this. I have waited to see if management would recognize my job performance and qualities as being promotable, but guess I'll have to toot my own horn.

First of all, I want to express how important my jobs are to me. I appreciate every opportunity CCC has given me. However, at this time, I am requesting a salary adjustment in relation to my responsibilities and job performance.

At review time last year, Samuel Short suggested a title change to justify a sufficient adjustment. I am not asking for a title change, per se, but for whatever is necessary to place me in a salary range comparable to others in the purchasing field. My present salary range is a minimum of $23,000 to a maximum of $36,800 (see Attachment #1). I am on the low end of this range, yet my reviews are excellent. As a means of comparison, I have assembled records to reflect similarities and differences (see Attachment #2). I have also assembled an outline of my duties arranged within the different areas for which I am responsible (see Attachment #3).

At one time, there were three people in the Purchasing Department, Jan Schick, Paula Samson, and Ralph Fredericks. During our highs and lows, Jan's and Ralph's positions were eliminated. Paula Samson remained to take over all purchasing duties on a full-time basis. During the last year that Paula was with the company, a total of 521 purchase orders were generated and Paula's salary was $27,200 (see Attachment #4). If Paula had remained with the company and received only a meager five percent (5%) increase per year, her salary would be $38,273.

In January of 19—, Paula Samson left the company and Richard Bickford was assigned to purchasing and remained there until his job was eliminated in September of 19—. At this time, I was assigned purchasing, along with my other duties, and have remained in this position for five years (see Attachment #5).

In conclusion, I am requesting a salary adjustment to $35,000/year. By performing multiple functions and positions, I am saving the company a great deal of money. Every area of my responsibility is run smoothly and efficiently. I believe that I have been a definite asset to the company and would like to continue to be an asset. I am only asking to be rewarded for a job well-done.

Thank you for your prompt consideration of this matter.

PART FOUR

NOTES AND COMMENTS ON SELECTED LETTERS

Notes and Comments on Selected Letters

Involve friends in your job-search, p. 11

The "friendship letter" penned by Dale Kreeger may be one of the best job-hunting letters ever written, because it can be modified slightly and used by nearly everyone. Dale first sent his letter to friends to look for a "real job." When he decided to go into business for himself, he rewrote the letter to sell consulting services. Many letters in this book borrow words from Dale.

Try to make your letter sound personal, one-of-a-kind, even if it will be mailed to several hundred friends. It takes time to write a "universal personal," but it's worth it. Don't send letters that sound cold and distant.

1.1 Announce new job, p. 32

It's difficult to sell consulting services to friends. You want their business, but you don't want to impose on them and ruin the relationship. Neil does a nice job of walking that thin line.

2.1 Clarify your career direction, p. 36

Your friends will help you chart your course, but you have to ask. Let them know what you need, and involve them— make it clear how important their ideas and opinions are to you. Most people like to feel valued and needed, to be called upon for advice and information. Give your friends the opportunity to help.

2.2 Ask for information, not for a job, p. 39

When writing to a stranger, it's better to ask for advice and information than to ask directly for a job. Most people don't like to reject others, so they resist speaking to job-seekers at all—and they rarely have a job opening. That's why it's easier to ask for information. Most people are willing to be helpful, if you make it clear you won't be pressuring them for employment.

2.3 Arrange informational interview, p. 42

Bud appealed to my ego, saying he liked one of my seminars. That kind of opening would probably get anyone a meeting with me—I like sincere praise. But Bud's final sentence *guaranteed* a meeting. He said, "I know your time is valuable so please be assured I won't ask for more than 30 minutes." If you assure people you won't waste their time, they will be more inclined to meet with you.

3.6 Find part-time work as trainer, p. 49

Perfect example of a well-planned "problem-solver" letter. Sally obviously spent a lot of time on this piece. She understands what my problems *might be*. Good guesswork on her part. She's sending the right letter to the right person. The letter is extremely persuasive without being hard sell. It says "I'm great" without bragging. If I had a big assignment and needed help, I'd certainly give Sally a call.

3.7 Find permanent part-time work, p. 50

Some people don't ever want to work full time. Clint Jones is one of them. (So is Nancy Thomas, the attorney whose letter appears on page 21.) Clint does a good job of telling his friends exactly what industries he wants to be involved with. Don't leave people guessing what you want to do. Target a specific market. Make some decisions about where you belong and communicate those decisions to your support group. It's a big mistake to keep your options *too* open.

4.1 Summarize your career in a letter, p. 54

Great example of a letter that briefly explains a 25-year career. Use this idea when caught without a current resume.

5.1 Leverage your contacts, p. 59

This letter produced a $100K+ job offer through an ex-high school friend.

5.3-5.6 Personalize letters to friends, pp. 61-64

One letter is seldom right for everyone on your list of "friends," so you may want to send tailored letters to various subgroups: one for consultants, another for close personal friends, for family, for former vendors, and so on. The more you personalize your campaign, the better it will work. Doug's letters are variations on Dale Kreeger's friendship theme.

5.7 Renew distant contacts, p. 65

Don't ignore the past. A contact is *anyone* who might remember you. It's better to write to someone who vaguely remembers you than to a total stranger. One senior executive client recently found a job through someone he had barely known in high school! In an earlier letter (page 60), Michael wrote to fellow-classmates he had never even *met*. (He got a lot of good responses, too.)

This letter's appeal is akin to that of the FEI letter (page 72): "We're all members of the same elite group." And most groups *do* think they're elite.

5.7 Contact old friends, p. 66

This letter produced a high-paying executive job.

5.11 Help from professional organizations, p. 72

Two of my accounting clients have landed jobs by contacting members of the Financial Executives Institute.

The first, Len Kenney, lives in Los Angeles. He wrote to 350 members of the FEI, nationwide. One day he received a call from a recruiter in Chicago who was looking for a controller in L.A., right close to home.

Len won the job and went to work for one of *INC* magazine's top 20 small companies. When he asked the recruiter, "How did you find out about me?" the search consultant said, "I called a candidate in Chicago to see if he was interested. He wasn't. But he said 'I have the resume of a *friend* right here.'"

Someone who had never met Len considered him a friend. Members of professional organizations tend to feel a sense of kinship with their peers. Paul Gutknecht's letter featured here (page 72) resulted in a job offer. That's a letter worth writing. Think about trying this with your own association.

5.12 Help from realtor, p. 73

The writer did not want to contact his realtor, whom he thought was mad at him. He had to be nudged repeatedly. The letter produced a Controller's job in a tight market.

5.13 Help from spouse's friends, p. 74

Contact your own personal network, but don't forget that your spouse or significant other has a different circle of friends. When the oil field was down, Tom Jacob got a good job through his wife. Her best friend's husband was a senior executive in a major oil company. You can take this one step further by asking your business friends to write to their key contacts on your behalf.

6.1 Tell recruiters where you fit, p. 78

This form letter is easy to use, and it gives recruiters the information they need. Your resume tells them where you have been, not where you want to be next. They have to figure out where to put you. This letter gives them an idea where you belong: by company size, by geography, by any requirement you care to mention. It's almost as simple as filling in the blanks.

6.1 Establish rapport with recruiters and headhunters, p. 79

Surprise! You have to sell yourself to recruiters the same way you sell yourself to employers. Recruiters must get tired of letters that say, "I've enclosed my resume for your perusal." This search letter has a bit more zip; it's a teaser.

Craig says, "I have strong marketable skills in which you would be interested." "What skills?" the recruiter wonders. If the candidate *thinks* he's highly marketable, he probably is.

Successful, self-confident candidates are much easier to place; they "show" better. Therefore, recruiters place them faster and earn more commission. They like that.

Craig says what he's selling: a rare combination of business savvy and design expertise. That's a big plus, as many artists are erratic.

Saying "at your earliest convenience, please contact me . . ." conveys a sense of urgency. Although closing with "Please contact me" is technically weaker (you generally want to state that you'll call *them*), the letter is so forceful and direct it still works.

6.4 Use response forms, p. 91

This letter produced a job interview.

7.1 Use two-column chart for want ads, p. 105

The left-hand column lists the requirements mentioned in the ad, and the right-hand column shows how you match those requirements. The clerk or manager reviewing resumes will quickly see that you fit, and they will screen you in rather than out.

7.6 Include testimonials, p. 117

Third-party endorsements often help a sales effort. They're seldom seen in job-search correspondence; therefore, a good addition.

7.6 Answer want ad, p. 119

Try to keep want ad letters short. Generally, one page is better than two, and two pages are better than three.

This is a well-written response to a want ad; it's obvious Ken has spent some time on it. A letter like this looks easy to write, but it isn't. It could take five hours to write this kind of concise, warm, friendly, professional letter. Tailor letters *only* to those ads you think fit you perfectly. Otherwise, you waste time, your biggest asset.

7.8 Answer important want ad, p. 127

Rick put a lot of work into this piece, which is more of a proposal than an actual letter. He spent several days writing it, and he had a lot to work with (for example, 200 letters of reference from celebrities who had performed in his facility). Save this kind of in-depth writing for those few jobs that are a perfect fit—your dream jobs. The letter did produce an interview.

7.9 Follow up on want ads, p. 132

If Keith didn't hear back from a want ad after two weeks, he sent this letter. He mailed about 30 letters and received a 60% response!

8.2 Draft your own reference statement, p. 135

Even if you're leaving your company on good terms, it's a good idea to draft a reference statement for your boss to review and discuss. That way the two of you will tell exactly the same story. It's not uncommon for bosses to be completely unaware of some of their employees' accomplishments.

8.3 Get reference from boss who fired you, p. 136

It's often hard to get a decent reference from someone who has just fired you. It often helps if you draft ideas for him or her to review, as Charles has done here. He outlines significant accomplishments, strengths as a manager and employee, reason for leaving, and personal characteristics—a great package.

Let your former boss know what you're saying and what you expect him or her to say. Negotiate a story the two of you can agree on. Don't just let them say whatever they want.

9.2 Sell your way into a company, p. 145

This is one of my all-time favorite letters, and it contains two of the best job-search lines I've seen: "Freedom to work more than 40 hours per week," and "Whatever it takes I can and will do."

Like all great letters, this one reflects the writer's personality: Linda is bright, creative, enthusiastic, *alive*. And she's successful. She mailed thirty letters, got three interviews and one job offer. Linda went to work in computer sales and was immediately fast-tracked. When the job soured, she rewrote her letter slightly, remailed it, and received another job offer. Today Linda is president of **The Final Word**, her own computer training company in Houston, Texas.

9.5 Show your track record, p. 148

Not all marketing people can write a sizzling letter, but Chris did. First of all, she had a winning headline, which is 90% of the battle according to John Caples in *Tested Advertising Methods*. Although her letter is heavily accomplishment-oriented, it doesn't sound "braggy." It also says exactly what she's looking for, something job-hunters rarely do. (Many mistakenly stay vague to "keep their options open.")

Being a good marketer, Chris wasn't out of work long. She attended two national health-care conventions and received a job offer immediately.

9.6 Sell your attitude, p. 149

I love this letter. Judy and I discussed marketing letters, and I sent her home to draft one. Normally, clients return with scattered ideas and a hodgepodge of notes, but Judy announced that she had completed a sales letter. I looked at this letter and felt it was really aggressive. I was about to suggest toning it down a bit when she told me she had already mailed it to 30 companies. Because it was too late to make any changes, I said, "Oh well, let's see what happens."

What happened was delightful. Judy received a dozen calls, and had several interviews and a few temporary consulting assignments. One interview produced the job she now holds (product manager for a high-tech medical company).

During salary negotiations, Judy showed me her offer letter. The president of the company wrote, and I quote, "We can offer you an exciting and challenging environment in which to work. If you are looking for a chance to step up to the plate and hit another home run (to use your analogy), this is the opportunity for you. We hope you will be the lead-off batter on our championship clinical sales team."

End of story. What a letter!

9.7 Sales letter offering help, p. 150

First of all, "Need Help?" is the perfect headline. I've never seen anything better. Who could say "no." *Everyone* needs help.

Scott follows with, "I love to repair . . ." I like to hire people who love what they do, don't you? They're fun to work with.

He's labeled himself a "craftsman"—not a handyman. Another plus. The word "craftsman" implies quality, perfection, and attention to detail. Then he says he "cares." That's important. Who would prefer someone lazy, undependable, and indifferent?

Last of all, he offers "free estimate or advice . . ." Free advice is another nice touch—the essence of good service.

Scott did not exactly fit the "real job" mold. He was creative, an independent thinker, a "do-it-yourselfer." He loved the idea of working for himself. We created a repair/remodeling company for him, and the "Need Help?" letter was the cornerstone of his advertising campaign.

This piece was used numerous ways: as a letter, as a flyer, and as a newspaper ad. It worked so well that within a couple weeks Scott had more business than he could handle.

This is a good structure for a marketing letter. If you change a few words, *anyone* from an accountant to a vice president of finance can use it. It's short and powerful. Try it.

9.10 Break a few rules, p. 153

This letter produced an interview and job offer as sales manager. In a follow-up letter to me, Bill said, "I was aware that this letter breaks most of the rules, but I decided to approach the prospective employer with a 'concept sale' rather than a 'brand sale.' That is, rather than sell myself, I felt I needed to convince a technically oriented business manager that what he really needed wasn't a better technological mouse trap, but a sales manager.

"My decision was based on my observation that engineers and other technically trained managers tend to think of business success largely in terms of technical excellence of their product, rather than as a result of the efforts of their sales force. Whether my assumptions or my approach were entirely correct I cannot say, but the letter worked."

10.1 Try the direct approach, p. 159

This letter produced a $100K+ job offer in the mortgage banking industry.

10.2 Appeal to the reader's ego, p. 162

An appeal to the reader's ego is one of the strongest approaches possible. It can't be beat, but you do have to be careful to keep it honest. Readers will react negatively to praise that sounds casual or insincere. So, when you really do respect and admire someone, tell them so. If executed properly, appeal to ego is an attention-getter business leaders can't ignore.

10.2 Create a sense of urgency, p. 163

This is the kind of persuasive writing that motivates employers to reach for the telephone. I modified it to approach **Ten Speed Press**, and it produced the contract to publish this book!

10.4 Target favorite company, p. 171

Craig has a "favorite company," and he says so. His letter told a story and showed honest admiration. Best of all, it worked. He interviewed with Caterpillar over the phone, but their corporate downsizing prevented his being hired. Try this approach with any company you truly admire.

10.5 Capitalize on industry growth, p. 173

When job-hunting, look for growing companies and industries. This letter could be modified to apply to *any* industry. For example, take out "outplacement" and plug in "hazardous waste."

The letter really begins with a disguised question: "Are you growing and expanding? If so, then perhaps my resume will be of interest." "Perhaps" is an important word here, a soft-sell. Many job-seekers come on too strong, telling rather than asking.

"My background covers all aspects from start up through national expansion" pretty well says it all: "I know what I'm doing."

"I hope to contact you directly . . . to determine whether an exploratory meeting is indicated," assures that the reader feels in control—Wesley is not going to call and demand an appointment.

You could probably get through to almost anyone using this letter. It's thoughtful and polite, and best of all, it's short.

10.6 Introduce yourself, pp. 174-175

Jim is a professional copywriter, so his letters are near perfect. They are smooth, casual, and easy-to-read—but also forceful and persuasive. What creative director in their right mind could say "no" to meeting him?

Jim is an interesting person. He has worked for advertising agencies in Denver and New York, and he recently completed a Ph.D. in psychology. That's a rare combination, and it intrigues employers.

10.9 Blitz employers, p. 179-181

Charles mailed three different letters, in the same order as they appear here. The first one caught my attention with the line "If your firm has any expansion plans in the Southwest . . ." This person clearly knew what he wanted. I liked that, but he didn't offer to call, and didn't ask me to do anything. That's a mistake.

The second letter includes a resume. That takes the mystery out of the situation, and could weaken a campaign. It feels like giving in and going back to the old "cover letter and resume" routine.

The *third* letter mistakenly says it's the *second* letter—I was tracking his campaign better than he was. "I solicit your comments" is a good start, but he needs to solicit them more actively. Call the reader, or ask them for some kind of reply. A good effort, but letters by themselves seldom do the trick. If you care about meeting someone, call and tell them *why*.

11.1 Increase response to your letters, p. 184

This is one of my favorite success stories. Jon Bartoshek worked for Safeway for 13 years driving a semi. A back injury prevented his continuing. He showed up in my office wanting to "go into construction management." It seemed impossible, but we looked into his background. Thirteen years earlier, Jon had owned a small tenant-finish construction company, the kind that builds out offices in leased space.

We took his construction experience and made it look "great big" on paper. We deleted the truck driving

experience altogether and came up with two marketing tools (not resumes).

Then Jon said, "By the way, I'd really like to relocate to Houston." (He was in Denver at the time.) We wrote a marketing letter, designed a reply form, gathered the names of commercial construction firms in Houston, and sent off a mailing.

Jon got three positive responses, took three interviews, accepted a job offer, and relocated his family to Houston. Since then he has relocated four times, and today he is project superintendent for construction of the newest and largest hotel in Miami Beach. Who says you can't change careers?

11.4 Guarantee a reply, p. 190

Letters have always worked well for me. I love writing them, and love seeing the results. I've used them for: 1) college course descriptions, 2) proposals, 3) getting new business, 4) collections, 5) thank you's, 6) getting media attention for myself and others, and for many other purposes.

I can always tell when a letter "feels right." Everything comes together and it "sings" (to quote a writing teacher). I just know in my heart it's going to work.

This particular letter was a great one. I was doing freelance PR and marketing for small professional firms—MDs, dentists, lawyers, financial planners—and decided I wanted more business. The letter was directed to medical doctors who are facing increasing competition.

The opening headline "Are you a good candidate for PR?" is ideal. But the bullets that follow are even better—because most of them must be answered, "Yes!"

Take this bullet, for example: "Are you already successful, desiring more success?" What physician is going to say, "No, I'm not successful. I don't want more success?"

I sent along a reply form, and got several positive responses. This letter could be changed to work for almost any consultant or service provider. Give it a try.

11.5 Sell benefits to the reader, p. 192

Few job-seekers have as difficult a situation as Jim. Laid off in a small rural town when the oil field crashed, he lost both his job and his home. His family relocated to Denver without really knowing what the future would hold. But Jim is an optimist, and for an optimist the future is always bright.

Here's how his letter was created. I asked him to talk about sales: his philosophies, his approaches, his values. I recorded everything he said. When he finished, we put his key ideas into a sales letter format. We targeted the letter only to companies in Jim's zip code. For an added bang, we added a "response letter."

The package worked beautifully. Jim got lots of calls and interviews. Best of all, he found the job he wanted close to his new home.

12.2 Use letters as flyers, p. 201

I found this handout on the information table at a convention. When I saw "Please turn me over" stamped in big black letters on a white sheet of paper, I couldn't resist. I turned the page and found this letter. The gimmick was good. I read the letter. It's short—that's a plus. But it's a bit too much "Here's what I want, here's what I need." It's too cold. When you're asking strangers to help, you need to be cordial. You need to give them a "reason why." Something offbeat like this might work if it were better written.

13.7 Say thank you for everything, p. 223

Nothing is too small to warrant a thank you note. Absolutely nothing. One of my favorite tricks is to invite someone to lunch, pay for the meal, then send *them* a thank you note. That's different!

14.2 Follow up after conference or convention, p. 228

Every person you meet at a conference is fair game for a follow-up letter. However, the letter has to offer them something: a thank you, an ego stroke, an article from a recent journal, something of interest.

14.5 Sell by saying "thanks," p. 233

A thank you note is really a sales letter in disguise. On the surface, you're writing to say "thanks." But underneath, you want something: a job, a consulting assignment, a media placement, another meeting.

Therefore, use the thank you note to sell. "I had almost forgotten how stimulating business luncheons are" translates to the reader as "You are a very stimulating person to be around." (Appeal to ego.)

Richard summarizes his life's work in *one paragraph!* He defines the market he's looking for (smaller organizations) and asks for referrals in a soft-sell way. He ends with a strong close ("I will call you") and signs off cheerfully.

Send a thank you letter to *every person* who offers you any kind of assistance in your quest for success. All the job-hunting books say to do so. Few job-seekers ever do.

14.9 Act on want ad replies, p. 245

Susan is a go-getter. She's always enthusiastic, and this letter shows it. Here's the situation: She has answered a want ad. The job fits her beautifully. So when the company merely acknowledges they have received her resume, she seizes the opportunity to do more selling. She writes back enthusiastically. That's the way to do it. Don't put these replies in manila folders and file them—not until you've taken action!

14.11 Keep selling after turndown, p. 251

In marketing, "no" doesn't mean "never." It means "not right now, maybe later." Use a turndown as a public relations opportunity—an opportunity to build goodwill. Respond in such a positive way the company actually feels bad for not hiring you. (Don't show anger and make them feel glad!) It's a long shot, but sometimes the person who got the offer doesn't work out. Then they call you.

14.12 Show your enthusiasm, p. 254

All of Brad's letters are "hot"—full of excitement and enthusiasm. They reflect the real person. Brad is full of life and energy. This letter ultimately resulted in a job offer. Brad is now Public Relations Director for Presbyterian/St. Luke's Hospital, dealing with the local and national media.

14.15 Show how you fit, p. 258

Following up after a telephone call? Don't say, "It was nice to talk to you, and I look forward to hearing from you again soon."

Sell them something. Here Tom shows similarities between his last job and the new job. Very important. Employers often can't see the similarities for themselves. You have to show them. The burden is on you. If you don't show them how you fit, someone else sure will.

14.16 Remind friends to help, p. 260

It's good to let your friends know you're in the job market. But after a month, they forget you. If they haven't heard from you, they assume you've found something. If you haven't, remind them.

The best reminder letter I ever saw was in the form of a newsletter. The job candidate, a CPA, sent a monthly humor- and anecdote-filled newsletter to all his friends and supporters. It was well written and great fun. There was only one problem. He was employed after only two months, so the newsletter ended.

14.17 Show persistence, pp. 263-264

Don't take "no" for an answer, because "no" doesn't mean never; it means "not right now." Keep all your options open. Never close a door on yourself. Just remember, marketing is . . .

1. Working magic.

2. Actualizing, making things happen.

3. Finding out what people *think they need* and giving it to them. (Not making them need what you've got.)

4. A pleasant "can do" attitude. Infectious enthusiasm ("I like you . . . I like your carpet, etc.").

5. Keeping all the doors open. Never closing a door. Never being rude, short, or unkind—no matter how disappointed.

6. Trying all the avenues.

7. Making it a job. Working your buns off. "With part-time efforts, you get part-time results."

8. Knowing what you want. Having written goals.

9. Meeting as many people as possible in as short a time as possible. (Visibility.)

10. Always following up.

11. Not accepting rejection.

12. Not making excuses.

13. Staying busy.

14. Not quitting until you reach your goals.

14.17 Make a second effort, p. 266

Persistence is the name of the game, and it's especially good to let them know you're extremely busy, having a great time, and about to be snatched up by the competition.

14.17 Close the sale, p. 267

How do you rush someone without seeming pushy? You want to seem interested and excited, not desperate. Michael's letter succeeds. He is one of the rare senior executives who can actually write well. His campaign was full of well-worded letters. You'll see many of them in this book.

14.17 Tell them you'll call, p. 268

Great letter, weak close. When you spend this much time to draft a letter, don't leave the outcome to chance. Executives are notoriously busy, so don't wait for them to call you. Often, they won't. Not because they don't want to, but simply because they don't have time.

When you draft a tailored letter to an important contact, you should end it strongly. In this case, "I'll call you to see if there might be something to talk about in this suggestion."

14.18 Ask for the job, p. 271

Michael has a way with words. He crafts the "thank you letter" beautifully, addressing three key issues:

1. The people. He says, in effect, "I like you and I like your people. We'd work well together."

2. The employer's objections: 1) the job's not big enough, and 2) not enough "hands-on."

3. The close. He says "I want to work here," and asks for the job. As a bonus, he keeps it short. I-really-want-this-job letters can drag on for three or four pages if you let them. Be sure you don't.

14.19 Drop a few names, p. 273

This letter produced a job offer.

14.21 List your capabilities, pp. 275-276

Employers are not only concerned about the past (what you have done). They are also interested in the future (what you will do). A list of your capabilities shows them what you *can do*, not what you have done. Many hiring managers find a list like this more interesting than the resume.

15.1 Approach consultants, p. 280

Greg tells me where he got my name. That's a good idea. It makes it seem like less of a shot-in-the-dark and also lets me know my advertising is working.

Greg writes a well-worded, well-organized, low-pressure letter. He covers a lot of ground in a short space: a) family situation, b) summary of strengths, c) job targets, and d) salary questions.

I would gladly have spoken with Greg, but unfortunately, he never called. (This is a mistake, by the way. If you promise to call, do so. If you fail to call, you convey the impression that you don't keep your promises. That can work against you. You don't want to develop a reputation in your network for lack of follow-through.)

15.4 Sell consulting services, p. 285

This is a warm letter that sells well. It's an example of an extremely persuasive letter that doesn't sound like a "sales letter." The format could be used by any consultant, or by almost any job-hunter.

15.4 Learn from the master, p. 287

Jay Levinson, author of *Earning Money Without A Job*, *Guerilla Marketing*, and *Guerilla Marketing Attack*, is one of the country's leading advertising experts. This letter produced great results for Jay, although he had to mail it 13 times to get results.

15.7 Leave consulting for a "real job," p. 291

It's difficult to leave consulting and return to a "real job." Employers often view you with suspicion ("If you're so great, how come you didn't make it as a consultant?"). The best way to handle this is to approach it directly, as Paul does here. Here are some valid explanations for leaving consulting:

1. I'm a team player, not a soloist.

2. I like to make things happen, not watch them happen.

3. I like to stick around to see that my recommendations are carried out.

4. I've proved I can do it alone.

5. Long-term relationships are important to me. I don't enjoy jumping from job to job.

6. I'm a manager, not a guru.

15.8 Create a one-page response form, p. 292

A two-page letter and response form combination works fine, but if possible, reduce it to one page. It's easier for the reader to handle, and therefore, gets better results.

16.1 Congratulate your friends, p. 294

Delightful example of a well-written note. Short and to the point. If your handwriting is beautiful, as Sharon's is, quick thank you notes are definitely the way to go.

16.3 Send gifts to key contacts, p. 297

Sending occasional gifts to important contacts establishes you in their minds as someone thoughtful and professional.

16.5 Stay in touch with your network, p. 299

After you've received a job offer—or while you're happily employed—it's easy to let your network grow cold. As I've said many times, since 75% of good jobs come from friends, that's a mistake. This newsletter is designed to help you keep in touch, even if briefly. It could be personalized with inside name, address, and salutation; that would be better.

16.6 You can never say "thank you" too often, p. 300

A perfect example of making the reader feel good by choosing thoughtful words.

17.1 Get media attention, p. 302-303

I once owned a small PR and marketing firm, and worked for professionals like lawyers, dentists, and financial planners. My competitors claim I've always gotten more than my fair share of media attention. And it's true.

During a recent recession I got tired of the press dwelling on the problems in Denver's economy. I thought "the brighter side of unemployment" would be an interesting story idea. I called the editor of a local weekly newspaper, explained my idea, and sent this short follow up. The idea resulted in the story called "Job Hunters Beware," and introduced me to Brad Bawmann, a great writer and friend.

Before that, I contacted all the television stations in Denver (see page 303). That letter netted four television appearances and a long-term relationship with one television station in particular. It's one of my best.

One key to successful media appearances is to brief the interviewer. Explain your background and suggest questions for them to ask. This reduces the chance that you will have to answer something off-the-wall.

18.3 Resign carefully, p. 312

Use a letter of resignation to create good will, and good references, for yourself. Make sure you don't leave "kicking and screaming." Your career might never recover.

19.4 Offer assistance to job-hunting friends, p. 318

Job-hunters need a lot of emotional support, and this letter offers it without being too sweet or condescending.

20.0 Ask for pay raise, p. 320

You often have to approach employers for raises, because they don't approach you. Be sure to provide evidence of key accomplishments, clear goals for the future, and peg your salary expectations to market prices, not to personal issues, like orthodontia or college tuition. Jean received a $5,000 salary increase using this letter and its supporting documents (not included).

ABOUT THE AUTHOR

William S. Frank, M.A., is Founder and President of **CareerLab**™, a national career counseling firm based in Denver, Colorado. Since 1978 he has been a consultant to the employees, managers, and senior executives of more than 100 major U.S. corporations, including **Ampex, AT&T, Coors, Honeywell, Kaiser-Permanente, Pentax, Schlumberger, Sears Roebuck & Company,** and **TRW.**

Mr. Frank is author of *The Job Search Time Manager,* published by **Ten Speed Press,** and he writes "The Career Advisor," a monthly column for the **Colorado Human Resource Association**—a professional organization for personnel managers. His articles have appeared in *The Rocky Mountain News* and *The Wall Street Journal's* "National Business Employment Weekly."

Bill Frank is Executive Producer of the 6-part video series, "Getting FIRED, Getting HIRED: Job Hunting From A to Z." He served three terms as a Board Member of **The Colorado Human Resource Association**—and he makes frequent guest appearances in the media as an expert on career advancement.

CareerLab® is a small team of business experts who provide career advice to individuals and outplacement counseling to corporations. Corporations hire CareerLab™ to make sure departing employees are re-hired quickly.

CareerLab's® individual clients typically are high-level business executives or professionals—like engineers, lawyers, and CPAs. Their corporate clients span all industries and all geographic locations.

9085 East Mineral Circle, Suite 300
Englewood, Colorado 80112
303-790-0505
303-790-0606 FAX
800-723-9675

CareerLab and "The Career Advisor" are registered trademarks of William S. Frank

INDEX

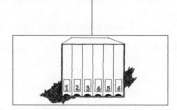

DEAR READER,

<u>WANTED: YOUR ADVICE, IDEAS, AND SUGGESTIONS.</u>

This book is not a one-time event. It is a process, not a product. It is a networking and communications tool, and as such it is never completed. It is always being changed and improved.

If you have job-search materials you think would help others, please send them to me. I'm interested in well-written resumes and job-search letters, especially those that produced interviews or job offers. I also collect job-hunting cartoons and forms or organizers that make the job search easier.

If I use your materials, you'll receive a $25.00 reward and a FREE copy of the next book containing your ideas.

Thank you kindly,

William S. Frank
President
CareerLab®
9085 East Mineral Circle, Suite 300
Englewood, Colorado 80112

$25.00 REWARD

P.S. Be sure to include your name, address, and telephone.